ISLAM AND ITS CHALLENGES
in the GLOBALISED WORLD

ISLAM AND ITS CHALLENGES

in the GLOBALISED WORLD

VOLUME 2

AHMAD AKIL BIN MUDA

PARTRIDGE

ISBN: Softcover   978-1-4828-5512-8
               eBook   978-1-4828-5511-1

Print information available on the last page.

To order additional copies of this book, contact
Toll Free 800 101 2657 (Singapore)
Toll Free 1 800 81 7340 (Malaysia)
orders.singapore@partridgepublishing.com

www.partridgepublishing.com/singapore

بِسْمِ ٱللَّهِ ٱلرَّحْمَـٰنِ ٱلرَّحِيمِ ﴿١﴾

**(In the name of Allah,
the Most Beneficent the Most Merciful)**

PROLOGUE

All the praises and thanks be to Allah, the Lord of the *'Alamin* (mankind, jinns and all that exist) and peace and blessing be upon the Prophet Muhammad (pbuh) as a Messenger of Allah, a compassionate, saviour and guider to the right path of Allah. He is an icon for human race to emulate and to be revered.

As it is now, the Muslim world is replicating the Western model to become progressive nations like them, but then would it be in line with the Islamic principles and Islamic world best interest? Probably the Muslim countries may progress into the developed nations, but if the development is only in the physical form without the spirit of Islam and its substance, naturally it would not lead to the enhancement of the genuine Islamic image.

Just to achieve developments alone without looking at the holistic Islamic human capital and values will not bring benefits to the Muslim community (ummah) and the Muslim world as a whole. Yes, developments and progress are essential and are part of Islam because Islam encourages Muslim to be progressive and advanced in every aspect of life. However, if the developments are in divergence of the Islamic way of life, then they will finally lead to transgression on the part of the Muslims overall in this temporal world. As such Allah will not bless the Muslims but instead they will receive His wrath not only in this world but also hereafter.

During the time Islamic Empire, it spread its wing throughout the world because of the charismatic and credibility some of its leaders and ulama (Islamic scholars). Nevertheless, Muslim ummah in the modern era of globalisation are disobedient (fasiq) lot unlike the Muslims of the past. Throughout the Islamic history, since the fall the Islamic Empire in Spain and the Ottoman Empire of Turkey, the Muslim ummah disintegrated, weak and subservient to the hegemonic non-Muslim powers, either West or East.

Conflict to dominate the world socio-economic, geo-politic and military supremacy continues to polarise. In the process of rivalry and political intrigues, developed countries manipulated and exploited the Muslim world and the other under-developed countries as well. The 'economy hit men' and 'corporatocracy' of the West subtly exploited to their best advantage the world economy through, for examples, the World Trade Organisation (WTO) and other various trade agreements led by United States of America. This does not mean that the Muslims are anti-Americans per se but the American policies, economically and militarily, are of much concern to the Muslim world, perhaps the rest of the free world as well.

Because of hegemonic power of America, Muslim countries are at its mercy so much so, it may be too unkind to say, that the Muslim leaders treat the Presidents of America like their 'Caliphs'. The fact is that many of the Muslims leaders are too happy to pay homage to them to get help, advice and blessing in almost in every aspect of life – economically, financially and militarily. In the eyes of Allah, it does not reflect well as the best people ever created by Him. On the other hand, there are certain non-Muslim countries daring enough to be at loggerhead with the West and yet they survive although with difficulty. This shows that the Muslim countries lack of moral fibres to stand tall on their own turf simply because their faith in Allah had diminished severely.

Globalisation, so to speak generally, is a tool created by the Western imperialists to control the world trade and the economy of other nations. Small and under-developed nations or the third world, including Muslim countries, are often under undue subtle pressure to accept regulations and agreements proposed with them, often than not much to their disadvantage in the long run. Nations whose recalcitrant leaders that defy them could possibly face some sorts of trade restriction in the world trade community.

It appears that the economic growth in most countries outside the Western world now is much better comparatively with that of the Western economies. Their economies, including the United States, have experienced little growth or stagnancy. Some of the European countries are facing recession and bankruptcy due to heavy debts, and have to be bailed out too. Their citizens sometimes resorted to street demonstration because of high cost of living that led to their hardship.

Through their subtle trade manipulation, they subsequently gain more than the small nation trading partnership counterparts. With their clever art of deception, they will continue to dominate other nations, economically and militarily. Their very aim is to keep and maintain their status quo in positioning themselves as world dominant powers.

Globalisation, in fact, already existed and recognised during the time of Islamic Empire. This is because Islam is a universal religion and is a way of life transcending all borders and cultures without discriminating any race or nations. Islam is borderless and relevant all the times. Islamic globalisation is a holistic one, enjoining people to do the righteousness and to always uphold justice for all in the right path of Allah. Islam is a religion of peace and moderation within the parameter of Islamic principles, and in this score it had spread easily throughout the world, no matter how much people dislike it.

The difference and the polarisation between the Christian West and the Muslim World are now becoming more transparent than ever before as already explained in volume 1. The incidents of burning al-Quran, ridiculing and humiliating the Prophet Muhammad (pbuh) and Islam in general by the anti-Islamist groups of the West, and the killing of thousands of innocent Muslims arising from the war against the so called Muslim 'terrorists' carried out by the West too on the Muslim world were transparent enough of their hatred towards Islam. On the other hand, the Muslims usually do not commit such degrading acts in the first instance. Such atrocities by the West created a deep-seated ill feeling and even to the extent of vengeance on the part of the minority hard core or radical Muslims towards them. Those uncivilised instances of cruelty committed by West directly or indirectly on the Muslims had given a green light or justification for the extremists to retaliate in a more radical way like the suicide bombing resulting in the killing of innocent bystanders as well.

The wounds inflicted by the Western powers in Iraq, Afghanistan, Syria, Libya, Yemen, Sudan, Somalia etc., including the long inordinate cruelty of Zionist Jews regime on Palestinians in Palestine, were bloody and are still bleeding. The sudden emergence of the ferocious ISIS in Syria and Iraq is the sequel of the atrocious action committed by the Western powers for so long on the so many innocent Muslims, not only in the Middle East but also elsewhere in the Muslim world. As such, the ISIS though initially bred by them in the proxy war intrigues or games, had turned against its creator and become an extremist organisation of vengeance that had become a force to be reckoned with and for which the whole world had gang-up, including the Muslim world as well, to contain its extreme ideology and tentacles from spreading to other parts of the world as well.

The usage of the catch-phrases by the West such as 'Islamophobia' and the branding of 'Muslims as terrorist' as a whole unjustifiably and frequently propagated throughout the world in the mass media against Islam and thereby affecting and slighting the feeling of friendly and moderate Muslims in general. This type of propagation is indeed very unhealthy and unjustifiably misrepresented against Islam.

The world rightly may condemn the so-called small numbers of Muslim radicals or 'Muslim terrorists' who out of revenge that had killed people, innocent or otherwise, either by suicide bombing or day-light killing etc. but the free world, however, should not condemn the overall of the majority innocent Muslims who have nothing to do with such dastard acts. However, ironically the world does not condemn the big powers, in their hunting down the terrorists or invading the defiant Muslim countries, that killed directly or indirectly thousands of innocent Muslim people simply because they are the super powers for which no small nations would dare enough to touch them.

It is a fact that the differences between Islam and other religions with regard to faith, moral, character, social, ethic, economy, politic, laws etc. are great. Therefore in this regard, there is no possibility that there would be a converging point between them. Notwithstanding, Islam as religion of moderation within Islamic context and principles, its followers, that is the Muslims can live side by side in co-existence with the others. Thus, in multi-ethnic and multi-religious society or country, there would not be a problem for the Muslims to live together harmoniously in peace provided there is a mutual respect with one another.

The disbelievers since the advent of Islam disliked Islam unless the Muslims follow them. As such, this hatred led them to always misrepresent about the virtues of Islam, thus influencing many people not only to be suspicious of Muslims but also to have negative impression towards Islam. The anti-Islamist groups, notably the Christian orientalists of the West, in their propagandas and books written by them gave false images about Islam without any relevant facts or proof. For example, they described Prophet Muhammad (pbuh) as a leader of robber gang, a clan leader who suppressed others, forced people to convert to Islam by swards, a sexual pervert and so forth. These were all falsehoods, insulting and incorrect. They also degraded Islamic culture and Islamic rituals. They misrepresented about history of Islam too. They conveniently forgot history that Islam brought civilisation to them through Spain and other European countries. They were for many centuries peacefully under the Muslim rule. Before Islamic enlightenment came to Europe, they were ignorant people and lived in the Dark Ages under the clutches of the feudal system and churches.

Islam is a religious faith believing in the Oneness of God (Islamic Monotheism) who is the Creator of the universe and its contents therein and to whom all shall finally return. Nevertheless the disbelievers reject all these, although they acknowledge that the universe as a whole together with its contents therein, do not exist by themselves. They deny about the Almighty Creator, that is, Allah the Almighty Who created this universe or the 'Alamin. Because of their arrogance and ungratefulness, they do not believe in Allah as the Creator and the Administrator.

As human beings, people should realise that they are just like tiny ants crawling in search of food etc. on the surface of this planet earth. They are no more than just like the flying termite species attracting to the beautiful neon light, but in the process of admiring it, they unnecessarily destroy or burn themselves by the heat of the light.

Human beings, even how genius they are, cannot create anything on their own. They even cannot create a fly. They are, by nature, so fragile and have no power whatsoever of their own and yet they are very ungrateful to Allah.

The purpose of Allah in creating human beings is to be His servants, to submit to Him alone and at the same time to be His caliphs as trustees to take care of the earth and its contents therein for their own benefits. They are not supposed to cause destructions to this beautiful world but to live therein together peacefully. Yet again, it is the Will of Allah (Sunnatullah) that not everybody would obey His ordainments. That is the ordeal or test from Allah to be faced by human beings. Whoever honestly submits to Him and to His commands will receive His blessing and much rewards in the Heaven hereafter as well as in this his world. On the other hand, whoever disobeys Him will get His wrath in this world and the world hereafter in the Hell Fire.

Muslim ummah in the modern world miserably failed in their obligations and responsibilities. They have betrayed Allah as promised. Their faith in Allah has been diminished and thus the Muslims become weak, spiritually and physically. Their leaders lack of credibility or integrity. They have become the servants to material world rather than the servants of Allah. Some of them even have sadly become the lackey of the disbelievers.

Consequently, it is the Will of Allah that the contemporary Muslim communities face suffering and misfortunes due to their own wrong doings. The wrath of Allah had befallen upon them for they do not help Allah in upholding and defending the sanctity of Islam. Muslim comradeship as brothers in Islam and the spirit of gallantry of the first Islamic generation as in the first war in Islam, the '**Battle of Badar'** that won by the Muslims was gone. Instead, the spirit of greed for worldly gains and pleasures had haunted them as in the lost war in the '**Battle of Uhud'**.

The crux of the whole presentation of these two volume-books is to create a spiritual awareness for the ailing souls and 'sick hearts' of the Muslim ummah as a whole. Changing paradigm by struggling hard or jihad in the spirit of Islamic principles for the betterment of their lives in this world and the world hereafter is the only way to succeed in this trying globalised world.

Without adhering to the Islamic principles in managing their affairs, locally or worldly, Muslims will not be able to achieve their victory as the best ummah ever created by Allah. Thus, in order to achieve success like the Muslims in past during height of the Islamic Empire, the present Muslims have no choice but to emulate, as far as possible, the attributes and the attitudes of the Prophet Muhammad (pbuh) and the subsequent great glorious Caliphs of Islam. Their faith in Allah, their good attributes and spirit of comradeship among the Muslims and their sacrifice for Allah catapulted them to victory in facing their adversaries. Insya Allah (God Willing) by emulating them, the Muslim ummah in this present challenging globalised world will be victorious in future.

These two-volume books may lack of substance in their contents and presentation. Certain words or phrases may also hurt the feeling of certain people or group of people. Being human and as a lay man, I therefore sincerely tender my apologies for any shortcomings.

Ahmad Akil bin Muda.
Petaling Jaya, Selangor, Malaysia.
January, 2016

CONTENTS

SYNOPSIS

Chapter 8. The Islamic organisation (OIC).

Muslim countries had gained their independence quite long time ago. However, economically, militarily etc., they are not. Most of the countries still much depend on the Western countries for survival.

The Muslims had lost their face and glory. They had miserably failed in managing their affairs. The OIC (Organisation of Islamic Cooperation) had led down the Muslim ummah.

The OIC and the Arab League as well are sick organisations. They failed in the job entrusted to them to consolidate and to unite Muslim ummah. They instead bicker among themselves for personal political interest. They do not have charismatic and effective leaders. They are unable to manage their affairs and therefore they become tools of the West.

In the world scene, Muslim ummah are not respected for they do not have the strength and capabilities. They are not united despite of being Muslims and having such large global Muslim population of more than 1.6 billion, inclusive of different sects, they are unable to harness their strength and power. These large human resources along with their riches of natural resources have the potential and the capacity to put them into good use to generate large economies and productivity of the Muslim countries thereby they can put Islam at the highest pedestal as well. Nevertheless, the contemporary Muslims countries absolutely failed in managing their countries.

The Muslims should not blame others for their failure. Their failure solely lies with them. There are too many fasiqun and munafiqun (disobedient and hypocrites) among the Muslims. Thus, Allah will never help them unless they transform themselves back into the fold of true Muslims by following the teaching of al-Quran and al-Sunnah.

Therefore, in view of the failure of the OIC, it is time for the Muslims in the South East Asian archipelago (that is, Malaysia, Indonesia and Brunei) to have a paradigm shift away out from the current rut of the Muslim world. They belong to the same ethnic groups and thus they can do wonders for the betterment of their people because they have overall more than 250 million people. The countries are rich in fertile lands and natural resources as well. Should they work together, with such huge population as a regional Muslim grouping, for example, Islamic confederation, union etc. like that of the European Union (E.U.) definitely they can stand on their own independently. Of course, they should not leave ASEAN.

Chapter 9. Jihad and Sacrifice.

Jihad is a sincere sacrifice for the sake or in the way of Allah. Jihad means struggle hard or striving hard in an effort to better oneself for example, to acquire knowledge, to enhance economy, to strengthen Islam, to defend the countries against enemies of Islam etc. The military effort against enemies of Islam is a form of jihad that should not be taken lightly. Scholars, however, differ in their interpretation of jihad because of its wide connotations.

Allah commanded the Muslims to go for jihad in the way of Allah when they are called to defend Islam. There are many verses in al-Quran about jihad. A war is not a Jihad if the intention is to force people to convert to Islam, to conquer other nations or to colonise them, to take territory for economic gain, to settle disputes, to demonstrate a leader's power etc. The act of extremism is out of jihad and Islam.

Jihad is continuous and relevant all the times. But in the modern world, Muslims not only become weak spiritually, economically and militarily but also spoil for personal gain, power and material wealth etc., therefore, the call for jihad has been diminished accordingly in its importance even though the Muslim world is being constantly bullied and harassed by the big powers of the disbelievers.

Chapter 10. The Disbelievers Vis-A-Vis the Believers

According to al-Quran, human beings broadly divided into two classifications, namely the believers and the disbelievers - inclusive the munafiqun (hypocrites). The disbelievers are categorised as the worst living creatures of Allah. They wage wars and killed millions of people from the time immemorial until to the present day. They also frequently break promises or covenants.

Allah said in surah At-Taghabun, verse (64:2):

هُوَ ٱلَّذِى خَلَقَكُمْ فَمِنكُمْ كَافِرٌ وَمِنكُم مُّؤْمِنٌ وَٱللَّهُ بِمَا تَعْمَلُونَ بَصِيرٌ

(٢)

"He is Who created you, then some of you are disbelievers and some of you are believers. And Allah is All-Seer of what you do".

Disbelievers always breach covenant. In surah al-Anfal, verse (8:56) said Allah:

ٱلَّذِينَ عَٰهَدتَّ مِنْهُمْ ثُمَّ يَنقُضُونَ عَهْدَهُمْ فِى كُلِّ مَرَّةٍ وَهُمْ لَا يَتَّقُونَ

(٥٦)

"They are those with whom you made covenant but they breach their covenant every time and they do not fear Allah".

The Muslims, therefore, should be very cautious about the disbelievers. However, it does not literally mean that the Muslims should make foe with them.

The world tyrants mostly were leaders of disbelievers who committed untold misery and cruelty on fellow human like Mao Zedong, Stalin, Hitler and so many others in comparison with the Muslims.

On the part of Muslims, they are enjoined to do good deeds and prohibited them from being extremists and transgressors. Thus, any wrong doings committed by Muslims, for example, corruption, abuse of power, cruelty, take interest, gambling, take one's life without right, extremism etc. are un-Islamic and out of Islamic principles. Nonetheless, if the Muslims are victimised, then it is obligatory upon the Muslim ummah to invoke jihad to protect Islam and its followers. Allah abhors Muslims that condone wrong doings.

The world powers are all disbelievers. They will do anything possible either by subtle deception in business or the use military muscles to threaten others, to enhance their economies or to maintain their status quo of their domains and supremacy over others.

Right now, Muslims cannot claim themselves as the best people ever created by Allah because most of them are no difference in their attributes with that of the disbelievers. They fear Allah not but they love mortal beings or material wealth more. If they fear Allah, they will not be in the position as they are now.

Chapter 11. The Ungrateful

Human beings should be grateful to Allah not only for creating them but also the universe and its contents therein for their use and enjoyment respectively. The Muslims should be much more thankful to Allah for choosing them to be the followers of the religion of Islam, particularly so for those who were born Muslims. Notwithstanding, there are ungrateful Muslims, though they were born Muslims they choose to be out of Islam, that is, to be infidel. However, in this free world and under the principles of universal human rights, no one can stop any Muslim to be apostate, although Islam prohibits it. It is a grave crime in Islam and is punishable by death.

The ungrateful Muslims are a plenty because there are many Muslims who do not practise Islam as it should be. Many of them not only do not worship Allah but also their moral character and their way of life are not much difference with that of the non-Muslims, except that they do not worship the idols or the cross. The rich idolise their money and those in power are corrupt and abuse their power. Some of the poor too are ungrateful of whatever they have had. In general, their Islamic faith has been diminished accordingly.

Muslim countries that are rich seldom offer help to others. The rich would rather live in excessive opulent and the super-rich elites having their bathrooms and toilet sets etc. made of solid gold or gold-plated, even their cars are gold-plated too. The super-rich even can afford to own a full sized Boeing 747 equipped with gold sinks, a Mercedes Benz covered with diamonds etc. They also have many unnecessary big palaces as well. In fact, they can buy anything in this world because they have much more money in their kitties unspent. They are real transgressors and ungrateful to Allah for His abundant endowments unto them.

The Muslim countries at present adopted secular system in some way or other in their governments rather than the Islamic system. They are very much comfortable with it. They prefer secularism because they can live with full freedom under the universal principle of human rights.

In world political scene, certain the Muslims collaborated with the big powers, in order to maintain their autocratic regime. In reality, they sold Islam and themselves with meagre worldly price to perpetuate their power and riches. Thus, the non-Muslim world looks low-down on the Muslims for not being able to manage their affairs accordingly.

Many Muslims wantonly ignored their obligatory duty towards Allah. It is little wonder, therefore, many instances of corruption, abuse of power, criminal breach of trust, adultery and other wrong doings committed by the Muslims themselves. Thus, their attributes are no difference comparatively with that of the non-Muslims.

Chapter 12. The Wrath of Allah.

People keep on committing wrong doings and evil deeds without any limit or conscience. They defy the commands of Allah. Thus, if any disaster or tragedy happens, it is a mean of warning and punishment of Allah to the human beings, believers and disbelievers, in this world as the result of their own folly, transgression and sins. When the wrath of Allah happens, it will come hard and nobody can escape from it.

Allah gives blessing and endowment to all, however there is a limit to it. A country may progress and become wealthy. When its people are rich, they live in opulent and more often than not, they start transgressing in extreme to the extent that they may become crazy in the search of vain desire and happiness and yet they will never feel happy.

When catastrophe comes, it destroys lives and properties. It is the Act of Allah due to human transgression and evil deeds. The disbelievers may reject it is as the wrath of Allah, instead they blame the global warming, climate change, natural disaster etc.

Allah will punish people who desert Him in this world and in the life hereafter. While alive, they seemed to be happy outwardly but inwardly they are surely not. Whether they are rich or poor, they will always feel scared, sceptic and unease of mind because their lives are empty and devoid of spiritual guidance. Al-'Aufy narrated a hadith from Ibnu Abas:

"Anything I give to My slaves, few or more, but they do not fear Me, they will never feel delighted and always live in difficulty".

Many Muslims, including their leaders, have abandoned Allah, al-Quran and al-Sunnah. Their leaders keep busy themselves, wrestling powers and wealth rather than looking after Islam and the welfare of their people. They fear and obey Allah not. Certainly, they will receive the worst torment in the Hell Fire than the ordinary masses in the world hereafter.

The Doomsday will surely be coming. It is a matter of when only. Whether one believes in it or not, many of the lesser signs of the Doomsday are happening now. The primary minor or lesser signs had manifested in the form of the general diminishing of religious observance on the part of Muslims and the increase of immorality and cruelty etc. overall in this world. When will the greater signs of the Doomsday and the actual day of Doomsday come? Only Allah knows best but when it comes surely it will be terrible beyond imagination.

Chapter 13. The Final Victory.

Muslim ummah would ultimately win over their enemies (disbelievers) and they would rule the world with Islamic syariah. Nonetheless, many people do not subscribe to this prophesy because the Muslim are currently weak. They considered this as a fantasy and it would never happen. However, the true Muslims believe that Islam will win ultimately because Allah said in surah al-Saff (61:9) and surah al-Ma'idah verse (5:56) as follows respectively:

$$\text{هُوَ ٱلَّذِىٓ أَرْسَلَ رَسُولَهُۥ بِٱلْهُدَىٰ وَدِينِ ٱلْحَقِّ لِيُظْهِرَهُۥ عَلَى ٱلدِّينِ كُلِّهِۦ}$$

$$\text{وَلَوْ كَرِهَ ٱلْمُشْرِكُونَ ﴿٩﴾}$$

"He sent His Messenger (Muhammad) with guidance and the religious of truth (Islam) and that to make it <u>victorious</u> over all other religions even though the mushrikun (polytheists, pagans, idolaters, and disbelievers) hate it".

وَمَن يَتَوَلَّ ٱللَّهَ وَرَسُولَهُۥ وَٱلَّذِينَ ءَامَنُواْ فَإِنَّ حِزْبَ ٱللَّهِ هُمُ ٱلْغَٰلِبُونَ

(51)

"And whosoever takes Allah, His Messenger and those believers as Protectors then the party of Allah (the Muslims) will be the <u>victorious</u>".

The clash of civilisations between the Muslim East and the Christian West had produced crises of values and identity. Polarisation between the liberal and the Muslim conservative is also of concern. It appears that the conservative is in a losing mode. Western culture is now thriving well and dominant in the Muslim world. More and more younger generation attracted to the free life style of Western culture. Disobedient to Allah has become more rampant. This is the real contemporary challenge that haunted the Muslims fundamentalists and the traditionalists. However, one thing is certain, no matter what challenge Islam is facing, Islamic fundamental is to stay and its principles and virtues would remain intact.

The enemies of Islam are waiting for the fall of Islamic morality and religion because moral decadent in the Muslim society is the linking bridge in bringing down the Islamic fundamental in the Muslim society. They will never stop in trying to extinguish the light of Islam for that is their universal aim. However, Allah is All-Knower, All-Powerful and His wrath as promised by Him will come hard on all the disbelievers and the hypocrites.

Islam will remain intact because Allah will protect Islam. Islam is the ultimate victor in the end with the emergence Imam Mahadi and then the Prophet Jesus (Isa) who would rule the world with Islamic syariah. That is the pledge of Allah and then the Doomsday will set in. When the Doomsday comes every living creature will die and then only to resurrect to meet Allah at the "Padang Mahsyar or Plain of Mahsyar" (The huge plain where mankind are assembled after death and the end of the world in front of Allah to be weighed for their sins and good deeds) for His judgement.

Chapter 14. Endless Tragedy.

Tragedies, again and again, have been happening on humankind arising from human craziness, affecting the believers and the disbelievers alike. However, the incidents are mostly affecting the Muslim ummah in particular and the others in general.

The crises among the world civilisations will never end although some people believed that it would. The contemporary Muslim ummah (communities) are now facing mounting challenges from their adversaries. Life would be difficult for the Muslims until and unless they return to the Islamic way of life based on the teaching of Islam as enshrined in the Holy Book of al-Quran and the al-Sunnah of Prophet Muhammad (pbuh).

Muslims nations lack of charismatic, capable and credibility leaders to lead and to close ranks for unity and work hard together to protect their turf. The Muslims need to sacrifice together to uphold justice for all in facing the vagaries of the villains. God willing, Allah will help them accordingly. Notwithstanding, beware of the wrath of Allah, if Muslims do not conform to His commands and to that of His Messenger, Prophet Muhammad (peace be upon him).

While the OIC or the Muslim world is in a state of dilemma and at loss of its focus and vision in the world politics vis-à-vis the ever powerful and domineering world powers, out of sudden in its midst an extremist and ferocious Islamist group called the ISIS emerged to claim territories in Syria and Iraq. This has caused the life of ordinary Muslims living in fear and difficulties.

This group came into being, out of vengeance, after the long inordinate suffering of Arab Sunni Muslims at the hands of the Shiites and the Americans and their allies in Iraq and Syria. The whole of the Middle East had become more chaotic after the United States of America unilaterally with the Great Britain invaded Iraq.

Then, again out of the blues the incident of the dastard act of killing by the ISIS 'lone wolf' in 'Charles Hebdo' office in France on January 6ᵗʰ 2015 shocked the world. The whole world vehemently condemned the ISIS extremist perpetrators. The carnage was the revenge against the sardonic French magazine that insulted and humiliated the revered Prophet Muhammad (pbuh).

Again, the downing of Russia civilian airline and the massacre in Paris on November 3rd and 13th 2015 respectively were much worst and greatly shocked the world, thus accentuated the war against the ISIS. According to the ISIS those acts were in retaliation against the nations that attacked them.

As the result of the incidents, the innocent minority Muslims overall in Europe, America and elsewhere are under 'siege' by anti-Islamist. Physical and mental assaults on Muslim individuals and burning of mosques etc. had happened though isolated. There were instances where the innocent Muslims, both men and women, were victimised and even to the extent of marching them out as passengers from the airlines they boarded due Islamophobia. But, ironically the atrocities inflicted on the Palestinians by the Israel Zionist Jews regime almost every day is being ignored by the free world.

In Southeast Asia too, the minority Rohingyas Muslims of Myanmar (Burma) had been facing prosecution by the inhuman government of the day for years. The government of Myanmar wants to get rid of Rohingyas. The government does not recognise Rohingyas as its citizen. The free world and the United Nation do not help them from the cruelty of Myanmar government. That is the latent human tragedy that is being faced by the Muslims in Myanmar, while the minority Muslims in the Christian Angolan government in Africa are also being victimised. It is reported that Angola is the first county in the modern world that had banned Islam.

CHAPTER 8.   THE ISLAMIC ORGANISATION

The Muslim world has an organisation, that is, the O.I.C. – "The Organisation of Islamic Conference (now Cooperation)" – established 48 years ago on 25th September 1969 at Rabat, Morocco, after the Arab-Israel war in 1967. Its Headquarters is in Jeddah, Saudi Arabia. It has 57 member-states. It is the second largest organisation in the world after the United Nations. Its first Secretary General was Tunku Adbul Rahman Putra al-Hajj (1970 -1974), the late first Prime Minister of Malaysia.

Its Charter was very noble ones, aiming inter alia to promote Islamic fraternity and solidarity through coordinating the social, economic, trading, scientific, cultural activities etc. among the Muslim countries, to eliminate discrimination and to respect human rights as stipulated in the United Nation Charters.

The objectives of the OIC were very commendable and holistic indeed. However, its inherent internal weaknesses are insurmountable due to large number of nation-state memberships of different ethnic groups, politics, economies and even religion – Sunni and Shiite Sect. Some of the states are rich and developing whilst the others are poor and underdeveloped. The critical issue facing OIC is its management and commitment of the leaderships in the OIC. It appears that it failed miserably due to lack of unanimity among the members.

There was, however, no mention in the OIC about military cooperation or collaboration in order to defend the Muslim countries in the event of military intrusion by foreign powers. Perhaps they were too weak to include this clause or under the pressure by the domineering Western powers to preclude such a clause. This is because the West would be very chary of such development especially with regard to unity and military cooperation among the Muslim countries.

Muslim population, albeit consisting of certain different sects, is now more than 1.6 billion or about 23.5% of the world population. Islam is therefore the world's second largest religion in term of its followers and if the Muslims are united they would be a great world force to be reckoned with.

Muslim cultures composed of a mixture of miscellaneous ethnic and language groups transcending nation-state borders throughout the world within the ambit of Islamic parameter. It is unique in itself but the faith in Islamic Monotheism is the same wherever the Muslims reside. Muslim culture, therefore, exists throughout the world wherever there are Muslim societies even though as a minority group in the non-Muslim countries. By the look of it, they seem to be very strong but in reality they are not due to their disunity despite of the fact that they are brothers in Islam. Politics, nationalism, clannish, culture differences, geographical distance etc. had torn them apart and the magic of the Islamic spirit of brotherhood as in the past is no more, even in the local politics simply because their faith in Islam had been diminished accordingly.

As a country, Indonesia has the largest number of Muslim population in the world. It is a secular state and does not declare Islam as the official religion. Second largest is Pakistan and the third is Bangladesh. China also has a large number of Muslim population but still a minority in the vast communist country.

Many member-states of the OIC are not only poor and under-developed but illiteracy is also high due to lack of educational facilities. Thus, in the realm of education and technology they are much behind the developed countries.

Large percentage of population also does not have access to medical facilities, safe drinking water and is lack of food as well. Half of the population lives below the poverty line classified as the most poor. No Muslim country is in the top list of the Human Development Index or in any other global economic indicators.

The OIC member countries possess 70 per cent of the world's energy resources and 40 per cent of other available raw materials but their GDP (Gross Domestic Product) is only 5 per cent of the world GDP.

Although Muslim ummah consist of various races, spread over vast areas of the globe and possessing enormous natural economic resources, Muslim countries, as already stated, miserably lag behind in development. Should they be able to manage and fully utilise their human and material resources and their spiritual power, Muslim ummah definitely can achieve an outstanding position in this world.

The immediate challenge facing OIC is its ability to establish a consensus on common ground or issues facing its various diversity backgrounds of the members. So far, often than not, this is the factor that it fails to achieve despite of the commonality of Islamic faith among its members.

The key challenge facing them is to surmount the problem as to how to unite them in diversity due to those differences. These are the underlying issues that divide the group. As a result, the OIC members often divided on many issues, especially for the last ten years or so where sectarianism differences had led to war within the regions between Sunni Muslims and Shiite sects. This religious difference is a disunity factor within the OIC. Thus, the OIC's credibility remains vulnerable, furthermore most member states are members of other regional organisations as well that are of more priority given than to the OIC itself. As such, the OIC's record of accomplishments is far from satisfactory, in fact unsatisfactory at all.

As mentioned above, the Muslims established the OIC not only to promote fraternity, solidarity and cooperation among them through coordinating positive connectivity, socially and economically, but also to reassert their identity in the world. However, this organisation has had little effect in achieving collaboration among Muslim nation-states. The collaborative achievement of any group needs a strong social band, in this instance is the Islam but unfortunately, it failed to create the bond unlike the Christian bond among the European nation-states in the EU (European Union).

It does not mean that the Muslim countries do not have a strong spiritual bond, but the stumbling block is due to the various differences in political ideology, inclination and alignment. Thus, this difference creates uneasiness and difficulty of sort out in the mix to manage such a big organisation.

After the independence the Muslim nation-states, after so long being subjected to suppression, they were much confused arising from the propagation of secularism, democracy, socialism, nationalism etc. Western influence undeniably had played a big role in shaping the thinking and political philosophy of the Muslims. In consequence, the Muslim ummah could not form any meaningful basis of group feeling and brotherhood in Islam. Thus, there is a strong feeling of nation-state identity and sovereignty, nationalism and individualism that had dominated the Muslim society of today. Dogmatic clannish attitude coupled with the difference of political ideology, political inclination and affiliation in this shrouded world politics accentuated the chasm of differences and division among its members. Furthermore, the overall Islamic faith among some of the Muslims has been corrupted beyond repair, again due to the influence of the Western philosophy, ideology, freedom and most of all materialism.

The OIC also runs on tight budget where contribution to the OIC fund is insufficient because some members cannot afford to contribute more, just like in the United Nations. In the UN, the United States and the other big powers who dominated the organisation contributed most. Similarly, Saudi Arabia and other Arab states contributed the most to the OIC. Therefore, directly or indirectly they have greater assertive voice or influence in the running of the organisation.

Therefore, the OIC needs a few strong and capable leaders to steer the OIC into the correct perspective in line with its objectives. Without strong and charismatic leaders of world standing in the OIC, the non-Muslim world, especially the big powers, will orchestrate the OIC like pawns. In such a scenario, the OIC holistic vision and mission will never be realised even in the future.

8.1. Disappointment.

As stated above, the objectives of the OIC were so holistic for the betterment of Muslim ummah overall. Nevertheless, the organisation lacks positive actions despite of its plans vis-a-vis the vision and mission it was first established. Summit after summit held and various declarations and resolutions were made, yet they did not move as expected.

To this present day, this organisation remains inactive, if at all it is not defunct. The members of the organisation could not move in unison because more often than not, it could not have the consensus on many local or global issues among the members. Thus, it remains silent and acts as a spectator only to any world big issues, even on issues affecting its member-states. In fact, most of the conflicts now are happening within the Muslim countries. The OIC has failed miserably to play the role of a mediator to pacify and to solve the conflicts between its members, and the following examples are representatives:

- The Iran-Iraq conflict (1980-89).
- The Iraq-Kuwait conflict (1990).
- Ahmad Queri of Hamas won election in Gaza, Palestine, on 25th January 2006. The Israel regime, the United States and many others did not recognise Ahmad Queri and forced him to resign.
- The United States or the coalition forces in 2003 invaded Iraq, unnecessarily victimising President Saddam Hussein and the innocent Iraqis.
- The spring (Jasmine) uprising in Tunisia brought down the government, ousting of long time President Zine El Abidine Ben Ali in January 2011.
- The Egyptian Revolution in January 25th 2011 overthrew the long reign autocratic Mubarak regime.
- The President Mohammad Morsi of Egypt, legitimately elected on 30th June 2012, overthrew by his general El Sisi on 3rd July 2013.
- The Libyan Revolution or Libyan Civil War, in which NATO and French Air Force supported Libyan rebels, ousted President

Muammar Gaddafi Muammar. The National Transitional Council "declared the liberation of Libya" on 23 October 2011 after Gaddafi was capture and killed by the mob.

- The Syrian Civil War due to atrocities of President Assad is on. The unrest began in the early spring of 2011 within the context of Arab Spring protests. Assad's forces responded with violent crackdowns. The conflict gradually turned from violent protests to rebellion and civil war until today with untold misery and exodus of refugees to Europe and elsewhere.

- In the mid of Syrian civil war, emerged the ISIS in Syria and Iraq, creating havoc in the region. The conflict became worst and had become a world problem.

- The civil war in Yemen remained unsettled. Politically, Yemen had never united for centuries. The current Yemeni Civil War began in 2015 between two factions – Shiite sect and the Sunni Muslims of Yemen. Southern separatists and forces loyal to the government of Abd Rabbuh Mansur Hadi, based in Aden, have clashed with Houthi (Shiite) forces and forces loyal to the former president Ali Abdullah Saleh. Al-Qaeda in the Arabian Peninsula and the ISIS are also involved. They controlled swaths of territories in the hinterlands and along stretches of the coast.

- The Palestine issue remained unsolved until today.

The above proved that the OIC was unable to play its role at all in helping to solve the problems affecting its own members.

On the issue of Palestine, the OIC left the Palestinian people alone to fight the Israel regime. The OIC as a collective body of Muslim countries does not able to help the Palestinians. Worst still, some of its members also all along played politic of survival and in cahoot with the West. The OIC feared of retaliation by Israel and its Western allies if it acted aggressively. In other words, they feared big powers rather than Allah despite of having Muslim ummah more than 1.6 billion people. Thus, it showed that the Muslim leaders loved material world and personal power more than Islam for they did not dare enough to invoke jihad against the kufar (disbelievers). In other word, they lack in Islamic faith, the political will and the fighting spirit against their adversaries.

Thus far at the present moment, no Arab countries or other Muslim countries have come forward to assist the Palestinians in their struggle against the Zionist Israel regime. Egypt, worst of all, has closed its borders, thus restricted and suffocated Palestinians movement.

The ordinary Muslim ummah are 'hopping mad' in their demonstrations condemning the Israel regime, but hopping alone will not help anything instead will get 'high blood pressure' only because their leaders are enjoying life and dancing along, wearing blinkers, with the big powers to save their own thick skins.

Pointing out to the Israeli aggressive action against the Palestinians in Lebanon in 1982, the then Palestinian leader, the late President Yasser Arafat, said that the Israel military besieged the PLO forces for 83 days in Beirut while no one extended any help or support. The PLO forces then besieged in Tripoli - a joint Arab-Israel blockade (pointing out to Syrian action against the PLO) - but neither the Arabs nor other non-Arab Muslims moved a finger. Thus, the OIC itself killed the Muslims.

Arising from the frustration, Yasser Arafat gradually alienated away from the original OIC decisions on the Palestinian issue and attempted to negotiate with Israel directly.

In fact, the process of negotiations with Israel by the OIC countries began in 1978. However, on September 17th, 1978 President Anwar Sadat of Egypt, an important member-state of the OIC signed alone an accord, known as the Camp David Accord sponsored by the United States, with Israel for which initially the OIC reacted angrily and suspended the membership of Egypt from the organisation "up to the time when the reason that provoked this suspension is eliminated".

It is interesting to note that within a few years, the OIC re-admitted Egypt without it abandoning its policy toward Israel. In reality, it seems that Egypt convinced the other OIC member states to adopt its policy of "reconciliation" toward Israel. This was because Egypt, the protégé of the United States, was powerful enough to exert its influence on other Arab members. The United States as a 'big brother' was behind Egypt, not only helping Egypt but also dictating its policy as well.

This reflects the weakness of the OIC for not being able to stand on its own and to have consensus among its member-states. When faced with strong adversaries, it recoils like snail sleeping in its soft shell.

Outside the Arab world, the Muslims ummah also faced similar problems, but the OIC let them alone facing the atrocities committed by the non-Muslims without helping them. Among the examples are the following:

- The United States of America and NATO - a band of big powers - after the Soviet Russia left Afghanistan, invaded Afghanistan on the pretext of maintaining peace. In the process of hunting the al-Qaeda mujahidin and other insurgents, they killed thousands of innocent Muslims. The puppet government installed by them was unable to maintain peace and until now Afghanistan is still unstable and in chaotic condition.

- In the Caucasian, the Soviet Russian regime invaded the tiny Chechnya that declared its independence. They committed untold miseries and atrocities on the Muslims population in Chechnya and elsewhere in the Soviet Union.

- Similarly, the Muslims in China, in India, etc. faced the same fate. For example, in 1983 in Assam state of India, Hindu fanatics massacred many Muslims villagers.

- In Bosnia, the Christians raped, tortured and slaughtered thousands of Muslims - a process of ethnic cleansing against the Muslims. With due respect, it was the United States and the UN that helped to restore peace in the area, although it was quite too late.

- In Southeast Asia too, similar problem faced by the minority Muslims in Southern Philippine, Southern Thailand and Rohingyas in Myanmar.

As stated above, the OIC in spite of its resolutions and commitments to support and promote Islamic solidarity, to protect their dignity and the independence of the Muslim community, when attacked by the aggressors it left the immediate Muslim victims to fight the enemies alone. The OIC members as an organisation did not dare enough to invoke jihad to defend the oppressed Muslims. It is of no point to have rhetoric fiery speeches and long prayers, simply because the Muslim nation-states overall did not have the political will to put at risk their national interests for the sake of other oppressed fellow Muslims.

In this kind of trying scenario, the Muslim ummah as whole is at sin for not being able to invoke jihad in the way of Allah to protect Islam and the Muslims when they are under duress and victimisation by their foes. But then it is not a passport for the Muslims to commit atrocities or to act in extremism whatsoever in fighting their adversaries.

As to the Christian West overall, they are united for their common cause, especially against the Muslims because they never like Islam. Therefore, wherever there is opportunity, they will try to put down the Muslims and stifle the growth of Islam. It is usual for them to have the feeling of jealousy towards the spread of Islam and the power of the Muslims. Furthermore, they are also ignorant about the virtues of Islam. The catchphrase of Islamophobia used by them was transparently showing their negative attitude towards the majority Muslims at large in general. This continuous hostile attitude against Islam does not reflect well on the good relationship between them and the Muslims.

The OIC, on the other hands, is always in docile mode despite of mounting hostility of the West. It failed to protect the virtues of Islam and the Muslim ummah. Its failure in handling the world issue affecting the Muslims is disappointing. Its failure to have a strong unity and cooperation among member-states as a strong force to be mobilised in time of need to face its adversaries is equally much disappointing.

On the economic front, the lack of economic progress and developments in the field of agriculture and manufacturing industries, trade and financial infrastructures, education, human capital resources etc. are the clear sign of the utter failure of the OIC. There is also a real shortage of Universities in Muslim world in spite of its large number of Muslim population comparatively with the developed and industrialised West. The performance of the OIC is therefore below expectation.

The Muslims countries in the OIC are rich in oil and other natural resources as well but their countries are in dearth of various human technical skills to develop those resources. Thus, they depend much on foreign expertise. Mismanaging of their countries is transparently seen, resulting in lack of governance, rampant incidents of abuse of power, corruption, lack of democracy and injustice and so forth. All these mismanagement resulted in hindering modernisation and development in most of the countries. But most of all, the lack of spiritual drive and intellectual strength based on al-Quran and al-Sunnah to put their countries back into the right track within the Islamic principles are the very key reasons for the weakness of Muslim countries.

Thus, on the whole the OIC not only does not have the spiritual strength but also political will and functional structural mechanism to help taking care and to protect its own member-states. They live in disharmony and in diversity instead of unity as preached by Islam. In order words, it disgustingly does not live up to its fullest potential as a nucleus or agent of change for the Muslim ummah to forge ahead in this present world.

To make matters worse, some of the members are also much in cohort with the Western world, rather than closing ranks with their Muslim brothers overall in the Muslim world. They look for the West to invest and thus the Arabs petrol dollars in billions or trillions parked and invested in Western countries. The rich Arabs trust the non-Muslim West rather than their brother Muslim countries to invest their money. This is really a sign of hypocrisy on their parts.

The God given oil riches should be managed and utilised holistically for development, not only of their own countries but also for other poor Muslim countries for the benefit of their people. How noble it is if the rich members of the OIC could help the poor member-states in providing better business opportunities, financial facilities or infrastructure for investment, ease of doing business and other opportunities and so forth instead of siphoning the oil money much for themselves and their cronies to enjoy. In this regard, it is a clear blatant transgression in managing the God given wealth and resources.

Should they invest their excess money in other brother Muslim countries, God willing Allah will bless them for they are helping in developing the poor Muslim countries. However, instead of helping the Muslims, their money is being utilised by the West to generate more profit, notably for the United State and the Jews. They in turn will use the money indirectly or directly to finance their war expenses against the Muslims. In this regard, the rich Arabs are directly not only in financing the West to develop their economies but also helping them to utilise the money to kill and humiliate the Muslims.

By right, the rich Muslim countries should be grateful to Allah for endowing them with abundance oil resources in their lands. As Muslims, they are duty bound to help the poor Muslim nations, for which they have enough money to do so, instead of making themselves super rich and making the rich Western countries to become richer. This is really a grave transgression in managing their riches.

It is reported that roughly about USD 1 trillion of Middle East funds parked in the Western financial centres in New York, London and Switzerland. The funds can easily be utilised to help bringing economic and education developments etc. in their own and other poor Muslim countries instead of building of unnecessary tall buildings for pride. Such being the case, it is not surprising that the rich Arab countries are in unstable position because many of their people dislike them. Allah also does not bless them for their un-Islamic action. Furthermore, they are autocratic governments and their survival much depends on the support of the big powers to guard their backyards.

As to the OIC, it is already known that it failed in its vision and mission. It had not achieved any praiseworthy achievement.

Although there were many summits held to make intensive analysis of the OIC failures and issued many ambitious action-plans for its accomplishment, but unfortunately all the pledges and declarations remained unaccomplished.

In summary, the OIC overall failed to respond meaningfully to any world crises. It failed to demonstrate any unity of thought and action apart from voicing high-sounding declarations at the end of each summit or conference. It failed altogether to contain the crises or avert the tragedies befallen on the Muslim ummah. It also failed to play the role in helping economic developments etc. of member-states. All this while it remains merely in name but as an organisation it becomes a silent spectator and dormant, while some of its member-states undermine and doing disservice to the solidarity of the OIC by being in alignment with the West or the East, as the case may be, instead of being united among themselves and being a neutral body in the world affairs.

8.2. Relevancy of OIC.

The OIC already aged 48 years since its establishment. It should have been matured by now and that the spirit of Islamic fraternity or unity among the Muslim member-countries should have been well developed and in place. Unfortunately, it is not so, in fact the Muslim countries are in disintegration and in disarray instead. The holistic objectives remain unfulfilled. Collectively it does not dare enough even to raise strong voice criticising against the Western powers in critical issues facing the Muslim ummah, let alone world issues.

The situation of Arab League which was established in 1945 in Cairo is also of not much different from the OIC, even though it has few members and of the same ethnic group. Being Muslims, there must be something wrong with them overall.

Prophet Muhammad (pbuh) was born an Arab. He came to this world to preach the religion of Allah (Islam) to all mankind in this world. From the Arab Peninsular, Islam then subsequently spread to the whole world. Yet the overall Arab countries of the modern day are disunited and weak. They distrust each other and often fight among themselves like in the olden ignorant time before the advent of Islam.

The OIC main objective was to liberate Jerusalem from Zionist Israel occupation and also to look into the welfare of Muslim ummah. Unfortunately, it turned out to be just as an organisation of Muslim elite leaders. Their rhetoric speeches and pledges fit for listeners in the coffee shop or coffee house only.

'Islamophobia', the catchword purposely created by the West to smear the image of Islam and Muslims in an effort to stifle the growth of Islamic Faith is regrettable. Open minded people would not play politics with religion to create fear among the public. One cannot condemn and write off the whole religion and its followers merely due to the heinous and despicable acts of certain known groups of people who have clearly hijacked and abused Islam for their own ends which is really nothing to do with Islam and the Muslims at large. Terrorist acts were motivated by many reasons, some of which were nothing to do with religion but for other causes. For instance, Ireland had to contend with issues between two denominations of Christians. Similarly the incidents of mass murder at the Sandy Hook elementary school and the McVeigh tragedy in the United States had no connection with Islam whatsoever. Therefore, smearing campaign against Islam by the catchphrase Islamophobia is unjustifiable.

Whenever and wherever terrorism incidents happened firstly, rightly or wrongly, they pointed fingers at the Muslims, particularly after the 11th September 2001 terror incident. Muslim leaders in the OIC as a body failed to vigorously ward off the negative 'Islamophobia' propaganda of the West but instead gives affirmative indicator to the West without giving cautious statement as to why such incidents and terrorism did happen in the first place. It appeared that as if the OIC is willing to let the overall Muslims to become a scapegoat, notwithstanding Islam is not a religion of 'terrorism'. Therefore, it gave a passport to the West to arrogantly brand the Muslims as 'terrorists' and to propagate 'Islamophobia' as a tool against the Muslims overall.

This sort of branding or generalisation on the Muslims by the West is very unfortunate befallen on the moderate Muslims generally. In countering the West, perhaps the OIC could also coin a negative catchphrase of "Christophobia" against the Christians or whatever the correct word may be. In fact, it serves the West well because the whole world is in a state of fear and under the surveillance by the big powers of the Christian West.

In reality, if one is honest in analysing the overall conflicts and anarchy in this whole world, was it the Muslims first of all that started them? Are the

Muslims generally the real 'terrorists'? Who are the real players behind all these games, terrorising the world? Who was instrumental in all these havoc or chaos if not the big powers of the divides – the West and the East - that had killed thousands of innocent Muslims and raged almost the entire Muslim world? Not to point fingers though, but even without going into details, the whole world knew who they were.

The Muslims faced inordinate problems with the Western Christian powers following the fall of Muslim empire. Since then, the Muslims were disunited. They were too weak to stop the onslaught of the belligerent West.

The Muslims looked to the OIC, as an organisation, to protect them but alas, it was too weak and it even did not dare enough to register collectively its strong displeasure against the big powers or the perpetrators. Thus, due to this ineffectiveness of the OIC, a certain group of frustrated Muslims who could not tolerate the nonsense, out of vengeance they became extremist 'jihadists', though small in numbers they created havoc by committing terrorism to vent their anger.

On the whole, they are just a meagre group of 'desperados' who fight for the unaccomplished justice in their lands – be Muslims or otherwise. Therefore, it is very unfair to blame the Muslims overall and brand them as terrorist whereas the big perpetrators are well praised as 'peace-makers' and 'saviours'.

In this scenario of the world craziness, unless the OIC members are honestly willing to unite to face together the present challenges boldly to demonstrate their political will to emphasise their role in the world affairs, the OIC will continue to fail its members. In fact, the current crisis in the Middle East should not had happened if the OIC is effectively playing a productive role to pacify the situation between the warring parties. It should build bridges of communication and discussion, and intelligent dialogues between conflicting parties.

In the current quagmire situation in the Middle East, where many parties and nations involved, it appears that the situation is becoming more serious and will be protracted until and unless a concerted effort is made among the nations involved to meet to settle the issue.

Aside from the inability of OIC to help solving conflicts in Syria and Iraq and elsewhere in the Muslim countries, the OIC also failed for so long to realise the importance of enhancing and exploiting to their advantage the big potential from the riches of Muslim countries. Through cooperation to exploit the rich God given resources in the member states, it can facilitate to develop whatever resources they possess to become a major economic power. Some of them might realise its potentials, but the majority of them, particularly the rich ones, are still wearing blinkers for not wanting to invest their money. They are just too happy to be the followers of the West and invest their money there to maintain their comfortable lives, let alone the feeling and the suffering of the other poor Muslim countries.

In view of the lackadaisical Muslim leaders to move forward for transformation, the Muslim countries are unable to get out from the clutches of the West - financially and militarily. Thus, in most issues affecting the Muslim ummah, the OIC as a group had refrained from making any independent strong stand in the world crises, because it did not want to directly offend its patrons and friends in the West that protected them. In this regard, one could transparently see that, for example, the protracted issue of Palestine directly facing the Arabs remained unresolved despite of the atrocity committed by the Israel Zionist regime. Certain of the Arab members even collaborated with the West to protect the Israel regime. The worst is Egypt that had the audacity to close its excess borders to suffocate and to weaken the movements of its Muslim brothers in Palestine.

But the worst shameful scenario was the episode in which the coalition forces unilaterally led by the United States with its ally, the Great Britain, invaded Iraq in 2003 to punish Saddam Hussein, a staunch Muslim Sunni and a champion for the Muslim Sunnis. The members of the OIC in this critical situation were divided, not in consensus and dilemma as to how to handle the grave situation affecting the Muslims due to the pressure of the United States. Thus, in the end Saddam Hussein was left alone that led to the total destruction of Iraq. To this day many Sunni Muslims considered Saddam Hussein died as a hero and a martyr. The invasion of Iraq was the nastiest scheme or mission to destroy the cradle of Muslim civilisation in the modern world history, successfully executed by the President Bush of the United States and the Prime Minister Tony Blair of the Great Britain in this 21st century.

The OIC is really a dead duck. It failed to defend Muslims and Islam against the Christian West perpetrators. The defeat of Saddam Hussein had led to open conflicts, not only in Iraq but also in Syria, between the Sunnis and the Shiites and the other minorities. With the emergence of the extremist ISIS, the situation became worse. With the involvement of big powers of the divide – the West and Russia – and their forces bombing sporadically targeting the ISIS and other insurgents in Syria and Iraq, resulted in the killing and displacement of millions of innocent civilians on the ground.

The region has become a big quagmire of untold misery to the people in the area. To this end, the OIC is just like a paralysed 'sick old man' suffering from 'chronic diabetes' disease. It had become powerless and 'legless' as if it had been amputated under Islamic criminal (hudud) law.

Away from the Middle East debacle, but still related to the OIC though in the Southeast Asia, it was interesting to note that the West felt hurt on the verbal instigation by the former Prime Minister of Malaysia, Tun Dr Mahathir when he called on the Muslim world during the OIC conference in October 2003 to boycott the Dutch products due to their film "Fitna" that humiliated Islam. It was apparent that he was disappointed with the inaction on the part of the OIC.

Arising from his boycott call, many negative comments hurled at him. To him those comments levelled at him were normal for he was famous for his straight talk and blunt comments on world and local issues as well. He was and is still a seasoned and experienced politician, admired both by friends and foes.

In connection with his call for boycotting the Dutch products, there was a very strong critic made against him but very relevant by a person using pseudonym 'venividici' who said:

"Muslims are idiots. Muslim countries are net-importers of food. Should we stop exporting the food, they would die starving. We

would see they would be starving in the streets of Malaysia, Pakistan, Bangladesh and so forth. We talk about a group of people who are ungrateful biting the hands that feed them".

What a shame to the Muslims overall, but like it or not it was a very relevant and interesting comment for the 'sleeping' Muslims to digest. It is a fact that the Muslim countries, including Malaysia, are not self-sufficient in food production to feed their own mouths. Therefore, the Muslim countries should not take it lightly but to take heed of the remarks by trying to produce enough essential food for themselves, in the first place, along with other industrial developments for export.

Of course, the Muslim countries, if they unite, they can boycott certain products but at the same time, they must be prepared and dare to face the consequences arising out of such action. The history of boycotting was not new, even the Prophet of Islam (Muhammad) himself and his followers at the beginning of Islam were once boycotted for three years by the Meccan Quraish kufar (idol worshipers) but they survived accordingly though with difficulties.

In this modern era, should there be any food embargo from the producing countries, the Muslim countries also, if need be as a form of retaliation, can even use oil as a weapon by invoking oil export embargo to those hostile countries concerned. But then, the Muslims must be prepared to sacrifice together to face any eventualities that would be forthcoming. In this regard, a strong OIC as an organisation can play a big role. However, it may not be the case due to disunity among the members, and for this the OIC is aptly, as some people had made satirically remark, that OIC stands for as 'O I See'. It fits its name. It is already dead and functions only as 'coffee shop' congregation of the Muslim elites.

Notwithstanding, the open and direct call by Dr Mahathir was daring and praiseworthy one. As a Muslim and a Malaysian seasoned states-man who championed to uphold the dignity of Muslim ummah, Muslims should support and appreciate for what he said.

As repeatedly said, the OIC failed to move in line with its vision and mission. Similarly, the United Nations had many noble intentions and mission too but in certain issues often failed to defend and uphold the rights of the oppressed due to chauvinist attitude of big brothers in the organisation. In other words, in certain areas, it is analogous to the failure of the OIC. It failed, thus far, to solve the Palestinian issue and other big issues affecting the Muslims and non-Muslim in general throughout the world. The UN members in the assembly and the permanent members of the UN Security Council also lack in authority to lead the world when faced with the hammer of the veto powers of the big five world powers. Thus, the United Nations itself does not have full democracy. However, with due respect to the UN, it does not mean that it is not affective at all, much credit to it in solving many world issues but it needs further refinements and changes.

The Middle East was once the cradle of civilization and the commercial centre of the world with the most cosmopolitan outlook. It is now under 'siege' and destruction at the hands and vagaries of the West. The sick OIC could not contribute much to help to alleviate and pacify the situation. Thus the disunity of its members has exacted its toll on the entire Muslim ummah.

On politic, the West while never stop lecturing Muslim countries on democracy and human rights but they themselves do not practise in earnest where it is due. They apply the policy of double standards. Where they have political interest, they support with no qualm the autocratic regimes in the Middle East. Indeed, it is very true as the Professor Noam Chomsky, a Crypto Zionist, rightly said in May 2011 that Washington and its allies would do everything in their powers to make sure that the people in the Middle East would not get regimes of their choice.

The Western powers are cagey of the Islamist power, especially in the Middle East, because their interest entrenched in the region would be in jeopardy. A strong democratic government that legitimately elected by the people will never tolerate the autocratic government like the Wahhabi Royal Saudi Arabia as an example to exist. Even a strong autocratic government will not be tolerated by the West, for instance the Saddam Hussein regime, for that the United Stated invaded Iraq to pin it down. The Western powers feared to lose their 'friends' that protected their oil interest there. The puppet autocratic governments supported by them would behave well. The truth is that the Western powers, including Russia and China all the way, are wary of a united Muslim world under a unified Islamist command.

On food production, the OIC noted long time ago about it. They were much concerned about the insufficiency of food production in all the member countries. The members are aware that they depended much on external sources to meet part of their food requirements, even though many of them possessed vast areas of arable and grazing land. In fact, the OIC countries have the potential to produce enough grain for their own people. However, thus far in this agriculture issue, it does not seem to be interested to pursue to develop this important industry to see that the Muslim countries are self-sufficient enough to feed their populations. The question is how long the Muslims can depend on the food imports from the big non-Muslim producers?

The OIC, indeed, needs to restructure itself, in form and substance, if it wants to be relevant and play a role as the United Nations of the Muslim ummah. The failure of its many resolutions suggested that the OIC could never be effective as an organisation because the components or member-states are 'more powerful' than the mother organisation (that is OIC) itself.

Fruitful cooperation and consolidation on the platform of the OIC can take place only if its members can give priority to problem solving of Muslim ummah vis-a-vis their own sovereign states. Muslim society needs to change its paradigm as it did under the Prophet Muhammad (pbuh), in whose time the ummah or communities replaced the tribes-fanatic, but not to the extent of discarding them. Likewise the Muslim ummah today needs to replace the strong nation-state racial sentiment but of course not to dismantle them. In the different analogy, it does not mean that nation-states need to be abolished but like the early Muslim community, modem Muslims need to temper down their race or clannish sentiment or identities and sovereignties so that every state stands on equal footing in the organisation. Thus, the OIC would become the 'mother and supreme' over and above the member nation-states. With such structural transformation, if can be formalised, perhaps the OIC may stay relevant and be more dynamic in handling any issues facing the Muslim ummah as a whole. As it is now, the OIC has become a mockery to Islam itself because of its sub-standard action and is surviving under 'paralysis in analysis' syndrome.

In fighting spirit, it also seemed that the members of the OIC to have conveniently forgotten or ignored the importance of jihad in the way of Allah (fisabilillah) against their enemies of which it would be touched on in chapter 9.

Based on the foregoing scenario of the past and current failures of the OIC in playing its role, is it still relevant? Perhaps, as a collective voice, whether forceful or not, it may be still relevant to exist on that score despite of its non-performance, but it needs revitalisation and overhaul like the mal-functioned engine, failing which it would be useless and for which it is better to discard and forget about it altogether. To let the OIC to remain in a state of dysfunction is a shame to Muslim ummah and a mockery to Islam itself.

8.3. Paradigm Shift.

It is already much said about the failures of the OIC. Negative though, but it is a fact which cannot be masked. It is an open secret of its failures and the Muslims at large are disappointed with it.

Looking objectively at the failures of the OIC as a big Muslim organisation, it is timely for Muslims nations in the South East Asian region, that is, Indonesia, Malaysia and Brunei to toy the idea of establishing an alternative smaller Islamic association in this part of the world. Furthermore, they are of the same ethnic group with the majority of them having the same Islamic faith and, therefore, it may be easier to look after their own affairs. It is also, probably, much easier to manage and co-operate within a smaller group. Therefore, in this regard, it is quiet pertinent for the Muslim countries in this part of this region to visualise the idea of forming an alternative regional association of Muslim countries in this archipelago instead of thinking about the failed OIC.

It is not a new idea any way for it was mooted long time ago, but due to political and ideology differences, it was not materialised. Now it is the time to invoke to continue the old vision but in is a new perspective in view of the current world scenario.

The Muslims in this archipelago need to get out from the current rut arising from the dysfunction of the OIC. Honestly, it is rather stressful and uncomfortable position for the Muslims in this region to face the ever growing hostility and challenges from others - politically, economically, religiously and even militarily. Therefore, these three countries can formulate something positively for the betterment and for the protection of their Muslim people. In term of population combined together, they have overall more than 250 million people to harness their potential.

These three countries are also rich in fertile lands and other natural resources as well, notably oil and other mineral resources. With such huge population coupled with abundant resources – human capital and natural resources - as a regional group working and cooperate together like that of the European Union (E.U.) definitely will give them an edge over others. Their economies and trades etc. can be developed and expended together and therefore they can stand on their own independently without much depending on the outsiders.

In this highly competitive and trying contemporary globalised world, it is worthwhile and beneficial for them to venture out and to crystallise the idea to form such an association to cooperate as a regional team vis-a-vis the ASEAN and other organisations. Of course, this new association should not abandon the ASEAN as a large economic cooperation as a whole.

Sceptics may criticise the idea as an economic digression or going backward in this globalised world. But if one looks at it positively, there is nothing disruptive, digressive or wrong with the idea at all, perhaps it is a healthy way of moving forward to excel within its domain without inveigling others. In fact, in the long run the idea would be beneficial for the Muslims in this part of the world. Again, it is important for the Muslims of the present generation to deeply think and fathom the consequences in the long term of their position in this part of the region vis-à-vis of the non-Muslim population if they do not unite.

Geographically, the Muslims in this region are being surrounded by non-Muslim nations, though currently they are friendly nations. Such being the case, it is an ideal idea to have a forward critical thinking to form their own grouping to ensure for the protection of their identity, turf and sovereignty. This is really meant for their survival as Allah said in the al-Quran that disbelievers would never like Islam unless the Muslims follow or submit to them.

These three Muslim nations are immediate neighbours and of the same ethnic and language group, having such a large population that are big enough to generate economies of large scale of their own for which definitely they would be able to survive among themselves.

If not wrongly quoted, Dr Mahathir, the ex-Prime Minister of Malaysia used to say that Malaysia should have 70 million people so that they can survive on their own economically. Now, with more than 250 million people combined in these three peaceful countries, they can create wonders to survive and to defend their own people.

In this new world order of the globalised world, the adventurous industrialised West or the East is busy trying to increase their dominance, either economically, militarily or both. It is therefore in the interest of the Malay Muslim ethnic groups, as a large community in this archipelago, to unite to ward off any untoward onslaught from outside forces - be it religious, cultural, economy and even military. In military strength, they may be well able to withstand foreign enemy excursion or intrusion, if any.

Probably, this new grouping can be in the form of association, union, confederation or commonwealth of Islamic nations of the South East Asia or whatever name may be, using the same existing currency or new currency, for example Gold Dinner. God willing (insya Allah) this noble vision, for the sake of Islam and Muslim ummah, would be able to realise, even in the short period of time if there is a political honesty and will of the leaders to do so.

Although Southeast Asia as a whole has the ASEAN, its composition consists of many nations of multi-ethnic and multi-religious groups unlike the European Union. Due to diversity nature of the ASEAN in its components and its policy of none-interference, it is not possible to have a very cohesive stand and close corporation without having to sacrifice or compromise of each member's national interest. Furthermore, in world politics, political inclination of certain members may not of the same wave length and alignment in the group.

In view of the above, a desire to have strong association of nation-states of the same religious and ethnic group is of paramount importance. Indeed, it is a realistic and holistic vision. It is a form of jihad as well. Trust (tawakkal) in Allah, hopefully with full of conviction it will be materialised with the blessing of Allah.

The Muslim world as mentioned above disgustingly weak in every field and therefore the Muslim countries in this region need to move fast to work out the idea or the proposition so that economically, financially, industrially and technologically etc. can be developed accordingly to enable them to progress and be developed countries. Though this would take time, eventually it would be realised and it would be time well spent. Islam enjoined Muslims to work hard and be patient in facing any eventualities. Therefore, as a start let the group right now move and consolidate its people to achieve the vision.

The countries have sufficient assets to deploy and organise and it would be for them to identify the resources available. This would entirely be possible if they start to think, to plan, to strategies and to take the first few critical steps forward. Even the first few steps can yield fruitful and positive results.

The big powers and other non-Muslim nations probably may voice dissention and may not welcome the proposition of such association because they also have their own political agendas as well in this region. Nevertheless, there should be a strong political conviction and political will of these three nations to stand tall against any objections or eventualities. There must be political jihad or struggle to achieve this noble vision as mentioned above. This paradigm shift may face many obstacles, but the Muslims in this region should be bold enough and hold fast to the Islamic principles as enshrined in the al-Quran and al-Sunnah of Prophet Muhammad (pbuh). They should never be in a wavering and nervous mode.

Perhaps again, this may be a long shot, but the people of this region should have visions and dare to change and to chart the blue rough ocean without fear. They should not behave like the Arab brothers in the Middle East, always fighting among them without end, so much so enabling the foreign elements and forces to come into the scene to meddle into their affairs, politically, economically and militarily. It is a real and living example of mockery and disservice to Islam.

As already stated, the land areas of these three countries are big enough, especially Indonesia, with plenty of resources and labour. Overall, their lands are fertile and good for agriculture. They are also rich in oil and other mineral recourses. With these resources, if properly and intelligently exploited, it can turn them into one of the richest countries economically in the world. The countries have large reservoirs of human capital resources to meet the modern demand by training them with knowledge of technical skills. With the large population coupled with technical skills, the countries can automatically generate sufficient and large internal economies that can look after the welfare of their own people and far beyond. There is no reason as to why these countries cannot formulate some sort of solid frame-works or infrastructures to cooperate and consolidate for mutual benefits of the people as a whole in this, so far, peaceful region.

In a short time to come, this new group will become an equal and respectable global partner for peace and prosperity in this part of the world, if not the whole world. In the world politics, probably it is better for this grouping to stay as a non-alignment group, but should stay put with the Muslim brothers, if feasible.

This vision may be a tall order, but there is nothing to stop them from crystallising and realising this noble idea. As stated above, the vision was not new and strange. It geminated on and off from time to time, but perhaps, due to political differences and interference, the idea was kept on shelve indefinitely. Certain powers will definitely chary about this kind of idea as evident in the Arab countries in the Middle East.

Nonetheless, why worry because there is nothing achievable without trying and sacrificing, even to jihad with life.

In the current scenario of many world or regional conflicts, involving Muslims and non-Muslims, it is therefore imperative to make paradigm change in the spirit of regional fraternity within the Muslim community or ummah to strengthen the bond among the Muslims in this region. This is a political jihad indeed. Let alone the adversaries. This vision of mutual consolidation is solely germinated on the realisation that the Muslim ummah needs to be resilient on their own in this current era challenges being faced by the Muslim nations.

It should be realised that development and progress based on the Western secular principles alone cannot bring forward the genuine Muslim ummah, let alone be at par with developed secular nations. The Muslims have to follow the footstep of the successful Muslims of the past by complying with the true teaching of Islam as enshrined in the holy al-Quran and the Sunnah of the Prophet Muhammad (pbuh), failing which they will not be able to come up in life again as before. Nevertheless, be aware of the destructive agents of the imperialist, secularist and liberalist for they will not rest on their laurel to stop this vision from being materialised.

Therefore, this unity and cooperation of the people of these three countries should be of priority. Development of holistic human capital in religion, modern technology and science should be of priority as well so that it will grow in line with the growth of the population and world challenge. The young intellectuals with the relevant expertise and skills can come to the fore to support this noble vision for survival of the Muslim nations in this region. A nation definitely needs development but must be in line with Islam as a progressive religion, not a backward religion as claimed by some of the ignorant and negative people.

This idea may be construed as a fantasy only by some, nevertheless, God willing there is nothing impossible if the people of these countries want to forge ahead, especially the younger generation, to take up the challenge. The spirit of brotherhood and jihad for the holistic transformation of the people has to come up to the forefront. The crux of the whole thing is that whether the Muslims of Malay ethnic groups of this archipelago are ready for that. If not ready, then they would never ever be ready.

With the positive attitude, the will to change to tune up with the changing global scenario will not remain as an illusion but an achievable reality. Certainly, visionary and critical thinking people of this region for the benefit of the ummah are not willing remain subservient to other powers all the time. This is not merely a day-dream, but it is an achievable one. The Muslim political divides due to different ideology should forget the differences and close rank so as to enable them to forge ahead together for the sake of Allah and survival of Muslim people.

Having so much said about Islamic fraternity and unity, one pertinent question comes to the fore is that why the Muslims are so passive and not feeling an iota of jealousy towards the success of the European Union (EU) of the Christian West?

Therefore, in this regard let the Muslims of Southeast Asia forge ahead to emulate the success of the EU. If the EU can succeed, God willing, there is no reason as to why the Muslims in this part of the world cannot succeed if there is a sincere intent to do so.

As the first step, the Muslim nations of the Southeast Asia should start moving right from now; do not wait because good and positive ideas often than not will fizzle out in no time.

Islam taught about peace, justice, moderation and fraternity among the Muslims from the beginning of its advent. Notwithstanding, the modern Muslims are suspicious and at loggerhead with each other. This is an anti-climax. It appears these people are willing to bear the wrath of Allah for they clearly go against the teaching of al-Quran and al-Sunnah. They are more interested in clanship or nationalism and power at whatever cause rather than the unity of the world Muslim ummah. In general, they are un-Islamic in their behaviour and practice. Thus, the Muslim ummah in this archipelago should wake up and change their paradigm to explore all the possibilities to chart their right path into the new horizon without fear.

8.4. Islamic Banking and Monetary Gold Dinar System.

While talking about the possibility of forming an Islamic organisation in Southeast Asia, it is also relevant to explore the possibility of using monetary Gold Dinar system, just like the European Union using Euro. Euro Pound has proved to be successfully used in Europe vis-a-vis US dollars.

During the time of Prophet Muhammad (pbuh) and during the Islamic Empire, the Muslims used Gold Dinar and Dirham monetary system. It once became an Islamic icon to show the strength of real wealth of the Islamic empire and dynasty. However, due to disunity and the diminishing Islamic practice by the later Caliphs and their followers, the great Islamic empire fell. Then the act of debasement of the dinar and dirham followed suit and therefore it died a natural death.

It is just ridiculous as to why the Muslims could not revive the use Gold Dinar system again in the contemporary Muslim world vis-a-vis the American Dollar and the Euro Pound. Probably, the real problem is the Muslim themselves for not wanting to revive it, especially the rich Arab countries that kept their oil money in the West. Again in this regard, the pressure from the West to bungle this dinar-dirham idea would be great, but God willing, if there is strong Islamic spirit and jihad among the Muslim ummah, this complex issue can be surmounted accordingly.

As regards the Gold Dinar, Abū Bakr ibn Abi Maryam reported that he heard that the Messenger of Allah said:

> **"A time is certainly coming over mankind in which there will be nothing (left) that will be of use (or benefit) save a Dinar (a gold coin) and a Dirham (a silver coin)."** Hadith from Ahmad bin Hambal.

This Prophet's prophecy clearly anticipated that the eventual collapse of the man-made capitalist Western paper monetary with interest system that is now though functioning but its value would be fluctuating off and on around the world was very true. This paper monetary system instability is unstoppable and will be finally flopped.

The world has witnessed recessions, inflation and economic collapse, off and on, in this modern day. This non-Islamic conventional monetary capitalist system will definitely not be able to contain itself to withstand the volatility of the paper monetary value, thus it would naturally collapse in one of these days, soon or in the near future. Only Gold Dinar and Dirham monetary system is the alternative one that can help to stabilise the world monetary system.

It is, therefore, already time for the Muslim countries to take a concerted effort to introduce the Gold Dinar monetary system in the Muslim world. If it is not possible to use the Gold Dinner currency for the entire Muslim world now, at least for the time being, use it first in the Muslim countries in the Southeast Asia. At the same time, slowly do away with the conventional financial banking system.

As a consequent of financial crises in Asia in 1997, the former Prime Minister of Malaysia, Tun Dr Mahathir Muhammad proposed to use Gold Dinar as legal tender in international trade transaction within Muslim world. Its purpose is to lessen reliance on American Dollar and at the same time to lessen the effect of dollar instability in international trading. Gold Dinar currency intrinsically tied down to gold value and therefore its value is much more stable comparatively with any paper currency without gold backing. His idea probably was not well taken-up by some of the rich OIC members then. However, Dr Mahathir intended to use Gold Dinar currency in Malaysia in 2003, but after his retirement as Prime Minister, the idea indefinitely was put off.

Dr Mahathir is dynamic Muslim leader in Malaysia. He was and is very vocal in his critique either in local politics or on certain world issues affecting the Muslims. He used to give strong critics or remarks towards the failure of Muslims with regard to political inertia, economic underdevelopment and lack of democracy or unrepresentative governments. He also strongly criticised as to the malaise afflicting the OIC. He too used to strongly criticise the West on handling the world issues particular pertaining to atrocities in Palestine and elsewhere in the Muslim world.

Touching again on the Gold Dinar currency, PAS (Islamic Party) Government of Kelantan, one of the states in Malaysia, launched their own Gold Dinar on 12ᵗʰ August 2010. They tried to give legal tender status to the Gold Dinar currency, but vetoed by the Federal Government of Malaysia for it was against the Federal Constitution. Nevertheless, it was daring one and noble effort on the part of Kelantan State Government in its attempt to use Islamic Gold Dinar currency. Though it was against the Federal Constitution, but if there was then a political collaboration and political will in this regard, the man-made constitution might be well amended accordingly to accommodate the noble overture of the Kelantan State Government.

As already stated that the Christian countries in Europe though with different ethnic groups, languages and economic standings were able to come up together to form European Union (EU) successfully with its own currency. In this regard, they are much better off in cooperation and unity than the Muslim counterpart despite of the never ending preaching about Islamic brotherhood or fraternity in Islam. The Christians of Europe political approach and strategy in respect of world affairs are exemplary and praise-worthy with regard to cooperation among themselves. Whereas, the Muslims instead of cooperation and consolidation, they quarrel among themselves in spite of believing in Oneness of Allah. Sometimes they quarrel on petty matters that are nothing much to do with the basic Islamic faith but out of egoism.

The Europeans are not only helping each other in economic sphere but also in defence because they are all members of the NATO. On the other hands, the Muslims just talk and see only. Their negative attributes are not because of Islam per se but they themselves have become disobedient and have diminished in upholding the very teaching of Islam.

Touching on Islamic finance and banking, it appears that it is well in progress and developing. If thing goes well, it is not impossible in the near future that the Islamic financial system will compete with that of the world conventional financial system.

The Islamic finance is now giving quite a challenge to the traditional Wall Street finance. Nevertheless, the Islamic finance is still a long way to go, but it has big potential to grow and to be a giant in the world market in the future because of the large Muslim population. It may one day in not far distant future it would be truly an alternative to Wall Street.

The Islamic finance has grown tremendously since it first emerged in the 1970's. Since then, the global Islamic banking assets had grown tremendously.

In the context of Malaysia, the Islamic finance industry has been in existence for over 30 years. The enactment of the Islamic Banking Act 1983 enabled Malaysia to set up the country's first Islamic Bank. Thereafter, with the liberalisation of the Islamic financial system, more Islamic financial institutions established.

Malaysia's long track of good record in building a successful domestic Islamic financial industry gives the country a solid foundation. Thus, this financial stability adds to the richness, diversity and maturity of the financial system of the country.

Currently, Malaysia has a significant number of full-fledged Islamic banks including several foreign owned entities. Conventional institutions have established Islamic subsidiaries and the entities are conducting foreign currency business as well. All financial institutions are given permission to conduct both ringgit and non-ringgit (Malaysian currency) businesses.

As Malaysia continues to progress in the industry, it invites foreign financial institutions as well to establish international Islamic banking business in Malaysia to conduct foreign currency business.

On international level of Islamic group, the Rapid Growth Markets (RGMs) Qatar, Indonesia, Saudi Arabia, Malaysia, United Arab Emirates and Turkey, recently known as "QISMUT", is expected to see their collective Islamic banking assets reach an estimated US$1.6 trillion in 2018.

The future success of Islamic banks in diversifying to build regional and global brands will be measured not only by growth of assets but more so by quality of growth. Excellence in customer focus and service, operational transformation and expanding international reach is the key factor to moving from merely providing a service to long-term sustainable growth.

Global Islamic banking assets are set to exceed $3.4 trillion by 2018, fueled by economic growth in core Islamic financial markets, according to specialists at Ernst & Young (EY).

EY's Global Islamic Banking Centre said the combined profits of Islamic banks broke the $10 billion mark for the first time at the end of 2013.

While the profit numbers for Islamic banks are impressive, they are still, on average, 15-19 per cent lesser than traditional banks in these markets. Reaching out into regional or world market and operational transformation, which are currently underway in several leading Islamic banks, will help to close this gap.

Nevertheless, despite of its growth, its total asset base of $1 trillion is still less than one per cent of global conventional banking assets.

Potential growth of the Islamic finance vis-a-vis the conventional system in the future is to stay and very positive and progressive if efficiently, ethically and transparently managed.

To transform the entrenched conventional financial system to the Islamic system is never an easy task. Nevertheless, currently it is progressing well to the acceptance of many, Muslims and the non-Muslims alike. Malaysia has played a leading part in this transformation without infringing the conventional system. Couple with this, it is high time for the Muslim world to introduce the Islamic Gold Dinar monetary system without much ado, especially in this Southeast Asia region.

Here, probably the OIC, if it is still surviving, can play an active role in propagating this Gold Dinar idea and Islamic financial system whole heartedly without feeling of stress and pressure from the Western world. It should stand tall to face any hassle from any quarters if at all in seeing the Gold Dinar monetary system goes through. This is the only way forward for the Muslims to progress to the future. It is now or never to make a paradigm shift for the sake of Allah and for the good of Muslim ummah.

CHAPTER 9.   JIHAD AND SACRIFICE

J ihad is a sincere sacrifice for the sake or in the way of Allah. Jihad means struggle hard or striving hard in an effort to better oneself and so forth, for example, to better inner-self towards Allah, to acquire knowledge, to enhance economic development, to strengthen Islam, to defend Islam and the countries against enemies of Islam. Military action against belligerent enemies of Islam is included when necessary. Scholars, however, differ in their interpretation of jihad because of its wide connotations.

The word jihad appears, in one form or another, 164 times in the al-Quran according to one count. Jihad is an Islamic term referring to the religious duty of Muslims to maintain and protect Islamic religion, self, family, property, society, country and so forth in the way of Allah. Jihad means to strive hard, to apply to oneself, to struggle or to persevere. A person engaged in jihad is called a *mujahid*, the plural of which is *mujahidin*. The word jihad appears frequently in the Quran often in the idiomatic expression of "striving in the way of Allah *(al-jihad fi sabil illah)*", that is to refer to the act of striving to serve the purposes of Allah in this world.

Jihad simply means an honest struggle and sacrifice in the name of Allah. It requires self-confident, firmness, bravery and determination to do virtuous deeds and to do away the wrongs or the satanic vain desires.

As stated earlier, Muslim scholars do not have consensus in their interpretation or definition of jihad. Nevertheless, generally jihad is a call to protect and defend Islam against it enemies and to enjoin to do the righteous deeds, and to go against or forbid the wrong doings or evil deeds and to excel oneself in this worldly life within the ambit of Islam principles.

From the above, jihad could be inferred for the mujahidin to have some of the following attributes:

- Realising the virtuous responsibility to carry it on at all the times.
- Holding the principle that jihad is for the cause of Allah only.
- The right objective or vision to uphold the sanctity of Islamic syariah.
- To have high spirit of struggle and sacrifice of self and property and always ready to face the risk with full of patience and trust in Allah irrespective of the outcomes to defend Islam.

Therefore, jihad is any virtuous deeds in the way of Allah such as jihad with the heart, mind, words and deeds, knowledge, writing (pen), weapons, self (life) and property. Allah said in surah al-Hujrat, verse (49:15):

إِنَّمَا ٱلْمُؤْمِنُونَ ٱلَّذِينَ ءَامَنُواْ بِٱللَّهِ وَرَسُولِهِۦ ثُمَّ لَمْ يَرْتَابُواْ وَجَـٰهَدُواْ بِأَمْوَٰلِهِمْ وَأَنفُسِهِمْ فِى سَبِيلِ ٱللَّهِ أُوْلَـٰٓئِكَ هُمُ ٱلصَّـٰدِقُونَ

⬡ ١٥

"Only those are the believers who have believed in Allah and His Messenger, and afterward doubt not but strive (jihad) with their wealth and their lives for the cause of Allah. Those! They are the truthful."

In surah surah an-Nahl, verse (6:90) Allah enjoined people to be fair, patient, help others, particularly the kinsfolks and prohibit any evil deeds as follows:

ﷺإِنَّ ٱللَّهَ يَأْمُرُ بِٱلْعَدْلِ وَٱلْإِحْسَٰنِ وَإِيتَآيِٕ ذِى ٱلْقُرْبَىٰ
وَيَنْهَىٰ عَنِ ٱلْفَحْشَآءِ وَٱلْمُنكَرِ وَٱلْبَغْيِ يَعِظُكُمْ لَعَلَّكُمْ تَذَكَّرُونَ ﴿٩٠﴾

"Verily, Allah enjoins al-adl (justice) and al-ihsan (patient in performing duties in full submission to Allah in totality) and giving (help) to kinship and forbids Al-fahsha' (all evil deeds) and al-munkar (all that is prohibited by Islamic laws) and al-baghy (all kinds of oppression). He admonishes you, that you may take heed."

In surah at-Taubah, verse (9:111) Allah loved the Muslims who loved Allah with their souls and properties to fight in the cause of Him. They kill or may get kill but Allah promised them Paradise and that is the greatest success.

ﷺإِنَّ ٱللَّهَ ٱشْتَرَىٰ مِنَ ٱلْمُؤْمِنِينَ أَنفُسَهُمْ وَأَمْوَٰلَهُم بِأَنَّ لَهُمُ ٱلْجَنَّةَ
يُقَٰتِلُونَ فِى سَبِيلِ ٱللَّهِ فَيَقْتُلُونَ وَيُقْتَلُونَ وَعْدًا عَلَيْهِ حَقًّا فِى ٱلتَّوْرَىٰةِ
وَٱلْإِنجِيلِ وَٱلْقُرْءَانِ وَمَنْ أَوْفَىٰ بِعَهْدِهِۦ مِنَ ٱللَّهِ فَٱسْتَبْشِرُواْ بِبَيْعِكُمُ
ٱلَّذِى بَايَعْتُم بِهِۦ وَذَٰلِكَ هُوَ ٱلْفَوْزُ ٱلْعَظِيمُ ﴿١١١﴾

"Verily, Allah has purchased of the believers their lives and their properties; for the price that theirs shall be the Paradise. They fight in Allah's cause, so they kill and get kill. It is a promise in truth that is binding on Him in the Taurat (Torah) and the Injeel (Gospel) and the Quran. And who is truer to his covenant than Allah? Then rejoice in the bargain that you have concluded and that is the supreme success."

To stress the point again that Islam is a universal religion of peace, justice and moderation in every aspect of life the Muslim does within the

34

parameter of Islam principles. It enjoins people to do good deeds and to inhibit from doing anything that Allah prohibited. Islam, therefore, abhors extremism, terrorism or transgression in whatever form whatsoever, be it in submission to Allah or in connection with fellow human beings and even to the fauna and flora, because the universe and anything contained therein is His creatures.

Nonetheless, the non-Muslim antagonists criticised Islam by saying that Allah's commandments are unfair since al-Quran contained dozens of verses promoting violence and that Allah ordered Muslims to kill disbelievers. However, they were grossly mistaken and therefore they were wrong to say so because the verses were pertaining to self-defence or protection of the Muslims against the onslaught of disbeliever intruders. In this regard, if one honestly looks at the world history the disbelievers, particularly the Christians, were far much worst in committing violence comparatively with the Muslims. The antagonists did not comprehend the verses but they simply tried to twist it literally to put Islam in bad light since they never like Islam anyway.

They also argued that the Quranic verses called for the Muslims to make war against the disbelievers in the name of Islam. Some verses, they pointed out, were with the command to chop off heads and limbs and kill infidels wherever they might be hiding. The Muslims who refused to join the war were hypocrites and Allah warned them that they would be in the Hell if they did not join the slaughter. They picked certain verses in isolation without looking into the back ground of the revelations like the verses in surah al-Baqarah etc. and one of the verses is verse (2:191) as follows:

وَٱقْتُلُوهُمْ حَيْثُ ثَقِفْتُمُوهُمْ وَأَخْرِجُوهُم مِّنْ حَيْثُ أَخْرَجُوكُمْ وَٱلْفِتْنَةُ

أَشَدُّ مِنَ ٱلْقَتْلِ وَلَا تُقَٰتِلُوهُمْ عِندَ ٱلْمَسْجِدِ ٱلْحَرَامِ حَتَّىٰ

يُقَٰتِلُوكُمْ فِيهِ فَإِن قَٰتَلُوكُمْ فَٱقْتُلُوهُمْ كَذَٰلِكَ جَزَآءُ ٱلْكَٰفِرِينَ

﴿١٩١﴾

35

"And kill them wherever you find them, and turn them out from where they have turned you out. And Al-Fitnah [disbelief and worshipping of others along with Allah] is worse than killing. And fight not with them at Al-Masjid-al-Haram (the sanctuary at Mecca), unless they (first) fight you there. But if they attack you, then kill them. Such is the recompense of the disbelievers."

As stated above, some of the verses were with regard to war and self-defence. It is preposterous to suppose that in war there would be no killing but to show mercy. If it were so, than it is not war. The war or the fight is for the cause of Allah against those who fight the Muslims, and therefore the Muslims have the right to kill them, otherwise the Muslims will be killed by them. However, in doing so, transgression is prohibited because Allah disliked transgression or extremism. Therefore, in this context, it is incorrect to say that Islam encourages violence and extremism. Although Allah is the most benevolent to all His creatures, He loves not those people who reject Islam for being ungrateful in refusing to worship Him alone because He is the One Who created them.

Since the disbelievers are ungrateful people and refuse to accept Islam, they cannot blame Allah for such ordainment. One should remember that Allah is the Creator of this entire universe and its contents therein. Therefore, all human creatures are His servants. They should worship Him and submit to Him alone without associating Him with any other things at all. They should follow His rules accordingly. It is as simple as that, period.

During Prophet Muhammad's life-time, and onwards to the present, the word 'jihad' was and is almost and always used in a military sense. Nevertheless, with regard to jihad as a 'holy war', there was no consensus in its definition because some scholars disagreed with the meaning of 'jihad' as 'holy war' since there was no such meaning in the Quran or authentic Hadith collections or in early Islamic literatures. However, some Muslim scholars, writers and translators of the Quran, the Hadith and other Islamic literatures translated the term "jihad" as "holy war". The terms used probably due to the influence of centuries-old Western propaganda. This could be a reflection of the Christians usage of the term "Holy War" to refer to the Crusades of thousand years ago. However, the Arabic words for "war" are "harb" or "qital," which are found in the Quran and Hadith. Notwithstanding, the concept of jihad was consensus among Islamic scholars that it would always include or involve arm struggle against the enemies of Islam.

Again on jihad, certain scholars said that jihad was divided into two classifications or meanings: an inner spiritual struggle (the "greater jihad") and an outer physical struggle against the enemies of Islam (the "lesser jihad") but this report or hadith was considered weak or falsehood.

This so-called Hadith of 'a greater and lesser jihad' considered weak because it was a later development originated from the 11th century book, 'The History of Baghdad', written by an Islamic scholar al-Khatib al-Baghdadi. Reference was made to Layth on the authority of 'Ata', on the authority of Abu Rabah, on the authority of Jabir ibn Abd-Allah, the companion of Prophet Muhammad, who said:

"The Prophet (pbuh) returned from one of his battles, and thereupon told us: 'You have arrived with an excellent arrival, you have come from the Lesser Jihad to the Greater Jihad - the striving of a servant (of Allah) against his desires.'"

The 'lesser' versus 'greater' jihad hadith and other similar narrations were weak and false as had been shown by many Islamic scholars. They serve no purpose in Islamic law or thought, and contradict sahih hadith (genuine hadith) and the al-Quran itself. Thus, a hadith or report saying about 'lesser and greater jihad' was a falsehood.

Therefore, this concept of a lesser and greater jihad has no validity within Islam. However, the report had been very influential among some Muslims, particularly the Sufis.

Most probably, the above hadith produced by certain scholars with the influence of the Western ideas to prevent the Muslims from military jihad against the belligerent Christian West at that time. Thus, instead of military jihad, Muslims became passive, introvert and focussed more towards devotion to Allah only, like the Sufism by forgetting the worldly needs of Muslim ummah. Forgetting the worldly needs is not the teaching of Islam because as the servants and caliphs of Allah, the Muslims are required to work and struggle hard to excel in both, worldly and spiritually.

As regards the holy war, there are so many references to jihad as a military struggle in Islamic writings and it is therefore incorrect to claim that the interpretation of jihad as 'holy war' is wrong.

While most Islamic theologians in the classical period (750–1258 A.D.) understood jihad to be a military endeavour, however after Islamic conquest stagnated and the caliphate broke up into smaller states, the military jihad diminished in its vigour or was made less important if not put-off altogether. Even when the Ottoman Empire carried on a new holy war of expansion in the seventeenth century, the war or jihad was not universally pursued by other smaller nation-states of Muslim countries, either they were too weak or captivated by nationalistic feeling rather than Islamic fraternity and unity. Probably, this was the reason that the Muslims did not make attempt to recover Spain or Sicily.

Again, when the Ottomans called for a jihad against Allied powers during World War I, their appeal did not unite the Muslim world or came to nought. From this experience, one could gauge that the dynamism of jihad had been diminished because their Islamic faith had been weaken in the first place. This is so even to the present day. Furthermore, the jihad call is more on personal interest and power rather than in the name of Allah or striving in the way of Allah *(al-jihad fi sabilillah)*.

The call for war or jihad in the way of Allah (fi sabililah) is only for justice against the evil and tyranny or suppressive ruler. In the 18th Century, the war between the Ottoman Turkey Empire with the Shafawi government of Iran was not the war in the way of Allah but for the sake of power or supremacy.

Earlier, in the middle of 15th Century the Ottoman Empire did not help the Muslim rulers in Spain against the belligerent Christians who conquered Granada in 1492 because both of the Muslim powers then had diminished in their Islamic practice but more inclined towards clanship or nationalism rather than helping the other Muslim brothers even though the Ottoman Turkey under Muhammad Al-Fateh had already conquered Constantinople by then in 1453. Tribalism or the spirit of nationalism had taken root over the spirit of fi sabililah. Thus, the last Muslim ruler in Granada capitulated to the Christian power.

The Christian conqueror forced the defeated Muslims to convert to Christianity and by 1502 Islam outlawed in Spain. They killed thousands of Muslims who refused to convert to Christianity or drove them out of Spain for good. By 1600 not a single Muslim was left in Spain. That was a great tragedy befallen on the Muslims in Spain simply because the Muslims were disunited and diminished in their faith in Allah at the time.

Since then there was no more universal spirit of brotherhood in Islam and in jihad. In the World War 1 (1914-1918), Turkey was in difficulties and called for war in the way of Allah (fi sabilillah) but it was of no avail because the Turkey government itself was very much diminished in its Islamic practice but more towards nationalism. Thus, it was natural (sunnatullah) that Allah would not help them.

The above is a good lesson for the Muslims of today to learn from it, but would they? They would not, because nationalism is more important than jihad in the way of Allah. They do not dare enough to risk their lives and sovereignty. That is the very reason the Muslims shun away from unity.

Within classical Islamic jurisprudence – the development of which dated back into the first few centuries after the Prophet's death – jihad was the only form of warfare permissible under Islam that might consist in wars against unbelievers, apostates, rebels, highway robbers and dissenters who renounced the authority of Islam. The primary aim of jihad as warfare was not the conversion of disbelievers to Islam by force, but rather for the defense and expansion of the Islamic state. The jihad was invoked by the head of the state but not by an individual.

In the broad spectrum, jihad is continuous as it was the command of Allah, not in theory only. One who dies in the way of Allah (fi sabilillah) is a martyr, whose sins remitted and would secure immediate entry to paradise. However, some argue that martyrdom is never automatic because it is within Allah's exclusive province or prerogative to judge who is worthy of that designation.

Briefly, jihad without going into details popularly used to describe generally into three different kinds of struggle or dimension:

- The internal-self spiritual struggle in upholding Islamic belief or faith to excel oneself to be closer to Allah to get His mercy, blessing and grace
- The struggle to build a good and prosperous Muslim society - economically, militarily etc.
- Holy war – the struggle to defend Islam, with military force if necessary, against its enemies.

As to holy war or simply war (harb or qital), Islam permits (some say directs) the Muslims to wage military war to protect the Muslims or Islam from their enemies when the Muslims or their territory are under attack. However, Islamic laws (syariah) set very strict rules in the conduct of such a war.

What can justify Jihad? There are a number of reasons but in al-Quran, it is clear that self-defence is always the underlying cause.

Permissible reasons for military jihad are as follows:

- Self-defence
- Strengthening Islam
- Protecting the freedom of Muslims to practise their faith
- Protecting Muslims against aggressors or oppression which could include overthrowing a tyrannical ruler
- Punishing an enemy who breaks an oath or covenant
- Putting right a wrong

A war is not a Jihad if the intention is to:

- Force people to convert to Islam
- Conquer other nations to colonise them
- Take territory for economic gain
- Settle disputes
- Demonstrate a leader's power

Although Prophet Muhammad (pbuh) engaged in military actions on a number of occasions, these were battles to survive, rather than conquest, and took place at a time when fighting among tribes was common.

Jihad is called for only to protect Muslims from aggressors and from cruelty. The Messenger of Allah (pbuh) called his adversaries first to come to terms and find ways to make peace with them. In the event that his adversaries threatened or invoked for war then the Messenger of Allah would prepare for war, but never would he wage the war in the first instance.

Thus, the essence of jihad is not to invoke war only. As stated earlier, jihad is a struggle and has a very wide meaning such as to contain the satanic vain greed and desire in oneself, to search for knowledge, to work for economic wellbeing and anything that is good for people. Therefore, it is grave misleading and incorrect to say that jihad is something that encourages war or terrorism, extremism or atrocity.

Suicide bombers to kill innocent people are not jihad but a form of extremism and terrorism. Nevertheless, Islam encourages or demands Muslims to invoke jihad to help Muslims who are under oppression or victimisation.

As regard to war, Allah said in surah al-Baqarah, verse (2:190):

وَقَـٰتِلُوا۟ فِى سَبِيلِ ٱللَّهِ ٱلَّذِينَ يُقَـٰتِلُونَكُمْ وَلَا تَعْتَدُوٓا۟ إِنَّ ٱللَّهَ لَا يُحِبُّ
ٱلْمُعْتَدِينَ ﴿١٩٠﴾

"And fight in the Way of Allah those who fight you, but transgress not the limits. Truly, Allah likes not the transgressors."

Thus, the Muslims are duty bound to defend Islam and fight against those who fight them but not be the transgressors. The above verse is very transparent for the Muslims to behave well within the limit allowable. Thus, extremism and terrorism are outside the teaching of Islam for this would taint the virtues or good image of Islam.

Although Islam is the religious of peace, Muslims are required to hold on seriously to jihad in case of war with non-Muslims. The call for jihad in the way of Allah is allowable only as the last resort and it should be subtly and judiciously executed, not to be carried away by emotion or unlimited anger that would result in unnecessary extremism, destruction and killing of innocent people.

From a story related by Imam Ahmad bin Hambal who received from Yunus bin al-Hassan who received from al-Aswad bin Sarii' who came to see the Messenger of Allah in order to go to war with him. They went to war and won. The fighting was brutal to the extent that they even killed children. The Messenger of Allah came to know about the incident and he said:

"What kind of act is this! This is an act of transgression by killing children. They killed future generation". Then a man said:

"O the Messenger of Allah, are not that the children that had been killed the children of non-believers?" The Messenger of Allah said:

"Not like that. Remember that those who are famous among you now are formerly the children of non-believers. Do not kill children. Every new born child is born in pure state of fitrah. Then his parents that make him a Jew, a Christian or Margian (Zoraostrian)". Hadith narrated by An-Nasaai.

That is the beauty, sincerity and the virtue of Islam. Killing or inflicting any injuries on innocent people is absolutely prohibited, including destruction of buildings etc. True Muslims will not kill children, women, old people and innocent people unlike the non-Muslims, for example in this present modern day warfare such as in Bosnia, Afghanistan, Iraq, Syria and elsewhere, where the disbelievers killed thousands of innocent Muslims by bombing, shooting and bayoneting, short of slaughtering by direct cutting the throats. Probably there could not be discounted altogether the instances of direct cutting the throats of the victims as well, knowing their hatred towards Muslims.

The true believers or Muslims, whatever happened, should be patient and not be feeble but keep on going and struggling hard without diminishing in trusting the fate in the hands of Allah. The unwavering faith in Allah is the weapon of inner strength that would finally lead to success.

As far as jihad is concerned, Allah said in surah an-Nisa' (4:74-76):

فَلْيُقَاتِلْ فِى سَبِيلِ ٱللَّهِ ٱلَّذِينَ يَشْرُونَ ٱلْحَيَوٰةَ ٱلدُّنْيَا بِٱلْأَخِرَةِ وَمَن يُقَاتِلْ فِى سَبِيلِ ٱللَّهِ فَيُقْتَلْ أَوْ يَغْلِبْ فَسَوْفَ نُؤْتِيهِ أَجْرًا عَظِيمًا ﴿٧٤﴾

"Let those (believers) who sell the life of this world for the Hereafter fight in the cause of Allah, and who so fights in the cause of Allah, and is killed or gets victory, We shall bestow on him a great reward."

وَمَا لَكُمْ لَا تُقَاتِلُونَ فِى سَبِيلِ ٱللَّهِ وَٱلْمُسْتَضْعَفِينَ مِنَ ٱلرِّجَالِ وَٱلنِّسَآءِ وَٱلْوِلْدَانِ ٱلَّذِينَ يَقُولُونَ رَبَّنَآ أَخْرِجْنَا مِنْ هَٰذِهِ ٱلْقَرْيَةِ ٱلظَّالِمِ أَهْلُهَا وَٱجْعَل لَّنَا مِن لَّدُنكَ وَلِيًّا وَٱجْعَل لَّنَا مِن لَّدُنكَ نَصِيرًا ﴿٧٥﴾

43

"And what is wrong with you that you fight not in the cause of Allah, and for those weak, ill-treated and oppressed among men, women, and children, whose cry is: 'Our Lord! Rescue us from this town whose people are oppressors; and raise for us from You one who will protect, and raise for us from You one who will help.'"

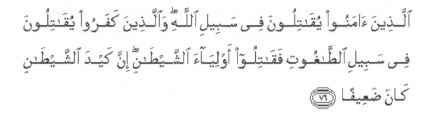

"Those who believe fight in the cause of Allah, and those who disbelieve, fight in the cause of taghut (Satan, etc.). So fight you against the friends of Satan; ever feeble indeed is the plot of Satan."

The Muslims who fight in the cause of Allah should be not afraid of their enemies. Their enemies are ever feeble for they are the friends of Satan.

The purpose of war is not for worldly gain but to fight in the cause of Allah (*fight fi sabilillah or war in the way Allah - it is analogous to holy war because if a jihadist were to die, he will die martyr*) against any cruelty or oppressors and whoever sincerely involved in it will get great reward from Allah in the world hereafter.

At the beginning of Islam, the pagan Quraish idol worshippers of Mecca oppressed and tortured the Muslims in Mecca that led to the plight, with the grace of Allah, of Prophet Muhammad (pbuh) to Medina. The above verses revealed while the Messenger of Allah was already in Medina but the verses would be continuously applicable forever, if such circumstances prevailed.

The mujahidin (those who engaged in jihad) fight with their lives for the cause of Allah, not for glory or the world vain desires, but sincerely because of Allah. They have their conviction that Allah will help them. Should they die, they die martyr and if they win, it is for the religion of Allah, not for pride or for the sake of power, for they would anyway die too later. This was the spirit of the mujahidin fighters in Afghanistan that was able to make the Russians combatant forces to withdraw from Afghanistan in May 1988.

Allah challenged the believers to fight in the cause of Allah against the enemies of Islam and to help the weak and the oppressed against the disbelievers who fight for the taghut (*friend of Satan that defied Allah and yielded to vain worldly desires for power and riches*). Nonetheless, in the present world, many instances where the honest people who dared to criticise the oppressive and wrong doings of the governments, especially of the autocratic regimes, had met with heavy punishment, including imprisonment or sentenced to death.

Notwithstanding, the truth and the right will always be prevailed, soon or later, over the falsehood and the wrongs. If at all the wrongs won, it would not last. However, in order to win over the wrongs, there must be a will to strive hard or jihad against all the wrong doings.

There are many other verses on jihad, for instance as hereunder, to protect the sanctity of Islam. The struggle to put things right and to uphold justice is something of noble cause although it is difficult to invoke but this struggle or jihad has to be kept on going.

In surat at-Taubah, verses (9:73-74), Allah said:

يَٰٓأَيُّهَا ٱلنَّبِىُّ جَٰهِدِ ٱلۡكُفَّارَ وَٱلۡمُنَٰفِقِينَ وَٱغۡلُظۡ عَلَيۡهِمۡ وَمَأۡوَىٰهُمۡ جَهَنَّمُ وَبِئۡسَ ٱلۡمَصِيرُ ﴿٧٣﴾

"O Prophet (Muhammad)! Strive hard (jihad) against the disbelievers and the hypocrites, and be harsh against them, their abode is Hell - and worst indeed is that destination".

45

يَحْلِفُونَ بِٱللَّهِ مَا قَالُواْ وَلَقَدْ قَالُواْ كَلِمَةَ ٱلْكُفْرِ وَكَفَرُواْ بَعْدَ إِسْلَـٰمِهِمْ

وَهَمُّواْ بِمَا لَمْ يَنَالُواْ وَمَا نَقَمُواْ إِلَّآ أَنْ أَغْنَىٰهُمُ ٱللَّهُ وَرَسُولُهُۥ مِن فَضْلِهِۦ

فَإِن يَتُوبُواْ يَكُ خَيْرًا لَّهُمْ وَإِن يَتَوَلَّوْاْ يُعَذِّبْهُمُ ٱللَّهُ عَذَابًا أَلِيمًا فِى ٱلدُّنْيَا

وَٱلْأَخِرَةِ وَمَا لَهُمْ فِى ٱلْأَرْضِ مِن وَلِىٍّ وَلَا نَصِيرٍ ﴿٧٤﴾

"They swear by Allah that they said nothing (bad) but really they said the word of disbelief and they disbelieved after accepting Islam, and they resolved that (plot to murder Prophet Muhammad) which they were unable to carry out, and they could not find any cause to do so except that Allah and His Messenger had enriched them of His Bounty. If then they repent, it will be better for them, but if they turn away, Allah will punish them with a painful torment in this worldly life and in the Hereafter. And there is none for them on earth as a wali (supporter, protector) or a helper."

In the above verses, Allah ordered the Messenger of Allah to be harsh towards the disbelievers and the hypocrites as well who were hostile or against Islam. Harsh here does not mean a passport to commit atrocities or extremism.

The following verse (9:29) Allah commanded the Muslims to fight the people of the Books:

قَـٰتِلُواْ ٱلَّذِينَ لَا يُؤْمِنُونَ بِٱللَّهِ وَلَا بِٱلْيَوْمِ ٱلْأَخِرِ وَلَا يُحَرِّمُونَ مَا حَرَّمَ ٱللَّهُ

وَرَسُولُهُۥ وَلَا يَدِينُونَ دِينَ ٱلْحَقِّ مِنَ ٱلَّذِينَ أُوتُواْ ٱلْكِتَـٰبَ حَتَّىٰ يُعْطُواْ

ٱلْجِزْيَةَ عَن يَدٍ وَهُمْ صَـٰغِرُونَ ﴿٢٩﴾

46

"Fight against those who believe not in Allah, nor in the Last Day, nor forbid that which has been forbidden by Allah and His Messenger and those who acknowledge not the religion of truth (i.e. Islam) among the people of the Scripture (Jews and Christians), until they pay the Jizyah with willing submission and feel themselves subdued."

The order to fight the people of the Books came only after the Muslims defeated the Arab pagans (idol worshipers) and the Jews. As more and more people embraced Islam, the Arabian Peninsula was secured under the Muslims' control and thus Islam became stronger.

There were three groups of enemies of Muslims then, the Meccan Arab Quraish idol worshipers, the Jews and, the Romans and the Arab Christians.

The Meccan Arab Quraish was defeated. The Jews were also defeated and chased out of Medina. The only remaining was the Christians of Rome that so long occupied Arab territories in the north (Syam) and the areas surrounded it. At the beginning, Prophet Muhammad (pbuh) wished to be friendly with the Christian big power of Rome, but when the Muslims became stronger, the Christians were wary about the expansion of Islam. They threatened to fight against the Muslims. News then came to the Prophet that the Roman Christian armies, including the Arab Christians, threatened to attach Medina.

Prophet Muhammad (pbuh) viewed it as serious and therefore called on the Muslims for jihad before the enemies reached Medina. Prophet Muhammad, with the strength of army of about 30,000 people, in the month of Rejab, ninth year after Hijrah (630 AD) marched to Tabouk or Tabuk (a place in the Northwestern Saudi Arabia) to fight the Christian power, the Roman-Byzantine that threatened to fight against the Muslims.

It was a very arduous long journey far away from Medina for a distance of hundreds of miles (about 610 kilometers) in intense heat. Prophet Muhammad (pbuh) was already old then. He was over 60 years of age. Some of the hypocrites joined in but lagged behind.

However, when the Muslim army reached Tabuk, the Byzantine armies were not there. He set camps next to water resources and waited for them there for about twenty days. The Byzantine armies did not turn up, thus, there was no actual fight between the Muslims and Christian armies.

On the way back from Tabuk to Medina, the hypocrites planned to kill the Prophet. There were twelve of them complotted to trap Prophet Muhammad (pbuh) at a narrow pass so that they could push him down a deep ravine to kill him. Their attempt however was not successful.

This expedition for war brought credit to the Muslim forces. They gained military reputation as strong force in the remote lands of the Arabian Peninsula. In consequence of which many non-Muslim Arab tribes abandoned their allegiance to the Roman-Byzantine and embraced Islam, thus enlarging the Muslim state. This was a foretelling sign of expansion of Islam and that the Islamic empire was in the making.

Looking at the above scenario, it was the Christians that looked for troubles because they never like Islam. In this current world, as living example, if all the Sunni Muslim countries gang-up together in jihad to support President Saddam Hussein against the American invasion of Iraq, would Iraq and Syria be in the quagmire as it is today? Of course, it is absurd to throw in such a question, but then it is a shame to put on record to show as to how the so-called Muslim leaders in the OIC in such a critical situation being faced by the Muslim brothers in Iraq behaved in such cowardice for not daring enough to throw a challenge against the unilateral American invasion. Thus the whole Muslim ummah again was put to shame in this world by the Christian West. May Allah save those leaders who chickened out to defend the Muslims in Iraq from His wrath in the hell fire in the world hereafter. Perhaps, it will not be too much to say that those leaders in the Middle East are currently facing the wrath of Allah in the Syria-Iraq quagmire.

These days, many Muslims talk about Islam as a religion of moderation and a peaceful religion as well, especially in the international forums, to put Islam in good light to the non-Muslims audience. It is good indeed, however, they usually omitted to stress the importance of jihad when the Muslims are under attack for the reasons best known to them, most probably not to offend the audience or they have 'weak hearts' as well. Nonetheless, they should not forget about this obligation on the part of the Muslims to retaliate or fight back 'in the way of Allah (jihad)' if the disbelievers humiliate or attack the Muslims. Again, perhaps the Muslims are too feeble to utter the word because they themselves do not subscribe to the fundamentals of the Islamic principles.

Many Muslims too, especially the liberalists, easily accused the Muslims as fanatic or dogmatic if they cry out for jihad to follow the food-steps of the Prophet Muhammad (pbuh). They are also not happy with the hostile attitude of Muslims who refused to acknowledge the disbelievers despite of the fact that the disbelievers and the hypocrites had shown disrespect towards Islam. If the disbelievers respect Islam, definitely the Muslims equally will respect them.

Prophet Muhammad (pbuh) himself frowned upon the disbelievers and hypocrites who showed displeasure towards him and Islam. But if they showed good manners and respect, the Prophet was equally pleased with them.

Professor Dr HAMKA, an Indonesian scholar (ulama), who said in his 'Tafsir Al-Azhar' to those people who were afraid to be accused as fanatic:

> "*That it was better for them to leave Islam if they were afraid from the accusation of being fanatic when the Muslims were under attack by the disbelievers and the hypocrites.*" (From Tafsir al-Azhar on surah At-Taubah, page 303).

From Ibnu Abas and others that the first permission Allah gave to Prophet Muhammad to fight against the disbelievers was as per His revelation in Medina in surah al-Hajj, verse (22:39):

أُذِنَ لِلَّذِينَ يُقَـٰتَلُونَ بِأَنَّهُمْ ظُلِمُوا ۚ وَإِنَّ ٱللَّهَ عَلَىٰ نَصْرِهِمْ لَقَدِيرٌ ﴿٣٩﴾

"Permission to fight is given to those (i.e. believers against disbelievers) who are fighting them, (and) because they (believers) have been wronged (victimised), and surely, Allah is able to give them (believers) victory."

The Muslims were weak and always victimised in Mecca by the Arab Quraish pagans then, as such the Muslims there had to be patient. However, subsequently with the grace of Allah, Prophet Muhammad (pbuh) and his followers migrated (hijrah) from Mecca to Medina. In Medina, the Muslim position was strong enough to defend themselves and this was the time Allah gave the permission to them to fight the disbelievers who harassed the Muslims.

Allah also permitted the Muslims to fight for Allah (jihad) against those disbelievers if they attacked the Messenger of Allah and his followers on their way to Mecca to do second little hajj or to re-do the little hajj (umrah) because the first little hajj was stopped by the Quraish kufar at Hudaibiyah. This was to inspire the pilgrims of the little hajj to fight any attack from the pagan Quraish because they might not keep their promise.

In the following verses (2:190-193) of surah al-Baqarah, [according to some interpretation, the verse (2:190) was the second time Allah gave permission for Muslims to go to war] in which Allah said:

$$ وَقَٰتِلُواْ فِى سَبِيلِ ٱللَّهِ ٱلَّذِينَ يُقَٰتِلُونَكُمْ وَلَا تَعْتَدُوٓاْ إِنَّ ٱللَّهَ لَا يُحِبُّ ٱلْمُعْتَدِينَ ۝ $$

"And fight in the Way of Allah those who fight you, but transgress not the limits. Truly, Allah likes not the transgressors."

50

وَٱقْتُلُوهُمْ حَيْثُ ثَقِفْتُمُوهُمْ وَأَخْرِجُوهُم مِّنْ حَيْثُ أَخْرَجُوكُمْ وَٱلْفِتْنَةُ

أَشَدُّ مِنَ ٱلْقَتْلِ وَلَا تُقَـٰتِلُوهُمْ عِندَ ٱلْمَسْجِدِ ٱلْحَرَامِ حَتَّىٰ

يُقَـٰتِلُوكُمْ فِيهِ فَإِن قَـٰتَلُوكُمْ فَٱقْتُلُوهُمْ كَذَٰلِكَ جَزَآءُ ٱلْكَـٰفِرِينَ

(١٩١)

"And kill them wherever you find them, and turn them out from where they have turned you out. And al-fitnah (disbelief and worshipping of others along with Allah) is worse than killing. And fight not with them at Al-Masjid-al-Haram (the sanctuary at Mecca), unless they (first) fight you there. But if they attack you, then kill them. Such is the recompense of the disbelievers."

فَإِنِ ٱنتَهَوْا فَإِنَّ ٱللَّهَ غَفُورٌ رَّحِيمٌ (١٩٢)

"But if they cease, then Allah is Oft-Forgiving, Most Merciful."

وَقَـٰتِلُوهُمْ حَتَّىٰ لَا تَكُونَ فِتْنَةٌ وَيَكُونَ ٱلدِّينُ لِلَّهِ فَإِنِ ٱنتَهَوْا فَلَا عُدْوَٰنَ

إِلَّا عَلَى ٱلظَّـٰلِمِينَ (١٩٣)

"And fight them until there is no more Fitnah (disbelief and worshipping of others along with Allah) and worship is for Allah (alone). But if they cease, let there be no transgression except against az-zalimun (tyrant and wrong-doers, etc.)"

According to narration by Ibnul Mundzir, Ibnu Jarir and Ibnu Abi Hatim from Ibnu Abbas who interpreted with regard to 'Allah likes not the transgressors' in verse (2:190) above were that the Muslims should not

51

kill women, children, old men and those who uttered salam (peace) and that they did not go against the Muslims with weapons.

In facing any eventualities, the Muslims have always to be prepared with all their arsenals and be ever ready as per verse (8:60) in surah al-Anfal:

وَأَعِدُّواْ لَهُم مَّا ٱسْتَطَعْتُم مِّن قُوَّةٍ وَمِن رِّبَاطِ ٱلْخَيْلِ تُرْهِبُونَ بِهِۦ عَدُوَّ ٱللَّهِ وَعَدُوَّكُمْ وَءَاخَرِينَ مِن دُونِهِمْ لَا تَعْلَمُونَهُمُ ٱللَّهُ يَعْلَمُهُمْ وَمَا تُنفِقُواْ مِن شَىْءٍ فِى سَبِيلِ ٱللَّهِ يُوَفَّ إِلَيْكُمْ وَأَنتُمْ لَا تُظْلَمُونَ ۝

"And make ready against them all you can of power, including steeds of war (tanks, planes, missiles, artillery etc.) to threaten the enemy of Allah and your enemy, and others besides whom, you may not know but whom Allah does know. And whatever you shall spend in the cause of Allah shall be repaid unto you, and you shall not be treated unjustly."

Thus, the Muslims should be strong and always be prepared and ever ready to uphold Islam because without the support of military power, jihad would be a futile effort and it would not serve its purpose other than only martyr. That was the rational that Allah did not allow the Muslims to fight the kufar Quaraish in Mecca then because the Muslims were few and weak then.

The duty of the every Muslim is to obey the command of Allah and His Messenger. Islam also enjoins Muslims do righteous deeds and to refrain from any evil or wrong doings. By doing so Allah would help them in their jihad in the cause of Allah as per His revelation in surah al-Hajj, verse (22:78) below:

وَجَـٰهِدُواْ فِى ٱللَّهِ حَقَّ جِهَادِهِۦ هُوَ ٱجْتَبَىٰكُمْ وَمَا جَعَلَ عَلَيْكُمْ فِى ٱلدِّينِ

مِنْ حَرَجٍ مِّلَّةَ أَبِيكُمْ إِبْرَٰهِيمَ هُوَ سَمَّىٰكُمُ ٱلْمُسْلِمِينَ مِن قَبْلُ وَفِى هَـٰذَا

لِيَكُونَ ٱلرَّسُولُ شَهِيدًا عَلَيْكُمْ وَتَكُونُواْ شُهَدَآءَ عَلَى ٱلنَّاسِ فَأَقِيمُواْ

ٱلصَّلَوٰةَ وَءَاتُواْ ٱلزَّكَوٰةَ وَٱعْتَصِمُواْ بِٱللَّهِ هُوَ مَوْلَىٰكُمْ فَنِعْمَ ٱلْمَوْلَىٰ وَنِعْمَ

ٱلنَّصِيرُ ۝

"And struggle hard (jihad) in Allah's cause as you ought to strive. He has chosen you (to convey His Message of Islamic Monotheism to all mankind) and has not laid upon you in religion any hardship it is the religion (Islamic Monotheism) of your father Ibrahim. It is He (Allah) Who has named you Muslims both before and in this (the Quran), that the Messenger (Muhammad) may be a witness over you and you be witnesses over mankind. So perform salat (prayer), give zakat (alm) and hold fast to Allah (i.e. have confidence in Allah and depend upon Him in all your affairs) He is your Maula (Patron, Lord, Protector, etc.), what an Excellent Maula and what an Excellent Helper."

According to al-Qurthubiy, some ulama interpreted the 'jihad' was "*jihad or struggle hard against the non-believers*" whereas some others interoperated as "*struggle or work hard to carry out all the ordainments of Allah and abstain all in injunctions of Allah*".

There were many hadith on jihad and a few of which are as follows:

"The best Jihad is the word of justice in front of the oppressive Sultan (ruler)". Hadith cited by Ibn Nuhaas and narrated by Ibn Habbaan.

In another hadith, the companion of the Messenger of Allah asked him about the best jihad. He replied:

"The best jihad is the one in which your horse is slain and your blood is spilled". Hadith also cited by Ibn Nuhaas and narrated by Ibn Habbaan.

Whereas Ibn Nuhaas also cited a hadith from musnad Ahmad ibn Hanbal, where Prophet Muhammad (pbuh) said that:

"The highest kind of jihad is the person who is killed whilst spilling the last drop of his blood".

While in Sahih al-Bukhari, the following hadith recorded:

Abu al-Yaman from al-Zuhri from Sa'id ibn al-Musayyab narrated from Abu Hurairah that the Prophet said:

"By Him (Allah) in Whose Hands my soul is: were it not for some men amongst the believers (Muslims) who dislike to be left behind me and whom I cannot provide with means of conveyance, I would certainly never remain behind any *Sariyah* (battalion, military unit) going out for *jihad* (armed struggle) in the path of Allah. By Him in Whose hands my soul is: I would love to be martyred (fighting) in the path of Allah and then come back to life and be martyred again, and then come back to life and be martyred again."

Muhammad bin Nashar from Ghundar from Sh'ubah narrated by Anas ibn Malik that the Prophet said:

"Nobody who enters Paradise likes to return to the world even if he got everything on the earth, except a martyr who wishes to return to the world so that he may be martyred ten times because of the honour and dignity he receives from Allah."

The inferences to the above verses and the hadith are obvious that jihad is a noble act commanded by Allah. However, again it is repeated here that after the fall of the Muslims in Spain the spirit of jihad had severely diminished. This change was attributed to the weakness of the Muslim ummah, either in faith or in its economic and military strength. As their capability to invoke jihad diminished, the Muslims turned into spiritual religious devotion influenced by Sufism. Thus, subsequently the concept of jihad had gradually worn off and had been largely reinterpreted in terms of Sufi ethics and sustained until to this very day. Even the word 'jihad' to certain people has a negative connotation probably they have inner fears and of lack of faith in Allah or ignorant.

It is obvious from the foregoing that jihad is a vast subject which encompasses various spheres of activity, all of which directed towards the betterment of own-self, society and country in the Islamic perspective. However, regardless of how legitimate a cause of jihad may be, Islam does not condone the killing of innocent people or terrorising the civilian population, whether by individuals or states. Such act of cruelty can never be termed as jihad because it is against the true teachings of Islam.

Allah commanded the Muslims to fight against their enemies, when required, in order to uphold Islam and justice. The Muslims of today do not invoke jihad although they have been harassed by disbelievers because they are disunited and weak. Furthermore, their jihad spirit and Islamic faith have been greatly diminished. Instead of fighting their enemies, the Muslim leaders become friends with them (the enemies) to save themselves. They fear Allah not but the enemies of Islam.

On unity, although Allah reminded Muslims to unite they heed not. They have returned to the olden days before Islam where fanatical spirit of nationalism, racism and clannish has taken root again by conveniently forgetting that the Muslims are brothers in Islam irrespective of race and colour. This kind of attitude is the very stumbling block that inhibits their unity and as one Muslim ummah.

During the Islamic Empire, Muslim ummah then were united and therefore they became very strong under the command of one supreme leadership. Notwithstanding, subsequently most of the leaders too succumbed to greed, worldly vain desire and power. They broke ranks and quarrelled which led them to disintegration. They became slaves of their own riches and power. They became ungrateful, arrogance, complacence, live in opulence, abusing their powers even to the extent of being cruel and oppressors on fellow Muslims. In consequence, they collapsed severely to the Christians West.

The Muslim populations combined at present are very large though but they are no more than the foams in the sea. Prophet Muhammad (pbuh) already hinted about this and it turned out to be very true indeed.

The protracted misunderstanding among the Muslim political divides aggravates the situation further to the detriment of Muslim fraternity and unity as a whole. Whereas, with due respect to the Western Christians, they unite and consolidate in diversity; they also forget their differences when come to fighting their common enemy.

Allah cautioned Muslims not to quarrel among themselves and should reconcile if they fall to fighting because they are brothers in Islam. In this regard, Allah said in surah al-Hujrat (49:9-10):

وَإِن طَآئِفَتَانِ مِنَ ٱلْمُؤْمِنِينَ ٱقْتَتَلُوا۟ فَأَصْلِحُوا۟ بَيْنَهُمَا فَإِنۢ بَغَتْ إِحْدَىٰهُمَا عَلَى ٱلْأُخْرَىٰ فَقَٰتِلُوا۟ ٱلَّتِى تَبْغِى حَتَّىٰ تَفِىٓءَ إِلَىٰٓ أَمْرِ ٱللَّهِ فَإِن فَآءَتْ فَأَصْلِحُوا۟ بَيْنَهُمَا بِٱلْعَدْلِ وَأَقْسِطُوٓا۟ إِنَّ ٱللَّهَ يُحِبُّ ٱلْمُقْسِطِينَ ۝

"And if two parties or groups among the believers fall to fighting, then make peace between them both, but if one of them rebels against the other, then fight you (all) against the one that which rebels till it complies with the Command of Allah; then if it complies, then make reconciliation between them justly, and be equitable. Verily Allah loves those who are equitable."

إِنَّمَا ٱلْمُؤْمِنُونَ إِخْوَةٌ فَأَصْلِحُوا۟ بَيْنَ أَخَوَيْكُمْ وَٱتَّقُوا۟ ٱللَّهَ لَعَلَّكُمْ تُرْحَمُونَ ۝

"The believers are nothing else than brothers (in Islam). So make reconciliation between your brothers, and fear Allah, that you may receive mercy or blessing".

The above is clear that Allah commanded that if two Muslim groups fighting against one other, then a third party of Muslims to take the responsibility to be the mediator to reconcile justly and equitably between the warring parties. If one of the parties refuses to make peace, despite of the presentation fairly made before them, and continue fighting against the other, then the mediator should take side and fight against the other party that refused to make peace until they surrendered. Nevertheless, at present the Muslims more often than not request the disbelievers be the mediator for them. This is clearly not in line with the commands of Allah. As such, it makes the situation in the Muslim countries to continue to be in difficulty, more complicated and unstable. Thus, the Muslim countries keep on continuing to depend on the non-Muslim countries.

What has been and is happening in the Middle East currently is the result of non-compliance by the Muslims to the command of Allah as stated above. Therefore, the wrath of Allah is severely befallen on them. The problem will not be solved unless they return to al-Quran and al-Sunnah. Believe or not, getting help from or collaborating with the disbelievers will not work. It will create more trouble to the Muslims instead of peace as is happening now right on the face of the Muslims in Syria and Iraq, the rest of the Middle East and in the Muslim world as a whole.

Allah commanded the Muslims when facing their enemy they should:

- Be braved,
- Always remember the name of Allah,
- Obey Allah and His Messenger,
- Not dispute with one another and
- Be patient lest they would become weak.

The above commands are registered in surah al-Anfal, verses (8:45-46) respectively as follows:

يَـٰٓأَيُّهَا ٱلَّذِينَ ءَامَنُوٓاْ إِذَا لَقِيتُمْ فِئَةً فَٱثْبُتُواْ وَٱذْكُرُواْ ٱللَّـهَ كَثِيرًا

لَّعَلَّكُمْ تُفْلِحُونَ ﴿٤٥﴾

"O you who believe, when you meet (an enemy) force, take a firm stand against them and remember the name of Allah much (both with tongue and mind) so that you may be successful."

وَأَطِيعُواْ ٱللَّـهَ وَرَسُولَهُۥ وَلَا تَنَـٰزَعُواْ فَتَفْشَلُواْ وَتَذْهَبَ رِيحُكُمْ

وَٱصْبِرُوٓاْ إِنَّ ٱللَّـهَ مَعَ ٱلصَّـٰبِرِينَ ﴿٤٦﴾

"And obey Allah and His Messenger, and do not dispute (with one another) lest you lose courage and your strength depart, and be patient. Surely, Allah is with those who are as-Sabirin (the patient ones)."

The verses are very clear. These verses revealed before the Battle of Badar where the Muslims won the war with the disbelievers of Quraish of Mecca although the Muslims under the command of the Messenger of Allah (pbuh) outnumbered three times by them. These commands are relevant and applicable all the time - in the past, now and in future.

The Messenger of Allah used to pray to Allah asking for help in trying period in encountering his enemies as follows:

"O Allah Who brought down al-Quran, moves the clouds and defeats the enemies! Defeat them and help us in fighting them." Hadith narrated by Bukhari and Muslim.

Therefore, to win in any encounter with the enemies of Islam, the Muslims should have no fear but fear and obey Allah and obey His Messenger.

Long prayers alone without preparation, hard work and struggle or jihad in the way of Allah will not do.

One of the reasons the Arabs could not win in their wars with the Israel simply because they did not unite and were disobedient lot. In fact, the Arabs were never able to unite and are still until today. This sort of negative attribute also prevailed or spilled into the OIC. Thus, the members of the OIC could not get consensus and therefore they could not act on any resolution in unison.

In the spirit of the above verses, the OIC should have been the one to lead the way as a mediator to reconcile the Muslim conflicting parties without involving the non-Muslims. Although at times the Muslims fight against one another, they are still believers and therefore they are still brothers that need time to cool off their satanic vengeance.

As Muslims they should hold fast to Islamic principles and stay undivided to get blessing and mercy from Allah. In surah Ali Imran, verse (3:103) Allah said:

وَٱعْتَصِمُوا۟ بِحَبْلِ ٱللَّهِ جَمِيعًا وَلَا تَفَرَّقُوا۟ وَٱذْكُرُوا۟ نِعْمَتَ ٱللَّهِ عَلَيْكُمْ إِذْ كُنتُمْ أَعْدَآءً فَأَلَّفَ بَيْنَ قُلُوبِكُمْ فَأَصْبَحْتُم بِنِعْمَتِهِۦٓ إِخْوَٰنًا وَكُنتُمْ عَلَىٰ شَفَا حُفْرَةٍ مِّنَ ٱلنَّارِ فَأَنقَذَكُم مِّنْهَا ۗ كَذَٰلِكَ يُبَيِّنُ ٱللَّهُ لَكُمْ ءَايَٰتِهِۦ لَعَلَّكُمْ تَهْتَدُونَ ﴿١٠٣﴾

"And hold fast, all of you together, to the Rope of Allah (i.e. al-Quran), and be not divided among you. And remember Allah's favour on you, for you were enemies one to another (during the time of ignorant before) but He joined your hearts together, so that by His Grace, you became brethren (in Islamic faith), and you were then on the brink of a pit of fire and He saved you from it. Thus Allah makes His ayat (proofs, evidences, verses, lessons, signs, revelations, etc.) clear to you that you may be guided".

The revelation of the above verse came down when the clan of Aus and Kharaj of Medina were on the verge of fighting between them, although they were close friends, due to instigation of the Jews who were envious of the closeness of the two clans. The Jews and the other disbelievers are doing the same thing today, but more in subtlety.

In the above case, when the messenger of Allah recited the verse, they immediately regretted and reconciled by forgiving each other. The verse, like any other verses, is relevant all the time. The Muslims should not blame others but themselves for their own folly for not obeying the command of Allah.

As far as Islam is concerned, there is no difference between the Arabs and non-Arabs and between the white and the black but the pious are the glorious ones before Allah. Unity, love each other and help one another in the way of Allah are sure ingredients for success. That was the scenario of the Muslim ummah during the height of Islamic Empire, hence Islam spread to Europe, Africa, India and so forth in this world.

When the Muslim power succumbed to the Christian West, the Christians became colonial masters. They purposely divided Muslim countries into smaller sovereignty nation-states, with the principle of divide and rule, in order to prevent the Muslims from unity. They feared that should the Muslims unite, they would surely rise again to challenge them. Thus far, it indeed proved that they succeeded in their past strategies in dividing the Muslims. Until now, they are maintaining the same strategies in orchestrating the Muslim world, thereby rendering disunity among the Muslims and their leaders in the OIC as well.

9.1. Relevancy of Jihad

Jihad is continuous and still relevant at all times, militarily or otherwise. Jihad on whatever forms it may be is ongoing all the time, especially against immorality and wrong doings.

Democratic system comparatively with that of Islamic system in many aspects is not compatible. In democratic system of government, although certain things are morally wrongs, they would consider them as right under human rights principles, merely because majority of the people in the society voted or approved them. For example, the practice of lesbian, gay, bisexual and trans-sexual (LGBT) is religiously and morally wrong under Islam, and other religions too, but now is considered as normal under the name of freedom and the principle of universal human rights. Thus, this abnormal practice becomes more popular now. Even some of the so-called the Muslim liberalists land support to this abnormal behaviour.

Previously the LGBT is strongly condemned by all religions. As far as Islam is concerned, it is a serious moral wrong and a great sin. Therefore, it is the duty of Muslims to stop it. It is a jihad or struggle to prevent this form of misbehaviour from spreading into the Muslim society.

On the point above, as an example, not every aspect the democratic system is suitable in Islam. Any act that religiously considered illegal or outside the parameter of Islam as ordained by Allah remains as it is forever. It is absolutely cannot be changed, even though majority of the people approve it. On the other hand, anything that religiously ordained as right it would remain as it is forever and no matter what even if majority of the people in the whole world want it otherwise. As such, there is neither absolute democracy nor absolute human freedom as envisage under the human rights. Therefore, Islam imposed certain limitation in anything within the parameter of Islamic principles as enshrined in al-Quran and al-Sunnah.

As already stated, everything has a limit. Human beings cannot penetrate the sky and beyond. Going to the moon and stars is not against Islam but it is nothing to shout about as far as Allah is concerned. Prophet Muhammad (pbuh), with the blessing of Allah, travelled even further up to the highest seventh sky, which is much higher than the moon, to meet Allah. Thus, as a servant of Allah, by nature one is weak and powerless and therefore has always to be thankful to Allah for all His endowments on this earth.

It is Allah Almighty Who controls everything in this universe, be it the fall of leaves from trees in the jungle, all of which in the knowledge of Allah. Therefore, one should not be arrogant but submit to Allah alone and obey His Ordainments, including the order of His Messenger, that is, the Prophet Muhammad (pbuh). Thus, the laws ordained by Allah cannot be altered or compromised except which are not absolute, but again it should be within the ambit of Islam. It sounds rigid though, but that is it because some of the laws are rigid which are beyond human interpretations and knowledge except Allah. It is only Allah Who knows the wisdoms behind all His laws meant for His creatures. For the believers or Muslims, take them as they are and believe in them, or leave them and become disbelievers or rejecters.

It is absolutely clear therefore that the Islamic system is not compatible with all the secular systems. In other systems – be the democratic, the autocratic, the communist, the military power etc. – those in power can enact and change any law that is only suitable to them vis-à-vis the Devine law, that is, al-Quran and al-Sunnah. Thus, those in power can influence people, whether through sheer brute force or otherwise, to give affirmative consent or action on any matter even though it goes against ethic, morality etc. As such, something of truth or good or virtuous may be put aside and considered as having no merit or standing when the majority or the power that be decides so. It may also summarily be dismissed without due process of law or totally ignored by those in power. Therefore, in these instances, the wrongs surpass the rights for which there is no such thing in Islam. The laws enshrined in the al-Quran and al-Sunnah cannot be circumvented by the majority rule or by the brute power. In this regard, when talking about jihad, it is duty bound on the Muslim to call for jihad (it does not mean to invoke war here) to struggle hard to put things right in life in the way of Allah.

Notwithstanding, the Muslims nowadays are much in love with worldly benefits and therefore, the call for jihad is not emphasised. While still believing in Islamic faith, many of them become modern ignorant in Islam and their faith overall has enfeebled.

When Iraq under the late autocratic President Saddam Hussein invaded and conquered Kuwait on 2nd August 1979, the whole world condemned him. Seven months later the Americans became world hero for capturing back Kuwait from Iraq. Ironically when this hero all along supported the illegal Israel regime, the world just kept quiet.

When another big power, the Russians, invaded Chechnya (Chechnya unilaterally declared independence from Russia) on 7th August 1999, no nation on earth, including Muslim world, did anything to protest or to stop the Russian carnage. The reason being the Chechnya is a small Muslim state overrun by the big non-Muslim state. As such, Chechnya, the tiny nation in the Caucasus, capitulated pathetically. Nonetheless, the Russian can conquer Chechnya but they would never be able subdue the Muslim Chechens because they are strong believer in Allah. They will keep on their jihad against the infidel Russians.

Similarly, in Bosnia when the Christians slaughtered Bosnian Muslims, neither the Muslim world nor the non-Muslims helped them. The perpetrators not branded as terrorists. Likewise, when the Burmese (Myanmar) committed similar atrocities or chased the Muslim Rohingyas away, the world did not seriously condemn and take action again Burma.

Despite of having more than 1.6 billion Muslims, they are just like the froth in the sea for they are unable to do anything to help or to invoke jihad against their adversaries as if jihad is irrelevant anymore. The Muslim power is no more there to check the big powers. Perhaps, in the near distance future a new Allah fearing Muslim group would emerge to buck-up the strength to invoke jihad in way of Allah (fi sabilillah) against the Muslim adversaries.

The world had witnessed that the Muslims were inordinately subject to onslaught by foreign soldiers, either from the air or the ground, on the Muslims' soils for such a long time such as in Afghanistan, in the Middle East and elsewhere on the pretext of hunting down the so-called designated 'Muslim terrorists'. In this regard, what is the different between the insurgents and the foreign soldiers? They are both killers, terrorising the population. Both sides have their own causes, but the victims are the innocent civilians. But the interference of the foreign powers in the first place is the inherent cause of the conflicts.

Arising from the continuous operations against the designated terrorists had led to many deaths, mostly innocent civilians. The groups of the hard-core Muslims could not tolerate such kind of cruelty. Therefore, they became insurgents but they resorted to 'radicalism in vengeance' to vent out their anger, some of them had become merciless suicide bombers. They called themselves 'the jihadists' against the foreign forces on their soils and their own oppressive regimes. In the process of their actions, they too intentionally or unintentionally killed the innocent bystanders as well. Thus, the terror fights between the two groups – **small terrorists** and **big terrorists** or whatever name may be branded - had become more intense and endless. Thus, many more deaths or injuries inflicted on the innocent local people and their properties destroyed as well.

The insurgents, be it jihadists or terrorists, commit the action as such because they are desperadoes to free their lands from intruders and the puppet regimes, the collaborators. That is their reasons and in doing so, they do it not for glory but for justice unaccomplished. To them, it is a 'jihad' or struggle against tyranny. So long as tyranny exists, the oppressed parties will not stop fighting for their rights and freedom.

Talking about this act of radicalism or terrorism, perhaps, one has to ponder outside the box, whether right or wrong, it is up to one's own interpretation depending on the circumstances of the case. Take for example of the scenario where the intruders or marauders, whoever they are, killed certain innocent persons or destroyed their houses or chased them away from their own houses and lands. They are defenceless and there is no people coming forward to help or to defend them. Since justice was not available to them, what would ultimately the victims, Muslims and non-Muslims alike, do?

Justice has to be done or is seen to be done. However, if justice is not done or not available to the victims they would naturally resort to certain action when opportunity arises, especially if their love ones or families were killed. Thus, to gain back their property or dignity they would take action by any mean, even to the extent of sacrificing their own lives or take other drastic action against the perpetrators though it may be barbaric. The anger of the persons subjected to the victimisation will not simply subside until they get back their properties or dignity. Such being the circumstances, would it be justifiable to blame them solely for their drastic retaliatory action? On the other hand, would the marauders or the aggressors who killed innocent people or confiscated properties and lands of others be scot-free from the blame simply because they have the power?

No sane human beings will tolerate injustice. People who have never experienced such traumatic incidents committed by the detractors may blame the dastard retaliatory acts by the victims, but does it change anything? It will not change a thing unless the perpetrators stop the carnage or atrocities.

Currently, look at the illegal Israel regime that keeps on killing the Palestinians even though most of the time they fought with stones and knives only and yet the Israelis retaliated with live bullets and even destroyed their homes. Even though the Palestinians fight with stones, they are not afraid because to them it is the jihad to liberate their lands. When a Palestinian killed an Israeli, they retaliated by using big guns and bombers to kill many innocent Palestinians and to destroy their houses. This is, indeed, the hypocritical world where the stronger powers used their might to dictate their terms on the helpless others. Honestly, is it fair?

Extremism and use of force of any sort on adversaries generally resorted to by people who are desperate due to oppression, injustice, victimisation and atrocities. When they have exhausted of all normal means available to stop it, they would resort to anything beyond imagination. In such trying condition, the feeling of hatred and vengeance surpasses the feeling of goodwill. So long as the situation remains as it is, there will be no hope to have peace.

It is natural that cruelty will breed cruelty, no matter how much people dislike it. Nonetheless, to resist or fight against wrong doings or cruelty is the responsibility of every able-bodied person - Muslims and non-Muslims alike.

As always expressed, Islam is a religion of moderation, peace and justice but there is limit to it. For example, if the sanctity of Islam and the right of Muslims are invaded or humiliated, then it is the duty of the Muslims to fight back in the way of Allah (jihad) to protect self-respect and the religion of Allah. Only the hypocrites, the disobedient, the ungrateful and the cowards will shun away from such duty.

Allah said in surah at- Taubah, verse (9:32):

$$يُرِيدُونَ أَن يُطْفِئُوا نُورَ اللّهِ بِأَفْوَاهِهِمْ وَيَأْبَى اللّهُ إِلَّا أَن يُتِمَّ نُورَهُ وَلَوْ كَرِهَ الْكَافِرُونَ ۝$$

"They (the disbelievers, the Jews and the Christians) want to extinguish Allah's Light (Islamic Monotheism) with their mouths, but Allah will not allow except that His Light should be perfected even though the kafirun (disbelievers) hate (it)".

The disbelievers always hate Islam and wish to extinguish it from spreading, either through negative propagation or through force. Thus, the Muslims have to continuously stand strong and struggle hard (jihad) to protect the sanctity of Islam against them. Nonetheless, the Muslims themselves firstly have to be good Muslims by following the Islamic principles fully in their everyday life before due respect be accorded to them by others.

Coming to jihad again, it may be relevant to mention briefly here the success story of the great Sultan Muhammad al-Fateh of Turkey, a staunch Muslim ruler who conquered the great Roman-Byzantine Empire in 1453 AD.

In this extraordinary episode, it indicated that Allah's help will come by only when the leader is a person of taqwa (a pious and Allah fearing) and always grateful to Him. In this regard, the world had seen the kind of devoted Muslims who conquered Constantinople (Istanbul), the seat of the great Byzantine Empire. The person or the leader was no other than the pious great Sultan Muhammad al-Fateh of Turkey.

The Muslim leaders in the secular world of today, by comparison most probably by the same age of the Sultan, might live in the life style of the West, playful and enjoy life as the case may be.

Briefly, the story of success of the Sultan Muhammad al-Fateh is as follows:

For eight centuries, the conquest of Constantinople was a dream by many Muslim commanders. Ever since the era of the Caliph Mu'awiyah Ibn Abu Sufyaan, there had been many attempts to conquer it, but none succeeded.

Every Muslim commander wanted to be the conqueror of Constantinople since the Prophet Muhammad (pbuh) said during the digging of the trenches in the battle of Khandaq (627AD):

> **"You will conquer Constantinople. Its commander is the best and its army (that will conquer it) is the best."** Hadith narrated by Imam Ahmad bin Hambal.

Muslims of the olden days believed the hadith and tried their very best to carry out the mission but unfortunately failed. However, the Muslims only succeeded after about 826 years later.

Who was then the person about whom the Prophet gave glad tidings (good news)? It was Muhammad Al-Fateh, the son of the Ottoman Sultan Murad II.

Muhammad Al-Faatih was born on 30th March 1432. His father trained him since childhood to be a pious and excellent Muslim to shoulder the responsibilities of the position of a Sultan.

Muhammad Al-Fateh memorized the whole of Quran, learnt the Hadith of Prophet Muhammad (pbuh), Islamic jurisprudence, mathematics, astronomy and the skills required for war. He was devoted Muslim and never neglected his prayers in his life.

He also learnt Arabic, Persian, Latin and Greek languages. He joined his father in his battles and conquests.

The good training influenced the character of the young prince and coloured his personality with Islamic morals and manners. His teacher managed to inculcate in his heart the spirit of jihad and the desire to be a person with high ambition, highly cultured, and had deep knowledge of the skills in war and combat.

After completing his preparations, the youthful Sultan Muhammad Al-Fateh of 23 years of age only then marched to Constantinople with an army of about three hundred thousand fighters. Huge cannons supported this army. The army besieged Constantinople and the Ottoman cannons started to fire their missiles at the fortified walls of the city days and nights. From time to time, the Sultan surprised the enemy with a new war plan until the city defenders lost control and their forces surrendered.

At dawn of Tuesday, 20th Jamadilawal, 827 A.H. (May 29th 1453 A.D.) the Ottoman forces managed to conquer Constantinople.

The Sultan arrived and he dismounted from his horse and performed thanks-giving prayer to Allah Who blessed him with the conquest. Then the Sultan addressed the people of the city who were still bowing and prostrating in tears:

> *"Stand up! I am Sultan Muhammad and I would like to tell you, your brothers, and all the people present that your lives and freedoms are protected."*

How noble was the speech. He was not arrogant but grateful to Allah for his success.

He changed Constantinople to **Islambul**, meaning the House of Islam. Later on, however the word viciously twisted to become **Istanbul**.

The Sultan was very tolerant and merciful with the people of the city, and acted according to the teachings of Islam. He commanded his soldiers to treat their prisoners of war in a good manner. He also allowed those who left the city when it was under siege to return home.

Thus, with the conquest of Constantinople and the realisation of the glad tidings as predicted by Prophet Muhammad (pbuh) completed accordingly.

Then Muhammad Al-Fatih decided to take Otarant as a base for his northern military operations until he could reach Rome. The European world was terrified because of this attempt and they expected the fall of the historical city of Rome into the hands of Muhammad Al-Fateh. However, he died young suddenly on 4th Rabiulwal 886 A.H. (May 3rd 1481 A.D.) while he was preparing to realise this dream. He was only 49 years old. Some reported that his death was due to poisoning arising from internal rivalry.

All Europe was very happy and rejoicing to learn about his death. The Pope of Rome ordered thankfulness prayer in churches as a means of expressing joy and happiness over the news.

During the reign of Muhammad Al-Fateh through his wise leadership and well-planned policy, the Ottoman State reached boundaries that it had never succeeded before.

All these conquests and achievements were due his loyal men and his adherence to the teaching of al-Quran and the al-Sunnah of Prophet Muhammad (pbuh).

Through high ambition, determination and abiding servant of Allah, he managed to realise his dream, and this made him one of the great Muslim heroes and one of the best conquerors in the world.

That was history. Would world history repeat itself? Of course, God willing provided the present Muslim leaders emulate the good attributes of those successful past Muslim leaders and willing to sacrifice for jihad. The problem is the present Muslim leaders mostly are ungrateful and follow the way of 'taghut' rather than Islamic principles.

What is taghut? Briefly, it is as follows:

Taghut denotes one who exceeds his limits, just like the Satan. The first stage is disobeying Allah without denying that one should obey Him, that is, fasiq, and the second is rejection of the very idea that one should obey Allah, that is, kafr (disbeliever). The last stage is the one that not only rebels against Allah but also imposes his rebellion against the will of Allah upon others.

In surah an-Nisa', verses (4:51, 60 and 76) Allah said respectively:

أَلَمْ تَرَ إِلَى ٱلَّذِينَ أُوتُوا نَصِيبًا مِّنَ ٱلْكِتَبِ يُؤْمِنُونَ بِٱلْجِبْتِ وَٱلطَّغُوتِ وَيَقُولُونَ لِلَّذِينَ كَفَرُوا هَٰٓؤُلَآءِ أَهْدَىٰ مِنَ ٱلَّذِينَ ءَامَنُوا سَبِيلًا ۝

"Have you not seen those who were given a portion of the Scripture? They believe in Jibt (magic, astrologer, saint etc.) and Taghut and say to the disbelievers that they are better guided as regards the way than the believers (Muslims)."

The above verse referred to an actual event in which a group of disbelievers in Mecca (idol worshippers) went to two eminent Jewish figures for counseling on the truth of Muhammad's teachings. The Jews told them that they were rightly guided comparing with the Muslims.

أَلَمْ تَرَ إِلَى ٱلَّذِينَ يَزْعُمُونَ أَنَّهُمْ ءَامَنُوا بِمَآ أُنزِلَ إِلَيْكَ وَمَآ أُنزِلَ مِن قَبْلِكَ يُرِيدُونَ أَن يَتَحَاكَمُوٓا إِلَى ٱلطَّغُوتِ وَقَدْ أُمِرُوٓا أَن يَكْفُرُوا بِهِۦ وَيُرِيدُ ٱلشَّيْطَٰنُ أَن يُضِلَّهُمْ ضَلَٰلًا بَعِيدًا ۝

"Have you (Muhammad) seen those (hyprocrites) who claim that they believe in that which has been sent down to you, and that which was sent down before you, and they wish to go for judgement (in their disputes) to the Taghut (false judges etc.) while they have been ordered to reject them. But Satan wishes to lead them far astray."

اَلَّذِينَ ءَامَنُواْ يُقَـٰتِلُونَ فِى سَـبِيلِ اللَّهِ وَالَّـذِينَ كَفَرُواْ يُقَـٰتِلُونَ فِى سَـبِيلِ الطَّـغُوتِ فَقَـٰتِلُوٓاْ أَوْلِيَآءَ الشَّـيْطَـٰنِ إِنَّ كَيْـدَ الشَّـيْطَـٰنِ كَانَ ضَعِيفًا ﴿٧٦﴾

"Those who believe fight in the cause of Allah, and those who disbelieve fight in the cause of Taghut (Satan etc.). So fight you against the friends of Satan. Ever feeble indeed is the plot of Satan."

What is the stand of the Muslims today? Often than not, they seek taghut leader for help. Thus, do not blame Allah; do not blame others but themselves for being humiliated in this current world.

Allah also said about taghut in surah al-Baqarah, verse (2:256):

لَآ إِكْرَاهَ فِى الدِّينِ قَد تَّبَيَّنَ الرُّشْدُ مِنَ الْغَيِّ فَمَن يَكْفُرْ بِالطَّـٰغُوتِ وَيُؤْمِنۢ بِاللَّهِ فَقَدِ اسْتَمْسَكَ بِالْعُرْوَةِ الْوُثْقَىٰ لَا انفِصَامَ لَهَا وَاللَّهُ سَمِيعٌ عَلِيمٌ ﴿٢٥٦﴾

"There is no compulsion in religion. Verily, the right path has become distinct from the wrong path. Whoever disbelieves in Taghut and believes in Allah then he has grasped the most trustworthy handhold that will never break. And Allah is All-Hearer, All-Knower."

The write path of Allah is distinct from the wrong path but many choose to follow the path of taghut. Muslims are sensitive if labelling them as 'taghut', although their attributes and behaviours are just like those disbelievers, the followers of taghut.

If the word 'taghut' is aimed at the government of the day, although the government lacks of governance and transparency, particularly in autocratic regimes, it may construe as anti-establishment and may be subject to criminal charges. Therefore, abuse of power, corruption and other mismanagement of the Muslim countries reigned supreme, thereby leading to lack of development and progress.

Jihad is a spiritual dynamism that needs to be continuous in order to put things right in the Islamic perspective. Whether people like it or not, it should be non-issue. Jihad is a way to show displeasure of evil deeds, either by heart (the weakest way of jihad), mouth or hands for the Muslims who care in the struggle in the way of Allah.

CHAPTER 10.   THE DISBELIEVERS
VIS-A-VIS THE BELIEVERS

In Islamic perspective, human being is categorised into two broad classifications, namely the **non-Muslims** [disbelievers inclusive the **munafiqun** (hypocrites)] and the **Muslims** (believers). In this regard, Allah said in surah At-Taghabun, verse (64:2):

هُوَ ٱلَّذِى خَلَقَكُمْ فَمِنكُمْ كَافِرٌ وَمِنكُم مُّؤْمِنٌ وَٱللَّهُ بِمَا تَعْمَلُونَ بَصِيرٌ

"He is Who created you, then some of you are disbelievers and some of you are believers. And Allah is All-Seer of what you do".

Allah gives His human creature the discerning mind to think between good and bad; beneficial and harmful and right and wrong. However, mind alone would not suffice to ensure it would lead to a good and righteous life. Therefore, Allah brought down His syariah (laws) through His Messengers and Prophets from time to time to guide their people.

The last Messenger of Allah on earth was Prophet Muhammad (pbuh) to give guidance for the whole mankind. He brought glad tidings, peace and blessing to the world from Allah. Nevertheless, it is the law of nature (sunnatullah) that not all people would believe in the preaching of the Prophets and the Messengers of Allah. Many of them would be disbelievers or rejecters. Allah will guide and give blessing only to those who are honestly searching for the truth because Allah is All-Knower and All-Seer. Allah created the universe and its contents are not for free but as test or trial for human beings to go through the ordeal in this temporal world before they return finally to meet Him in the world hereafter forever.

Briefly, the characteristics of disbelievers, hypocrites and believers are as follows:

i. The characteristic of disbelievers.

There are many verses in al-Quran describing the attributes about the disbelievers. Some of the verses are as below:

• Disbelievers (non-Muslims) are arrogant and antagonism – Sad: (38: 2):

$$ بَلِ ٱلَّذِينَ كَفَرُواْ فِى عِزَّةٍ وَشِقَاقٍ ۝ $$

"Nay, those who disbelieve are in false pride and antagonism."

• Disbelievers are close-minded – Al-Baqarah: (2:6):

$$ إِنَّ ٱلَّذِينَ كَفَرُواْ سَوَآءٌ عَلَيْهِمْ ءَأَنذَرْتَهُمْ أَمْ لَمْ تُنذِرْهُمْ لَا يُؤْمِنُونَ ۝ $$

"Verily, those who disbelieve, it is the same to them whether you (O Muhammad) warn them or do not warn them, they will not believe."

• Disbelievers are greedy – Al-Baqarah: (2:96):

وَلَتَجِدَنَّهُمْ أَحْرَصَ ٱلنَّاسِ عَلَىٰ حَيَوٰةٍ وَمِنَ ٱلَّذِينَ أَشْرَكُوٓاْ يَوَدُّ أَحَدُهُمْ لَوْ يُعَمَّرُ أَلْفَ سَنَةٍ وَمَا هُوَ بِمُزَحْزِحِهِۦ مِنَ ٱلْعَذَابِ أَن يُعَمَّرَ وَٱللَّهُ بَصِيرٌۢ بِمَا يَعْمَلُونَ ﴿٩١﴾

"And verily, you will find them (the Jews) the greediest of mankind for life and (even greedier) than those who ascribe partners to Allah (and do not believe in Resurrection - Magians, pagans, and idolaters, etc.). Every one of them wishes that he could be given a life of a thousand years but the grant of such life will not save him even a little from (due) punishment. And Allah is All-Seer of what they do."

- Disbelievers are deaf, dumb and blind – Al-Baqarah: (2:171):

وَمَثَلُ ٱلَّذِينَ كَفَرُواْ كَمَثَلِ ٱلَّذِى يَنْعِقُ بِمَا لَا يَسْمَعُ إِلَّا دُعَآءً وَنِدَآءً صُمٌّۢ بُكْمٌ عُمْيٌ فَهُمْ لَا يَعْقِلُونَ ﴿١٧١﴾

"And the example of those who disbelieve is as that of him who shouts to the (flock of sheep) that hears nothing but calls and cries. (They are) deaf, dumb and blind. So they do not understand."

- Disbelievers are evil – Al-A'raf: (7:177):

سَآءَ مَثَلًا ٱلْقَوْمُ ٱلَّذِينَ كَذَّبُواْ بِـَٔايَـٰتِنَا وَأَنفُسَهُمْ كَانُواْ يَظْلِمُونَ ﴿١٧٧﴾

"Evil is the likeness of the people who reject Our ayat (proofs, evidences, verses and signs, etc.) and used to wrong their own selves."

75

- Disbelievers are like animals – Al-Furqan: (25:44):

$$أَمْ تَحْسَبُ أَنَّ أَكْثَرَهُمْ يَسْمَعُونَ أَوْ يَعْقِلُونَ إِنْ هُمْ$$
$$إِلَّا كَالْأَنْعَامِ بَلْ هُمْ أَضَلُّ سَبِيلًا ﴿٤٤﴾$$

"Or do you think that most of them hear or understand? They are only like cattle; nay, they are even farther astray from the path (that is, even worse than cattle)."

- Disbelievers are unclean – At-Taubah: (9:28):

$$يَتَأَيُّهَا الَّذِينَ ءَامَنُوٓا إِنَّمَا الْمُشْرِكُونَ نَجَسٌ فَلَا يَقْرَبُوا الْمَسْجِدَ الْحَرَامَ$$
$$بَعْدَ عَامِهِمْ هَـٰذَا وَإِنْ خِفْتُمْ عَيْلَةً فَسَوْفَ يُغْنِيكُمُ اللَّهُ مِن فَضْلِهِ إِن$$
$$شَاءَ إِنَّ اللَّهَ عَلِيمٌ حَكِيمٌ ﴿٢٨﴾$$

"O you who believe, verily, the Mushrikun (polytheists, pagans, idolaters, disbelievers in the Oneness of Allah and in the Message of Muhammad) are najasun (impure). So let them not come near Al-Masjid-al Haram (at Mecca) after this year, and if you fear poverty, Allah will enrich you if He will, out of His Bounty. Surely, Allah is All Knowing, All Wise."

- Disbelievers are perverse – At-Taubah: (9:30):

$$وَقَالَتِ الْيَهُودُ عُزَيْرٌ ابْنُ اللَّهِ وَقَالَتِ النَّصَارَى الْمَسِيحُ ابْنُ اللَّهِ ذَٰلِكَ$$
$$قَوْلُهُم بِأَفْوَاهِهِمْ يُضَاهِئُونَ قَوْلَ الَّذِينَ كَفَرُوا مِن قَبْلُ قَاتَلَهُمُ اللَّهُ$$
$$أَنَّىٰ يُؤْفَكُونَ ﴿٣٠﴾$$

"And the Jews say: 'Uzair (Ezra) is the son of Allah, and the Christians say: Messiah is the son of Allah. That is a saying from their mouths. They imitate the saying of the disbelievers of old. Allah's Curse be on them, how they are deluded away from the truth?"

• Disbelievers are the worst of creatures - Al-Anfal: (8:55):

إِنَّ شَرَّ ٱلدَّوَآبِّ عِندَ ٱللَّهِ ٱلَّذِينَ كَفَرُواْ فَهُمْ لَا يُؤْمِنُونَ ۝

"Verily, the worst of moving (living) creatures before Allah are those who disbelieve (kufar), so they shall not believe."

• Disbelievers breach covenant – Al-Anfal: (8:56):

ٱلَّذِينَ عَٰهَدتَّ مِنْهُمْ ثُمَّ يَنقُضُونَ عَهْدَهُمْ فِى كُلِّ مَرَّةٍ وَهُمْ لَا يَتَّقُونَ ۝

"They are those with whom you made covenant but they breach their covenant every time and they do not fear Allah".

• Disbelievers are misapprehension – Al-Anfal: (8:65):

يَٰٓأَيُّهَا ٱلنَّبِىُّ حَرِّضِ ٱلْمُؤْمِنِينَ عَلَى ٱلْقِتَالِ إِن يَكُن مِّنكُمْ عِشْرُونَ صَٰبِرُونَ يَغْلِبُواْ مِائَتَيْنِ وَإِن يَكُن مِّنكُم مِّائَةٌ يَغْلِبُوٓاْ أَلْفًا مِّنَ ٱلَّذِينَ كَفَرُواْ بِأَنَّهُمْ قَوْمٌ لَّا يَفْقَهُونَ ۝

"O Prophet (Muhammad!), urge the believers to fight. If there are twenty steadfast persons amongst you, they will

77

overcome two hundred, and if there be a hundred steadfast persons they will overcome a thousand of those who disbelieve, because they (the disbelievers) are people who do not understand."

• The disbelievers are the most contemptible - Al-A'raf, verse (7:179):

وَلَقَدْ ذَرَأْنَا لِجَهَنَّمَ كَثِيرًا مِّنَ ٱلْجِنِّ وَٱلْإِنسِ لَهُمْ قُلُوبٌ لَّا يَفْقَهُونَ بِهَا وَلَهُمْ أَعْيُنٌ لَّا يُبْصِرُونَ بِهَا وَلَهُمْ ءَاذَانٌ لَّا يَسْمَعُونَ بِهَا أُوْلَٰٓئِكَ كَٱلْأَنْعَٰمِ بَلْ هُمْ أَضَلُّ أُوْلَٰٓئِكَ هُمُ ٱلْغَٰفِلُونَ ﴿١٧٩﴾

"And surely, We have created many of the jinns and mankind for Hell. They have hearts wherewith they understand not, they have eyes wherewith they see not, and they have ears wherewith they hear not (the truth). They are like cattle, nay even more astray! They are the heedless ones".

Other than the above verses, in surah al-Bayyinah, verse (98:6) Allah also said that the disbelievers were the worst living creatures:

إِنَّ ٱلَّذِينَ كَفَرُوا۟ مِنْ أَهْلِ ٱلْكِتَٰبِ وَٱلْمُشْرِكِينَ فِى نَارِ جَهَنَّمَ خَٰلِدِينَ فِيهَآ أُوْلَٰٓئِكَ هُمْ شَرُّ ٱلْبَرِيَّةِ ﴿٦﴾

"Verily, those who disbelieve (in the religion of Islam, the Quran and Prophet Muhammad) from among the people of the Scripture (Jews and Christians) and al-mushrikin (idol worshipers) will abode in the Fire of Hell for ever. They are the worst of creatures".

Allah described them as such and therefore in order to counter Islam, many orientalists and Christian missionaries studied and made research on al-Quran and al-Sunnah with the intention to corrupt and to misrepresent about Islam and Prophet Muhammad (pbuh). Their libraries are full of books written by them for the students to use as their reference in their studies in the hope to mislead the Muslims students to be critical about Islam.

Some of the orientalists created a false image of Prophet Muhammad by portraying him as a robber gang leader, mad leader, stupid, sex pervert and spreading Islam with sword and so forth.

Some of them also accused Prophet Muhammad wrote al-Quran. If he was stupid how he could recite the revelation of the al-Quran. There was even a ridiculous accusation that Prophet Muhammad liked eating pork. Because his servant stole his pork, he prohibited other people from eating it.

With regard to breaking of covenant, even during the time of Prophet Muhammad the Jews used to break agreements. By the Charter of Medina, the people of Medina agreed to support each other in case of war. Nevertheless, the Jews broke the covenant, not only not helping the Messenger of Allah in fighting with the infidel (kufar) Arab Quraish of Macca but they attempted many times to kill Prophet Muhammad (pbuh). In the battle of Khandaq they also collaborated with the Arab kufar. Because of the betrayal by the Jews of Bani Quraizah, Prophet Muhammad (pbuh) punished them. The male Jews in the tribe were beheaded and all the Jews were chased out from Medina for good.

On why the disbelievers are the worst creatures, Syaikh Muhammad Abduh said:

"They are rejecters or heedless of truth after knowing it although there were evidence, guides and signs of truth ever present. They denied the truth although their own souls accepted it, thereby they soiled their own souls and they also spoiled souls of others".

As human beings they have the natural senses given by Allah but they do not use these faculties to think and see this universe laid before them, as a sign of the ever present of the Almighty Creator (Allah). They can see the surrounding, the trees, the fruit trees bearing fruits, the forest, the birds, the sun and the moon and so on, but they question not and think not of the Creator although their own soul accept it. Who created the human beings, including themselves, if not the Creator? It is preposterous to think that human beings are the descendent of monkeys, as Charles Darwin absurdly envisaged. It is also preposterous to think that no one created those things but they happened or grew by themselves. Thus, Allah described those people just like cattle for they cannot use the natural senses to think about the Creator (Allah).

ii. The characteristics of hypocrites (munafiqun).

The hypocrites have many traits as prescribed in Al-Quran and al-Sunnah.

A munafiq (plural - *munafiqun*) or a hypocrite outwardly looked normal as usual and seemed to practise Islam but actually inwardly disbelieving (*kufar*). In other words, a hypocrite outwardly concealed the disbelief but in reality from the inside the person is a rejecter of Islam. Therefore, it is difficult to pin-point a hypocrite person.

The al-Quran has many verses on the hypocrites, explaining the attributes and attitude of the hypocrites, namely in surah al-Baqarah, verses (2:8-20) and other surah as well but not narrated here.

The hypocrites seemingly behave and pretend to be just like the ordinary Muslims, but in their hearts, they are not. They are the destructive elements of Islam from within whereas the disbelievers against Islam from the outside. Therefore, the hypocrites are very dangerous. They are more dangerous to Muslims than the non-Muslim enemies. They often appeared to support Islam, but in reality they hate and betray Islam. Hence, the Muslims have to be wary about them.

In surah al-Munafiqun (hypocrites), Allah explained their traits. They pledged that they were believers but they were not. They gave false oaths to cover-up their hypocrisy to avoid from being punished as disbelievers. They could communicate well as if they were believers, but in their hearths they are actually not. Allah said in surah al-Munafiqun, verses (63:1-5) as follows:

إِذَا جَاءَكَ ٱلْمُنَٰفِقُونَ قَالُوا۟ نَشْهَدُ إِنَّكَ لَرَسُولُ ٱللَّهِ وَٱللَّهُ يَعْلَمُ إِنَّكَ لَرَسُولُهُۥ وَٱللَّهُ يَشْهَدُ إِنَّ ٱلْمُنَٰفِقِينَ لَكَٰذِبُونَ ١

"When the hypocrites come to you (O Muhammad), they say: "We bear witness that you are indeed the Messenger of Allah." Allah knows that you are indeed His Messenger and Allah bears witness that the hypocrites are liars indeed."

ٱتَّخَذُوٓا۟ أَيْمَٰنَهُمْ جُنَّةً فَصَدُّوا۟ عَن سَبِيلِ ٱللَّهِ إِنَّهُمْ سَآءَ مَا كَانُوا۟ يَعْمَلُونَ ٢

"They have made their oaths a screen (for their hypocrisy). Thus they hinder (men) from the path of Allah. Verily, evil is what they used to do."

ذَٰلِكَ بِأَنَّهُمْ ءَامَنُوا۟ ثُمَّ كَفَرُوا۟ فَطُبِعَ عَلَىٰ قُلُوبِهِمْ فَهُمْ لَا يَفْقَهُونَ ٣

"That is because they believed, then disbelieved, therefore their hearts are sealed, so they understand not."

وَإِذَا رَأَيْتَهُمْ تُعْجِبُكَ أَجْسَامُهُمْ وَإِن يَقُولُوا تَسْمَعْ لِقَوْلِهِمْ كَأَنَّهُمْ خُشُبٌ مُّسَنَّدَةٌ يَحْسَبُونَ كُلَّ صَيْحَةٍ عَلَيْهِمْ هُمُ الْعَدُوُّ فَاحْذَرْهُمْ قَاتَلَهُمُ اللَّهُ أَنَّىٰ يُؤْفَكُونَ ۞

"And when you look at them, their bodies please you; and when they speak, you listen to their words. They are as blocks of wood propped up. They think that every cry is against them. They are the enemies, so beware of them. May Allah curse them! How are they denying (or deviating from) the right path."

وَإِذَا قِيلَ لَهُمْ تَعَالَوْا يَسْتَغْفِرْ لَكُمْ رَسُولُ اللَّهِ لَوَّوْا رُءُوسَهُمْ وَرَأَيْتَهُمْ يَصُدُّونَ وَهُم مُّسْتَكْبِرُونَ ۞

"And when it is said to them: "Come, so that the Messenger of Allah may ask forgiveness from Allah for you", they turn aside their heads, and you would see them turning away their faces in pride."

According to a hadith by Abu Hurairah (sahih Bukhari) that the prophet Muhammad said:

"The signs of a hypocrite are three:

- **Whenever he speaks, he tells lie.**
- **Whenever he promises, he always breaks it (his promise).**
- **If you trust him, he betrays it. (If you give something in trust to him, he will not return it)."**

The above hadith narrated by Bukhari, Muslim, at-Tharmizi and an-Nasaai.

During the time of Prophet Muhammad (pbuh), the leader of the hypocrite in Medina was Abdullah bin Ubay. There was no hypocrite in Mecca.

As pointed out earlier, the conflict between the Muslims and the disbelievers started since long time ago since the advent of Islam in Mecca. It continues until the present modern day. The disbelievers applied the time-tested Roman imperial formula of divide et impera (divide and rule) policy. This is the key of their success in dividing and taming the Muslims.

In connection with the disbelievers as the worst creatures, to prove the points, just a few of the following examples of their cruelties may be representative, though repetitious. This does not mean that the believers or the Muslims are angels, but comparatively they are as a whole not as bad as the disbelievers. The examples of their atrocities are as follows:

- The crusaders (Christians) in 1099 AD conquered Palestine and mercilessly killed about forty thousand Muslims. On the other hand, when the Muslims retook Palestine in 1187 AD by Sallahuddin al-Ayubi (Saladin), the Christians as well as the Jews were free with full freedom to practise their religions.

- The barbaric Mongol under Houlako Khan with the help Shiites invaded Iraq in 1258 AD. They plundered Baghdad and killed over a million of Muslims. They also burned down thousands of books of knowledge and threw them into the river.

- The Muslims ruled Spain for about 700 years and succeeded in establishing Islam there peacefully without prosecuting the Christians. However when the Christians in 1492 succeeded in overthrowing the weak Muslim rulers there, they tortured and killed the Muslims. They forced the Muslims to become Christians and those who refused either were killed or chased away from Spain. They burned Islamic books and converted mosques into churches. Because of the atrocities, even until today not many Muslims found in Spain.

- The Germans under Hitler in the World War II also were very cruel causing millions of death. They also killed thousands or a million of Jews, although they were long settled there. They exterminated thousands of Jews by putting them into the poisonous gas chamber.

- After the end of world war the 2nd in 1942, the Christian West chased away many Palestinians from Palestine and confiscated their land to give it away to the Zionist Israel (Jews). The Jews chased away many of the Palestinians and also killed many of them. Many of the Palestinians became refugees until today.

- Russians inflicted heavy atrocities, killing millions of Muslims in Chechen and others in the Caucasian mountains for umpteen years, even until today. The Muslims were freedom fighters for their homelands. They wanted to be separated from Russia.

- The political scenario in the entire Middle East is always unstable and chaotic. The Christian West played damaging role in the Middle East by interfering in their affairs, so much so the entire region became unstable. United States backed the autocratic regimes of Saudi Arabia and Egypt etc. The United States supported the autocratic regime of President Mubarak of Egypt for almost 30 years. Dissidents - Islamist and nationalist groups – mercilessly crushed. Mubarak was the America's protégé or puppet in the Middle East.

Mubarak fell through popular revolution on February 11, 2011. Mohamed Morsi of Muslim Brotherhood was elected. He became the President of Egypt for a year only on 30th June 2012 to 3rd July 2013. He was unseated on 3rd July 2013 by a military coup led by his army general Abdel Fattah el-Sesi, also a protégé of US.

Soon after the fall of Mubarak Egypt, Muammar Gaddafi regime in Libya also fell. The mob killed him. The West had a hand in Libya's affairs.

- Earlier on in 2003, the United States and the Great Britain invaded Iraq, thus resulting in the civil war quagmire in Syria and Iraq.

- In the infamous Bosnian war, on March 1st 1993 to December 14th 1995, the Christians not only tortured but raped women and slaughtered thousands of innocent Muslims. They committed the crime of genocide or ethnic cleansing. United Nations monopolised by the West did not do anything to save the Bosnian

Muslims. Only after so many Bosnian Muslims were killed, then UN intervened, with the help of the United States, to stop the carnage.

- The Japanese too were very cruel when they invaded China and South East Asia in the World War II. They killed and raped thousands of Chinese, Koreans, Philippines, Indonesians and Malays as well. They inflicted much hardship on the local people.

- In the South East Asia, the British, Dutch and American colonialists left 'cancerous spots' in the southern Philippines, southern Thailand, Burma and Kashmir etc. where never ending arm conflicts between the non-Muslim government and the displaced Muslim minorities. These peoples keep on demanding for self-government or autonomy that resulted in thousands of people killed.

The Muslim inhabitants in those regions are poor and often subjected to discrimination. The problems happened because when those countries got their independence by means of people's revolution or negotiation, new boundaries hurriedly drawn-up by the colonial masters, resulting some of the people displaced under the jurisdiction of different countries. Probably, the boundaries deliberately so demarcated with ulterior motives so that the inhabitants eventually would fight for their autonomy or self-government, thus retarding development in those areas.

However, the situation in Timor-Leste (East Timor), formally an Indonesian territory, was quite different simply because its population are Christians. The conflict there was settled quite easily due the interference of the Western Christian powers, whereas the problems in southern Philippines and Thailand and Burma (Myanmar) whose population are Muslims remained unsettled. The Western powers simply do not want to interfere in those areas because politically, religiously and economically do not benefit them.

The above episodes discounted some the most evil or tyrant individual leaders of disbelievers in the modern history who inflicted untold miseries on fellow human, a few them are cited as follows:

1. Mao Zedong.

Mao Zedong (1893-1976), a Chinese communist leader of China for decades, held absolute power over the lives of one-quarter of the world's population, was responsible for an estimate of 70 million deaths, more than any other leaders. He was said to have systematically killed millions of people during his ill-fated social programs of the Great Leap Forward and the Cultural Revolution. During the period of the programs, millions of people starved to death. The estimated deaths on the programs alone were about 20 million.

During the Culture Revolution, the Red Guards killed intellectuals and Mao's political adversaries that were responsible for many millions of death.

Overall, his policies and political purges from 1949 to 1976 caused the deaths estimated between 40 to 70 million people.

2. Joseph Stalin.

Joseph Stalin (birth surname: Jughashvili, 18 December 1878 – 5 March 1953) was the leader of the Soviet Union from the mid-1920s until his death in 1953.

Josef Stalin was the first Secretary of the Communist Party. After Lenin's death in 1924, he became the leader of the Soviet Union.

Stalin new economic policy in food production was a total failure in Ukraine that resulted in great famine across the country. It was widely believed that Soviet policies caused the famine there and designed as an attack on Ukrainian nationalism. The total number of casualties within Soviet Ukraine estimated between 3 to 10 million. During the late 1930s, Stalin launched another paranoid initiative called the Great Purge (also known as the "Great Terror") to kill off mercilessly the people who opposed him.

The trials and executions of those former Communist leaders in the great purges together with man-made famines had led to an estimate of at least 20 million deaths.

3. Adolf Hitler.

Adolf Hitler (20 April 1889 – 30 April 1945) was an Austrian-born German who was the leader of the Nazi Party and Führer (leader) of Nazi Germany from 1934 to 1945. As the absolute dictator of Nazi Germany, Hitler was at the centre of World War II in Europe and the Holocaust.

He gained support by promoting values like German nationalism and anti-Semitism. Hitler was obsessed with power. He hated most the Jews and others as well and wanted to dominate Europe. Hitler frequently denounced international capitalism and communism as being part of a Jewish conspiracy.

Hitler and the Nazi regime were also responsible for the killing of an estimated of 19.3 million civilians and prisoners of war, including an estimated of 6 million Jews. This did not include million soldiers and civilians died as the result of military action in the European Theatre of World War II. The number of civilians killed during the Second World War was unprecedented warfare, and constituted the deadliest conflict in human history.

4. Leopold II of Belgium.

Leopold II was the second King of the Belgians (born on 9 April 1835 – 17 December 1909). He believed in colonialism and chiefly remembered for the founding and exploitation of the Congo Free State as a private venture.

He created a colony called the "Congo Free State", enslaved its people, and forced the indigenous populations into forced labour, created a bustling rubber industry and abused his workers grievously.

Under his regime, millions of the Congolese people died. Modern estimates claimed that the death ranged from two to fifteen million with a consensus estimate around 10 million. Human rights abuses under his regime contributed significantly to these deaths.

Reports of deaths and abuse led to a major international scandal in the early 20th century and Leopold ultimately forced by the Belgian government to relinquish him from controlling the colony to the civil administration in 1908.

The tragedy would not happen if other European colonial nations did not authorise him at his claim to the Congo Free State to improve the lives of the native inhabitants at the Berlin Conference of 1884–1885.

5. Pol Pot.

Pol Pot (19 May 1925 – 15 April 1998) born Saloth Sar (Khemer) was the leader of the communist movement in Cambodia. He attempted to "cleanse" the country under his policy of agrarian collectivisation. He forced city folk to relocate to collective farm projects. He forced them into hard labour resulting in the death of millions of people. Pol enslaved his own people, did not feed them well, gave them little medical care and executed many of them.

The combined effects of executions, strenuous working conditions, malnutrition and poor medical care caused the deaths of approximately 25 percent of the Cambodian population. In all, the estimated death ranged from one to three million people (out of a population of slightly over 8 million) died due to the policies of his four-year premiership.

Pol Pot died in 1998, while under house arrest by the Ta Mok faction of the Khmer Rouge. Since his death, rumours circulated that he committed suicide or was poisoned.

The above were a few examples of tyrant leaders of disbelievers in the modern history.

There are, of course, many other tyrant leaders that caused millions of death. The latest tyrant leader of lesser extent may, perhaps, include George W. Bush, the ex-President of the United States of America who invaded Iraq in 2003. The invasion supported by his ally British ex-Prime Minister, Tony Blair and it was without the sanction of the United Nations.

The invasion toppled the government of Saddam Hussein and inflicted untold misery to the people of Iraq. The incursion not only destroyed Iraq and its civilisation overall as well but killed and displaced thousands of innocent Iraqis. Its aftermath or sequel led to havoc and great quagmire in Iraq and Syria with emergence of the belligerent and extremist ISIS.

The Bush Administration based its rationale for war principally on the assertion that Iraq possessed weapons of mass destruction and its immediate threat to the United States. However, subsequently the accusation proved to be unfounded and was heavily criticised internally and internationally.

Saddam Hussien was on the loose but subsequently pathetically captured in December 2003. The kangaroo Shiite military court three years later sentenced Saddam to death and executed him accordingly.

Thus, this is the modern sin committed by ex-President George W. Bush. He is the greatest cheat and liar that led to unnecessary conflict in Iraq causing roughly about a million or more of death toll overall.

However, following the power vacuum after Saddam's demise and the mismanagement of the occupation forces led to not only widespread sectarian violence between the Shiite and the minority Sunni Muslims but also a lengthy insurgency against the United States and its coalition forces.

The United States responded with a troop surge in 2007 and with that directly reduced the level of violence. The United States President Barack Obama formally withdrew all combat troops from Iraq by December 2011.

The Iraqi government remained ineffective, thus worsening sectarian tensions between the Shiite and the country's Sunni minority. The situation became worst when out of a sudden, in the summer of 2014 the Islamic State of Iraq and the Levant (ISIL) launched a military offensive in Northern Iraq and declared an Islamic caliphate, thus eliciting another military response from the United States and its allies.

The financial cost of the war has been more than £4.55 billion ($9 billion) to the United Kingdom alone. In March 2013, the total cost of the Iraq War estimated to have been $1.7 trillion by the Watson Institute of International Studies at Brown University. Critics have argued that the total cost of the war to the United States economy estimated to be from $3 trillion to $6 trillion, including interest rates by 2053.

Being the leaders of big powers, George W. Bush and Tony Blair escaped from any criminal charges against humanity and human rights. If this kind of crime committed by the leaders of small nations of the third world, they would surely be arrested and charged in the International court of Justice.

The above are just a few points to show how bad is the disbelievers in inflicting atrocities on fellow human beings, Muslims or otherwise, wherever they have interest or the opportunity to interfere. It proved that their cruelties were as such from the time immemorial until now. They killed people without mercy, irrespective of religions of their victims. Nevertheless, thus far they killed Muslims more than the Muslims killed them.

The disbelievers are ever prepared and ever ready with all military might available to use when the need arises. All the sophisticated weapons and other military arsenal of today belong to them whereas the Muslims depend on them for the supply of weapons, mostly made of second-class or outdated ones with exorbitant prices too. Some Muslims leaders used the weapons to turn on their own citizens.

The big powers of disbelievers of the divides have the capacity to control the world. They control the air space and the high seas. At present, Muslim powers are almost non-existence. The United States of America has military facilities or personnel stationed in Japan, Australia and Philippines, including the small island of Singapore at the southern tip of the Peninsular Malaysia.

Nevertheless, the presence of the United States may be required for the sake of political stability in this region as a military power balance in the Far East vis-a-vis the emergence of Chinese military power. The rivalry and ever explosive relationship between the regimes of North Korea and South Korea is also another problem that needs the support of big powers to prevent any untoward incident that may flare-up between them.

Under the present circumstances in South East Asia, the presence of the United States may be timely in order to contain the disquieting issue from escalating further that may undermine the stability in the region. China of late has flexed its muscles by unilaterally usurped and built-up by land reclamation on certain of the disputed territorial areas of the Spratly island chains by building air strips etc. much to the chagrin of other claimants.

The Spratly Islands territorial dispute is an ongoing for a quite long time between the Philippines, China, Malaysia, Taiwan, Vietnam and Brunei. The Spratly Islands consisted of a group of islands associated with "maritime features" (reefs, banks, cays, etc.) located in the South China Sea. The dispute is characterised by diplomatic stalemate and the employment of low-level military pressure techniques (such as military occupation of disputed territory) in the advancement of national territorial claims of ownership. All except Brunei occupy some of the maritime features of the Spratly Islands.

With regard to weapons of mass destruction, the world big powers have nuclear weapons, not only to safeguard themselves but also to have the power edge over the others. They highly distrust other countries, particularly nations that do not get along in line with their policies. Such being the case, these big powers keep on making surveillance on the other countries to ensure that they do not build weapons of mass destruction or nuclear weapons like them.

They stockpiled those mean weapons, ready to be used whenever the need arises. This stockpiling of nuclear weapons is very unfair state of affairs but they claimed it is for the sake of keeping world peace.

The United Nations per se is not effective in this regard because it does not able to control and destroy all nuclear weapons that belong to the big powers. The double standards of having nuclear weapons and veto powers reserved for the big powers only indicated that democracy in the United Nations is not alive. Being super powers they dictate their terms on the weak others. In reality, they do not want peace and harmony but they prefer instability so they can dominate the world economically and militarily. Small, poor and weak nations have no choice but to fall in line and abide by their rules otherwise life would be difficult for the small nations. Those are the attributes of the disbelievers.

The Muslims should be rightly emotional about all this, but emotional alone without working hard and wake up from their slumber and struggle hard (jihad) in the way of Allah for success will not do. The main problem is that most of the Muslim leaders are in the same boat with the disbelievers. In fact, in many instances the Muslims are of little difference from the disbelievers in their action and behaviour.

Probably, the conflict in the Middle East would not be protracted for such a long time if it is not the result of the outside forces interfering in the affairs of the Middle East, but being big powers they are waiting for such opportunity to get involved to ensure that the region is unstable and the Muslims become weaker so that the Muslims will always remain under their tutelage. Nonetheless, it is unfair to solely blame the disbelievers because the Arabs themselves have invited the West to come in to help solving their problems in their own backyards.

iii. The Characteristics of Muslims (believers).

As far as Muslims are concerned, it is undeniable that some of the Muslim leaders are also cruel, either in the olden days or in the modern world because their faith in Allah had been much diminished. Therefore, in managing their affairs too they do not subscribe accordingly to the true Islamic teachings. They are no angels though, but comparatively they are not as evil as the disbelievers. Many of the Muslim leaders and scholars are pious and Allah fearing people.

As to the Prophet Muhammad, the Messenger of Allah, his character was beyond reproach. He was infallible because Allah always protected and guided him. As to his four glorious close friends, Abu Bakr, Umar, Othman and Ali, they were all pious companions and of exemplary characters too. But to the Shiite, they branded them except Ali as infidels.

In the glorious al-Quran, many verses described the attributes and virtues of Muslims. Perhaps, the summary of which under surah al-Mu'minun, verses (23:1- 10) below may be representative:

قَدْ أَفْلَحَ ٱلْمُؤْمِنُونَ (١) ٱلَّذِينَ هُمْ فِى صَلَاتِهِمْ خَاشِعُونَ (٢) وَٱلَّذِينَ هُمْ عَنِ ٱللَّغْوِ

مُعْرِضُونَ (٣) وَٱلَّذِينَ هُمْ لِلزَّكَاةِ فَاعِلُونَ (٤) وَٱلَّذِينَ هُمْ لِفُرُوجِهِمْ حَافِظُونَ (٥) إِلَّا

عَلَىٰ أَزْوَاجِهِمْ أَوْ مَا مَلَكَتْ أَيْمَانُهُمْ فَإِنَّهُمْ غَيْرُ مَلُومِينَ (٦) فَمَنِ ٱبْتَغَىٰ وَرَآءَ ذَٰلِكَ

فَأُوْلَـٰئِكَ هُمُ ٱلْعَادُونَ (٧) وَٱلَّذِينَ هُمْ لِأَمَانَاتِهِمْ وَعَهْدِهِمْ رَاعُونَ (٨) وَٱلَّذِينَ هُمْ عَلَىٰ

صَلَوَاتِهِمْ يُحَافِظُونَ (٩) أُوْلَـٰئِكَ هُمُ ٱلْوَارِثُونَ (١٠)

1. *Successful indeed are the believers.*

2. *Those who offer their solat (prayers) with all solemnity and full submissiveness.*

3. *And those who turn away from al-laghw (vain talk and falsehood)*

4. *And those who pay the zakat (alms).*

5. *And those who guard their chastity (i.e. private parts, from illegal sexual acts).*

6. *Except from their wives or (the captives and slaves) that their right hands possess, for them they are free from blame.*

7. *But whoever seeks beyond that then those are the transgressors.*

8. *Those who faithfully true to their amanat (trusts and duties) and to their covenants.*

9. *And those who strictly guard their obligatory daily prayers (daily five times compulsory prayers).*

10. *These are indeed the inheritors (of the Paradise)."*

As the believers (Mu'minun), they are looking forward for success in life, not only in this world but also in the world hereafter. Therefore, genuine Muslims briefly, in line with in the above verses, have the following characteristics:

- They worship Allah sincerely, in heart, words and actions, with full of submissiveness and solemnity. They always remember and fear Allah.

- They abstain from vain or useless talk or listening to non-beneficial worldly things or non-spiritual sense.

- They dutifully pay zakat (alms). Zakat literally means to purify or to cleanse by giving to charity a portion of their wealth, subject to certain conditions prescribed by the syariah.

- They safe-guard their chastity (their private parts) against unlawful liaison except with their wives and their legal bondmaids according to the prescribed laws.

- They discharge their trust faithfully covering everything that they undertake to perform or to take care under the trust.

- They fulfil their covenants or promises.

- They diligently and strictly perform all their obligatory five daily prayers.

- They always maintain good relationship with Allah and their fellow humankind and other creatures of Allah.

The above are some of the characteristics or attributes of the true Muslims (Mu'minun). Of course, there are many other obligations the Muslims would have to observe in order for them to be more successful in life here in the world and hereafter. They are the ones who will inherit the Paradise. In other words, the true 'al-falah' (success) is to gain the inheritance of the Paradise of Allah or to enter the havens of Allah with His blessing.

It is a fact that the behaviour and moral character of most of the Muslims in the modern world are a far cry from the above verses. Nonetheless, Allah is Most Merciful and Most Forgiven and therefore if the Muslims repent and ask for forgiveness, insyaallah, He will give His blessing and pardon them.

10.1. Deception and Supremacy.

The world had seen since long time ago that the Christian people in Western countries ventured out to colonise most part of the world with their military might in search of riches and to expand their domains. Even after those countries gained their independence from them, the West still subtly continue to dominate their economy, apart from their military supremacy. To have their global supremacy, they all along have their strategy either by subtle deception or direct head-on competition or even war with their rivals.

The world powers want to maintain their status quo and at the same time to increase their domains wherever possible. They are ever vigilant to contain any new emerging power that would undermine them, especially the Muslim power. Being disbelievers as such, they would never allow the Muslims to surpass them again. They do not want history to repeat itself. Thus, the confrontation between the disbelievers and the Muslims will continue indefinitely.

Just look at the political situation in the Middle East, as a real living example. One could see that any strong Islamic government elected democratically or for that matter a strong independent autocratic Islamic regime will not last long. They know that strong Islamic regime will not easily bow to any big power because Islamic government has different philosophy with that of the Western or Eastern system. Thus, they would do anything to sabotage or to destabilise the country. Therefore, they destroyed Iraq under Saddam Hussein. They undermined the legally elected President Mohamed Morsi of Egypt by collaborating discretely with a pro-West general and installed him as a secular President in place. They have to do so lest their political and business interest there would be in jeopardy. For so long already, the Middle East region is overcrowded with them, not so much to protect the Arabs but to protect their political and oil interest there.

Again, coming to the world scenario, the United States of America and Russia as well are playing the big 'brothers' bullying the present world globally. They are the world 'policemen' on their own right to control the world. Probably, in the near future, China will also follow suit as a super power in its own right from Asia to flex its muscles in the world scene, if not the world at least in Asia.

On the eastern front in Eastern Europe, Russia too had shown its high-handed action in bullying Ukraine by annexing Crimea from it. On papers, Russia now may be not as powerful as before after the breakup of the Soviet Union but is still a big power to reckon with. The tension appears to be ongoing between the West and Russia. With the involvement of Russia as well in the quagmire in Syria and Iraq in waging war against the belligerent ISIS heightens the conflicts further in the region. The United States relationship with China is also not that cordial especially after China usurped parts of Spratly Island chains as its own to expend its territory domain southwards.

The downing of a civilian Malaysian airline MH017, flying in the airspace over Russia-Ukraine disputed border, killing 283 passengers and 15 crew on board, appeared to be shot down by Russian made surface-to-air-missile on 17th July 2014 was a very controversial issue, although there was evidence that the Russian-backed Ukrainian separatists were responsible for the downing of the Malaysia Airline. However, thus far the separatists and Russia denied it.

In July 2015, Malaysia proposed a United Nations resolution to set up an international tribunal to prosecute those suspected of being behind the downing of the plane. The proposal gained a majority on the UN Security Council, but it was vetoed down by Russia.

On 13 October 2015, the Dutch Safety Board (DSB) released a final report on their investigation into the incident, concluding that the airliner was downed by a Buk surface-to-air 9M38-series missile with 9N314M warhead launched from Eastern Ukraine.

However, the Russian government again disputed the report but instead blamed the Ukrainian government for the incident. Russia said that Ukraine "bears full, total responsibility" for the crash because it happened in Ukrainian airspace. This is in fact a blaming game tactics but so far it appears that nothing much can be done.

On the economic front, the West had the subtlety in manipulating the world economy. They have their 'economy hit men' and other agents to exploit the world economy. They have the forte and the art of deception in this game as well.

This economic competition and exploitation, according to the writer, John Perkins, in his book: 'Confession of an Economic Hit Man' he said that the 'Economy Hit Men' were highly paid hired professionals to defraud the nations of the world, involving trillions of American Dollars. Through the World Bank, the United States Agency for International Development (USAID) and other foreign aid organisations, they put funds into the large conglomerates and pockets of many rich families and elites of the countries that owned and controlled natural resources on earth as corruption payments.

Their modus operandi is through manipulation of financial reports, manipulation of election and rigging, corruption, intimidation, sex and murders and so forth. They employed the same strategy and tactic as before during their old colonial days but with a new sophisticated subtlety that is more deadly in this era of globalisation.

Big oil companies discharged as they like the toxic oil wastes into the seas, rivers and rain forests that could kill human, fauna and flora and the native inhabitants (aborigines) and their cultures in the forests. These greedy people did not take into consideration much of the damage done to environment and pollution arising from it, leading to human suffering as well, so long as they can make more money.

According to him, some of the American themselves, in fact, are poor lot too. About 12 million families live in difficulties to up-keep themselves. Nonetheless, the United States of America spent billions of USD, being the war cost in Iraq, to get oil riches there. The United Nations estimated that if half of the cost spent in the war were to use for fresh water, food, sanitation facilities and basic education, it would be enough to provide for every person on the surface of this earth.

In their endeavour to enhance their global economic empire, the Americans use their subtlety of deception in obtaining economic benefit from the world economy through not only their economy hit men but also through the system of closed-knitted conglomerates. In this manipulation, they make use of big conglomerates, banks and the government agency, collectively known as 'coporatocracy'. They have strong financial and political support. The government works hand-in-hand with the big corporations to control the world economy. In this scenario, the government has dominant interests in the economy, but the big corporation partners control the businesses.

In most of the world trade agreements or partnerships, the United States of America always leads the way. The latest example is the much talk about the US-led Trans-Pacific Partnership Agreement (TPPA). Broadly, it is quite similar to the agreement between the United States and the European Union that is, the Transatlantic Trade and Investment Partnership (TTIP).

The Trans-Pacific Partnership (TPP) is a trade agreement among twelve Pacific Rim countries concerning a variety of matters of economic policy which was reached on 5 October 2015 in Atlanta after 7 years of negotiations. It would be signed in Auckland in February 2016.

The agreement goal overall is to promote economic growth; support the creation and retention of jobs; enhance innovation, productivity and competitiveness; raise living standards; reduce poverty; and promote transparency, good governance, and to enhance labour and environmental protections.

The countries participated in this Trans-Pacific Partnership (TPPA) consisted of Pacific Rim countries – Australia, Canada, Chile, Peru, Japan, Singapore, Malaysia, Brunei, Vietnam, Mexico and the United States - which seeks, among other things, to address issues that can promote comprehensive market access by eliminating tariffs and other barriers to goods and services, trade and investment in order to create new opportunities for workers and businesses, a common framework for intellectual property, trademarks, copy rights and patents, enforcement standards for labour law and environmental law, establishment of an investor-state dispute settlement mechanism etc. Trademarks may be visual and auditory have been granted exclusive use for trade. Copyright granted at a length of life of the author and plus 70 years, thus it makes willful circumvention of the protections illegal. It is a sweeping trade deal that affects some 40% of the global economy.

This is no ordinary trade deal but to suit American-Asia policy, within the heart of ASEAN region as an economic and military strategy to counterweight the power house of China for the benefit of the United States generally. It is, therefore, no accident that China is excluded. However, it is also interesting to note that the other members of ASEAN - Philippines, Thailand, Laos, Cambodia, Indonesia and Burma – are excluded in the agreement. South Korea is also not in the list. Their exclusion may lead to inimical intra-ASEAN harmony.

It sounds good though, but there is a far-reaching implication provision in which global corporations could sue governments in private tribunals organised by the World Bank or the United Nations to obtain compensation from them for loss of expected future profits due to government interference or actions. Leading critiques who advocated for free trade and trade liberalisation sharply criticised the inclusion of the non-trade provision ostensibly free trade agreement. Thus, TPP seems to be a 'managed trade regime that put corporate interest first'.

Negotiations conducted much in secrecy and many voiced their criticism and objection. It appears that it is part of a global race to boost the profits of large corporations and Wall Street by out-sourcing jobs; undercutting workers' rights; dismantling labour, environmental, health, food safety and financial laws; and allowing corporations to challenge the country's laws in international tribunals rather than their own court system. If TPPA is such a good and fair deal, the administration or the negotiators should have the courage to show the people exactly what is in the deal, instead of keeping the contents of the TPPA a secret; but instead they just only show to the public the extract of it without the long-winded fine prints.

Overall, the clearest winners of the Trans-Pacific Partnership Agreement would be American agriculture, along with technology and pharmaceutical companies, insurers and many large manufacturers that could expand exports to the other nations participated in the treaty.

Some are concerned about TPPA's impact on healthcare in countries - developed and less developed - including potentially increased prices of medical drugs due to patent extensions, making cheaper generic product unavailable which could threaten millions of lives. However, some supporters of TPPA are disagreeable on this.

It is such a complicated negotiation with full of intricacies in which if it is not transparently negotiated and without certain safeguards, in the long term, it will benefit America more than those participating nations. Politically, technically and financially, the Americans are soundly far ahead of others. The real contents of the agreement are not transparently disclosed and therefore the ordinary masses are in the dark until after the agreement is signed. Its effect will not be known until after some times to come. By then, the agreement may give certain negative impact on the economies of the certain participant countries, for which it may too late to have any remedy. Thus, many people have opposed it. Many demonstrations also held protesting against the TPPA agreement.

The agreement would allow the United States to open up markets everywhere for its own benefit. Being a big economic power, with its economic advantage and expertise, it would control the businesses in the participating countries and eventually the political landscapes of those participating countries as well.

The opponents of TPPA maintain that the certain aspects of the agreement texts may create trouble from the perspective of regional stability, economic feasibility, social justice, and national sovereignty, although advocates of the deal have attempted vigorously to allay public criticism and fear. The TPPA obliges signatory countries to reshape their national laws and economic policies to conform to a neo-liberal agenda set by giant multinational corporations, to the benefit of local elites at the expense of the region's working classes and poor.

It is quite mind boggling because it would affect the business environment overall for those participating countries concerned.

The economic policies pushed by the US and its allies – backed to the hilt by multinational corporate interests – are demonstrably against the public good and show disregard for national sovereignty and political independence of the participating countries.

Overall, this TPPA is the subtle American ideas to dominate or colonise the world economy on negotiation table without the need to flex its strong muscles. It is, in fact, overshadowing the key functions of the World Trade Organisation (WTO), a comparatively more level playing field or even platform for discussing global trade. It is a neo-economic-political colonisation, indeed.

It is undeniable that with the economic endeavour and strategy in manipulating the market, world economy develops but it makes the elite groups and big corporations reaping the benefits much more than the ordinary masses. They become richer, but the majority poor masses remain poorer with cost of living keeps on increasing. They exploit the common people or poor masses to the maximum. Thus, the world economic and business culture becomes like a 'big machine' that is always moving, requiring every minute of input of large amount of raw materials it can acquire in order to get the machine working to the optimum. The aim is to maximise production and profit for the capitalist. When the raw materials are exhausted, the machine and the structure will burn down itself into destruction, leaving the poor masses in quandary. In the different analogy, when the natural resources depleted, those countries will suffer tremendously. The capitalist will run away with their money. Thus, the ones who suffer most are the poor people.

In this challenging globalised modern world, like in the olden days, the strongest and the fittest will win. In this regard, history proved that global empire did not last for long as at the end of the day, it would succumb and disintegrate by its own folly. It destroyed many world cultures in the process of military and economic expansion. No nation can stand strong for long by exploiting other people.

A good example is about the colonisation of America by Britain. It could hold America only for several decades. The Americans wanted freedom. When they knew the British trick in exploiting them, they revolted against the British and chased them away for good, although they were of the same stock and language. This example applies to any nation for that matter.

The system used by the British in America during its rule before, it is now duplicated by the United States of America itself until it becomes a big world power. America with its sophisticated technology and subtle manoeuvring wants to perpetuate its world dominance. However, one of these days, America would suffer or suffocate itself with its own manipulation.

Now, people of contemporary world have already realised of the American manipulation in cahoot with the shrewd Zionist Jews. Therefore, it is up to other leaders of the world to co-operate together to challenge and to put a stop to its craziness.

In this regard, do not the Muslims and their leaders realise of the treacherous attributes of the disbelievers? Al-Quran had already warned the Muslims about this and therefore, would the Muslims still easily want to cooperate with the disbelievers and trust them without safeguarding their own interest and turfs?

The Muslims may live in coexistence peacefully with the disbelievers and be always good to them, especially in this globalised world, but then there is a limit to it to ensure that the Muslims are not subservient to them. To this end, it is time for the Muslims to struggle hard or jihad to excel themselves in every sphere of life so that they can become a power of their own. Nevertheless, again, to put it in the correct perspective, Islam does not teach violence and extremism to its followers to obtain anything in their favour in their endeavour.

As always stressed, Islam is a religion of universal peace, a religion of moderation, justice and a virtuous religion. Thus, any wrong doings or transgressions are un-Islamic. Therefore, it is obligatory upon the Muslim ummah to invoke jihad to protect Islam and its followers in facing its aggressive adversaries. Allah abhors Muslims that condone the wrong doings and let it be as it is without taking any remedial actions to inhibit the misdeeds. If a Muslim cannot afford to stop the evil deeds by hands or by words of mouth, then at least by heart to show one's dislike of the misdeed.

The Muslims now are in quandary due their disunity. The disbelievers have a field day to play their dirty games in the uneven field against the Muslims. Although Allah commanded the Muslims to unite, irrespective colour or race, they miserly failed in this. Therefore, this is the struggle for all the Muslim ummah close rank otherwise it is a sin on all of them. As far as the disbelievers are concerned, the Muslims and Islam are their foes throughout life because they hate Islam unless the Muslims follow and submit to them. The Muslims therefore should never take them as leaders because they are not sincere towards Islam. They would somehow betray Muslims. Like it or not, that is the truth.

CHAPTER 11. THE UNGRATEFUL

Allah created human beings and jins to submit to Him only. Allah also created the universe with its contents therein for mankind to make use, enjoy and to look after them accordingly. They should not create mischief therein and cause destruction to this beautiful world. Human beings therefore should be grateful to Allah for all those endowments.

The Muslims should be much more thankful to Allah for choosing them to be the followers of the religion of Islam, particularly so for those who were born Muslims. Notwithstanding, there are ungrateful Muslims, though they were born Muslims they choose to be out of Islam, that is, to be infidel. They choose to be disobedient, hypocrites and apostates. However, in this free world and the under the principles of universal human rights, no one can stop any Muslim to be as such, although Islam prohibits it. An apostate in Islam is a grave crime and is punishable by death.

The ungrateful Muslims are aplenty. One could find easily everywhere that many Muslims do not practise Islam as it should be, either in worshiping and submission to Allah or about their mannerism and their way of life. Their life styles are not much difference with that of the non-Muslims, except that they do not worship the idols or the cross. The rich idolise their money, those in power abuse their power and corrupt whereas many of the poor likewise not much different in their life style. The lack in Islamic faith and the failure to apply Islamic syariah in the Muslim countries had contributed much to the moral decadent in the Muslim societies.

This subject matter of Islam is very sensitive to discuss, especially on Islamic syariah, even in the Muslim society. To the secularists, liberalists and pluralists, this subject matter is outdated and not relevant in the modern society because to them religion is an individual matter that needs no reminder or interference. They are advocators for the universal human rights principle.

Some of the Muslims are not ignorant in Islamic religion, but they do not practise Islamic principles in earnest. Protagonists of human rights principle had succeeded in undermining and corrupting their mind. In other words, the West had succeeded in its strategy to dilute the Islamic faith and in corrupting Islamic culture among the majority of the Muslims, especially those educated in the West. The Western culture had widely pervaded into the Muslim societies, even in the city of Mecca and Medina.

The fact that human beings are ungrateful expressed by Allah in the al-Quran in surah al-Hajj, verse: (22:66):

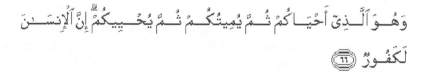

"And it is He, Who gave them life, and then will cause them to die, and will again give them life (on the Day of Resurrection). Verily mankind is indeed an ingrate."

It is clear therefore human beings overall, either disbelievers or believers, are ungrateful to the blessings of Allah except those pious ones who have received guidance from Allah.

When a person is good health, he misuses it. He becomes oblivious to the blessings of Allah. When he is sick, he complains. When he is rich, he is arrogant like Korah (Qarun), already mentioned on page 191 volume 1 book. Allah bestowed him much money which he kept in treasury safes that it took many keepers with difficulty in carrying the keys of his treasury. The verse is repeated below:

$$\text{قَالَ إِنَّمَا أُوتِيتُهُ عَلَىٰ عِلْمٍ عِندِيٓ أَوَلَمْ يَعْلَمْ أَنَّ ٱللَّهَ قَدْ}$$

$$\text{أَهْلَكَ مِن قَبْلِهِۦ مِنَ ٱلْقُرُونِ مَنْ هُوَ أَشَدُّ مِنْهُ قُوَّةً وَأَكْثَرُ جَمْعًا وَلَا}$$

$$\text{يُسْـَٔلُ عَن ذُنُوبِهِمُ ٱلْمُجْرِمُونَ ٧٨}$$

"He (Qarun) said: 'This has been given to me only because of knowledge I possess.' Did he not know that Allah had destroyed before him generations, men who were stronger than him in might and greater in amount (of riches) they had collected. But the Mujrimun (criminals, disbelievers, polytheists, sinners, etc.) will not be questioned of their sins (because Allah knows them well, so they will be punished without account)." [al-Qasas, verse 28:76]

Qarun (Korah) was not thankful to Allah despite the bounties Allah bestowed on him to make use of the blessings to perform good deeds to attain a piety and blessing in the next abode (the hereafter). He was ignorant and arrogant for he could not perceive the Divine Blessings and said instead that he got the riches due to his own knowledge.

Qarun finally punished by Allah. Allah made the earth swallow him up with his abode. Those who yearned for his place only the day before began to say as per verse of the same surah of al-Qasas (28:82):

$$\text{وَأَصْبَحَ ٱلَّذِينَ تَمَنَّوْاْ مَكَانَهُۥ بِٱلْأَمْسِ يَقُولُونَ وَيْكَأَنَّ ٱللَّهَ يَبْسُطُ ٱلرِّزْقَ}$$

$$\text{لِمَن يَشَآءُ مِنْ عِبَادِهِۦ وَيَقْدِرُ لَوْلَآ أَن مَّنَّ ٱللَّهُ عَلَيْنَا لَخَسَفَ بِنَا وَيْكَأَنَّهُۥ}$$

$$\text{لَا يُفْلِحُ ٱلْكَٰفِرُونَ ٨٢}$$

"And those who had desired for his position the day before began to say: 'Know you not that it is Allah Who enlarged the provision or restrict it to whomsoever He pleases of to His slaves. Had it not been that Allah was Gracious to us, He could have caused the earth to swallow us up (also)! Know you not that the disbelievers will never be success.'"

Human kind is not only ignorant but also unjust to his own self, for example, if a Muslim does not pray or fast then he is unjust to himself. When a person kills someone or robs him of his money, he is doing a disservice to himself, then to the other person too. Committing a sin is just like drinking poisoned water in which if a person drinks poison, he is hurting himself. The same logic is applicable to any misdeeds. Ungrateful to Allah is part of it.

Again, man is an inordinate being because he considers himself free from need or self-sufficient. Allah said in surah al-'Alalak, verse (96:6-7):

$$ كَلَّا إِنَّ ٱلْإِنسَـٰنَ لَيَطْغَىٰ ﴿٦﴾ $$

"Nay! Verily man does transgress all bounds (in disbelief and evil deed etc.)."

$$ أَن رَّءَاهُ ٱسْتَغْنَىٰ ﴿٧﴾ $$

"Because he considers himself self-sufficient."

Human beings feel self-sufficient when they enjoy the status of wealth and health etc. When a man has no money or is down, he is in sullen mode, impatient and frustrated. To illustrate the point, one of the companions of Prophet Muhammad (pbuh) was quite poor. He asked the Prophet for help. The Prophet gave him some money. Soon he became rich. He used to pray behind the Prophet (pbuh) before but as his money increased, his worship decreased. Therefore, one day the Prophet asked that man to pay the money back. When he paid it back, soon he became poor again and started to attend the mosque regularly. It shows that when a person is rich, he would most likely forget to remember or obey Allah.

People place reliance and trust on Allah only when they are in trouble and in difficulty but when they are off difficulties their reliance on Allah diminished. They think they have become self-sufficient, strong and need no God. In this regard, Allah said surah Yunus, verse (10:12):

وَإِذَا مَسَّ ٱلْإِنسَـٰنَ ٱلضُّرُّ دَعَانَا لِجَنبِهِۦٓ أَوْ قَاعِدًا أَوْ قَآئِمًا فَلَمَّا كَشَفْنَا عَنْهُ ضُرَّهُۥ مَرَّ كَأَن لَّمْ يَدْعُنَآ إِلَىٰ ضُرٍّ مَّسَّهُۥ ۚ كَذَٰلِكَ زُيِّنَ لِلْمُسْرِفِينَ مَا كَانُوا۟ يَعْمَلُونَ ۝

"And when harm touches man he invokes Us, lying down on his side or sitting or standing. But when We have removed his harm from him, he passes on his way as if he had never invoked Us from a harm that touched him. Thus it seems fair to the transgressors that which they used to do."

From the above verse an inference can be made, for example, when calamities befall on them, they turn to Allah by observing all the religious rituals and try hard to be close to Almighty Allah, but once the calamities are over, the feeling of being close to Allah waned or gone.

Man is also impatient, greedy and niggard or stingy being as stated in surah al-Ma'rij, verses (70:19-21) and al-Isra', verse (17:100) respectively as follows:

۞ إِنَّ ٱلْإِنسَـٰنَ خُلِقَ هَلُوعًا ۝

"Verily, man was created very impatient."

108

إِذَا مَسَّهُ ٱلشَّرُّ جَزُوعًا ﴿٢٠﴾

"Irritable (discontented) when evil touches him."

وَإِذَا مَسَّهُ ٱلۡخَيۡرُ مَنُوعًا ﴿٢١﴾

"And niggardly when good touches him".

قُل لَّوۡ أَنتُمۡ تَمۡلِكُونَ خَزَآئِنَ رَحۡمَةِ رَبِّيٓ إِذًا لَّأَمۡسَكۡتُمۡ خَشۡيَةَ ٱلۡإِنفَاقِ وَكَانَ ٱلۡإِنسَـٰنُ قَتُورًا ﴿١٠٠﴾

"Say (to the disbelievers): 'If you possessed the treasure of the Mercy of my Lord (wealth, money, provision, etc.), then you would surely hold back (from spending) for fear of (being exhausted), and man is ever miserly."

A wealthy person is selfish and stingy if he is not helping the needy. He is ungrateful to Allah for the wealth bestowed on him. Similarly, a knowledgeable person who keeps it for himself and not imparting his knowledge to others is also part of an ingrate attitude. For example, if a knowledgeable Islamic scholar refuses to impart his knowledge unless he is paid well over certain amount of fees for forty minutes or less than one hour lecture for listeners in a mosque or public places is also considered as an ingrate to impart the Islamic knowledge to others. These days, this ingrate attitude is quite common on the part of certain knowledgeable persons or ulama, whose intention is to make money only. This excessive material inclination is analogous to commercialising their Islamic knowledge for worldly gains, popularity, glamour or monitory rewards. They are just like the other celebrities, like the artists or other motivators, rather than preaching humbly in earnest for the sake of Allah.

Nowadays, despite of many Islamic scholars that disseminate Islamic knowledge to the Muslim society, the moral behaviour of the society keeps on diminishing. The influence of Western culture is overwhelming and is too difficult to contain in this cyber and digital age. Therefore, moral decadent in the society has set in.

No doubt, the preacher may very well attract many audience or participants per se as seen in the TV or elsewhere but more often than not its effect is nought because the 'brain-computers' of the listeners will not compute or absorb the input, as if garbage in and garbage out. This is because in imparting Islamic knowledge, no matter how noble or pious it looks, if the intention is not as noble and not in earnest in the way of Allah but for monetary gains, it will not work as most probably it is devoid of blessing from Allah. It is analogous to a rhetoric public speaker that pulls crowd only, but soon it will be forgotten. In other words, it will not motivate people to change for the better. It is just like the foams of the 'poisonous' coca cola drink, it will soon fizzle out into the air after drinking it.

May be this is a small sign, among the other signs, that preludes to the fast approaching of the end of the world. Some of the Islamic scholars seem to be proud of their religious knowledge and overly motivated to get quick reward by commercialising their Islamic knowledge.

Similarly, the ruling elites of the government of the day may give pep talk or long rhetoric speech to their people, asking them to be honest and be good citizens but on the other hand, the leaders themselves misbehave or do not lead the way by example or do not walk their talk. Thus, it would be meaningless and of no consequence.

In this current globalised world or 'village' with its sophisticated ICT and the cyber age, there is no news that is secret any more. It is in a matter of split seconds, the whole world would know about any news but the only thing is whether the news is reliable. Falsehood or fabricated news abound, especially if it comes from the disbelievers or the sinners (fasiq i.e. disobedient). Therefore, one has to be discerning in hearing, seeing or reading it. Scrutinising of its authenticity is of paramount importance, whether from the true disbelievers or disobedient (fasiq) believers, especially from political people or foes because they are more or less of the same category when come to propagation of their political belief and agenda. Their main agenda is to gain power by any means, legal or otherwise; everything goes including many millions of dollars of money politic secretly changing hands to buy votes. These are all the works of the greedy, dishonest and ungrateful people for want of power.

On news brought about by sinners (fasiq), Allah cautioned the believers in His revelation in surah al-Hujrat, verse (49:6):

يَٰٓأَيُّهَا ٱلَّذِينَ ءَامَنُوٓاْ إِن جَآءَكُمۡ فَاسِقُۢ بِنَبَإٖ فَتَبَيَّنُوٓاْ أَن تُصِيبُواْ قَوۡمَۢا بِجَهَٰلَةٖ فَتُصۡبِحُواْ عَلَىٰ مَا فَعَلۡتُمۡ نَٰدِمِينَ ۝

"O you believers, if a fasiq (a sinner or disobedient who violates Islamic law) comes to you with news, verify it, lest you harm people in ignorance, and afterwards you become regretful to what you have done".

In affirming news or in witnessing any incident, one has the responsibility to ensure of its truth. In surah al-Isra', verse (17:36) Allah said:

وَلَا تَقۡفُ مَا لَيۡسَ لَكَ بِهِۦ عِلۡمٌۚ إِنَّ ٱلسَّمۡعَ وَٱلۡبَصَرَ وَٱلۡفُؤَادَ كُلُّ أُوْلَٰٓئِكَ كَانَ عَنۡهُ مَسۡـُٔولٗا ۝

"And follow not (i.e. say not or do not or witness not) that of which you have no knowledge (e.g. one's saying: "I have seen," while in fact he has not seen, or "I have heard," while he has not heard). Verily, the hearing and the sight and the heart of each of those you will be questioned (by Allah)".

Whatever one says or witnesses, or commits crime, one is responsible for it. One may conceal it but at the end of day, the truth will prevail, even in this world over the falsehood, because no one can run away from the law forever. Those people who create falsehood are indeed ungrateful lot for disturbing peace and making other peoples' lives in misery.

Not helping others to get out of poverty is also a sign of ungratefulness. Allah bestowed them riches but many rich Muslim people and rich Muslim countries let the Muslim brothers in the other part of Muslim countries live in poverty. They do not help those suffering people but instead they live in excessive opulent life style. It is not a matter of envy, but a matter of responsibility on the part of the rich to help the poor.

Muslim countries if well managed would be economically and militarily strong, but in reality they are not because most of those in power are lack of credibility. The incidents of corruption, abuse of power and lack good governance in the government are common. Their desire and greed are beyond bound and again, it is due to their lack of devotion and ungrateful attitude towards Allah.

The human livelihood, including human rights worldwide, is constantly under threat and abused. Allah abhors all these as explained in the whole chapter 5 of the volume 1 book. Indeed, the world has become a place of unhealthy competition as it is today is due to never ending of human satanic desire and greed.

In the non-Islamic industrialised world, they are equally concerned about poverty and injustice. Since the end of the World War 2, they formed an organisation in the name of 'Oxfam' to help alleviating peoples' suffering resulting from the war. Oxfam was founded at 17 Broad Street in Oxford, Oxfordshire, England, in 1942 as the *Oxford Committee for Famine Relief* by a group of Quakers, social activists and Oxford academics.

This noble organisation then spread over to other countries which had become an international confederation, consisting of many organisations working in approximately 94 countries worldwide to find solutions to poverty and what it considers injustice around the world. Its ultimate goal is to enable people to exercise their rights and manage their own lives. Oxfam works directly with communities and seeks to influence the powerful, to ensure that poor people can improve their lives and livelihoods and have a say in decisions that affect them.

Oxfam's programmes address the structural causes of poverty and related injustice and work primarily through local accountable organizations, seeking to enhance their effectiveness.

Oxfam recognises the universality and indivisibility of human rights in the following terms:

- the right to a sustainable livelihood
- the right to basic social services
- the right to life and security
- the right to be heard
- the right to an identity

Oxfam believes that poverty and powerlessness are avoidable and can be eliminated by human action and political will. The right to a sustainable livelihood, and the right and capacity to participate in societies and make positive changes to people's lives are basic human needs and rights which can be met. Oxfam also believes that peace and substantial arms reduction are essential conditions for development and that inequalities can be significantly reduced both between rich and poor nations and within nations.

The mission of Oxfam is very noble one. But then if the Muslims, of course the non-Muslims too, follow the teaching of al-Quran and al-Sunnah of Prophet Muhammad (pbuh) by paying zakat (alms), impart of some their wealth to help the poor and do not live in excessive extravagant, poverty will, to some extent if not all, can be alleviated accordingly. In connection with this, see page 198, under 5.3 (wealth in Islamic perspective) in the volume 1 book.

According to Oxfam, the wealth of the richest one percent of population is equivalent to the rest of the world combined. This is the result of a system which allows the rich unfettered representation without taxation.

The global 1 per cent would soon own more than everyone else on the planet put together. Inequality has been at the centre of domestic and global political lingering concern and debates. The dangers inherent in the yawning gap between the filthy 'undeserving rich' few and those struggling to get by are really serious and profoundly ugly. But then, instead of healing the scars on the face of the global economy, it seems that the richest have pulled further away from the rest of the ordinary general population.

It is recognised that investment, trade and profit are essential to economic development and is a way of eradicating poverty. But, the truth is that it would not be able to reach that goal unless the extreme and widening inequality is honestly tackled.

While as a whole, the world celebrates the fact that millions of people have escaped extreme poverty, but since 2010, the wealth of the few richest persons has increased accordingly. Instead of trickling down to the poorest as economists promised, wealth is being sucked up to the top.

The economists need to look beyond textbook economics and take account of the fact that the wealthy have more resources and opportunity to influence policy makers, and are therefore more likely to benefit from laws, regulations and economic policies and practices that favour their interests. This is where Islamic way of tackling economic woes to manage God given wealth is found in al-Quran and Sunnah. Islam shows the way, but being ungrateful and greedy humankind as they are, they will not subscribe to it.

One could also see the exorbitant of executive pay, accompanied by reductions in taxes for top earners, while wages for so many others, especially the already low paid have stagnated or fallen. It can be seen in the financial sector which now accounts many billionaires globally survived due to government bailouts when its bets went bad. Perhaps, most of all it is reflected in the condoning tax havens which allow the richest individuals and biggest multinationals to avoid paying their fair share to society. Tax dodging is a form of corruption. Poor people would be deprived of their fair share in relying on the state healthcare, schools and other vital public services. It is people who are poor, sick and hungry that suffer most.

To close the gap between rich and poor, governments around the world need to tackle seriously and meaningfully the poverty problems to see that those who work earn a living wage; to invest in public services which can help assisting the poor; look at the gaps of income between men and women, and offer more supportive aids to those who cannot work to ensure the poorest benefit from economic growth. They also need to take on the vested interests which defend tax havens and extreme tax avoidance. Too many of the rich and powerful virtually pay no taxation today.

Aside from the above, as already mentioned, the rich Muslims are many but most of them are thankless to Allah. They live and lead their life as they like and untouchable. They are so rich to the envy of many people. Some of them even have their bathrooms and toilet sets etc. made of solid gold or gold-plated, even their cars are gold-plated too. The rich even can afford to own a full sized Boeing 747 equipped with gold sinks, a Mercedes Benz covered the whole body in diamonds etc. They also have many big palaces as well. In fact, they can buy anything in this world because they have much more money in their kitty unspent.

Other than the above the rich Muslim Arab countries built unnecessary the tallest buildings (already cited in volume 1 book, chapter 5), competing among themselves to show off, but the other extravagance, for example, the tallest Christmas tree in the luxurious Emirates Palace hotel. It decked out a 43 foot-high Christmas tree with about $11million worth of precious jewellery from a local jeweller. Diamond necklace-and-earring sets, strings of pearls, and emerald and ruby bracelets - 181 pieces in total - are strewn between the gold and silver balls and bows. The priciest piece is a diamond set costing about $1 million.

It already the home of the world's first gold ATM (It installed a gold ATM near its lobby, where customers can buy bullion). It also holds a Guinness world record for serving up the most expensive shot of alcohol - at some $2,000 for a Hardy Perfection cognac.

What are they up to? It is just like another Korah within the midst of the Arab world. May Allah bless and save them so as not to be swallowed by the earth.

With regard to riches, Islam does not prevent Muslims to acquire wealth but Islam prohibits amassing such riches alone for own self excessively without helping others as stated above. Using cutlery and utensils made of gold and silver are also prohibited. Islam also prohibited Muslims to sit on pure silk spreads in their houses. Islam too forbade men to use golden pen, golden watches, gold cigarette cases and lighters etc. and wearing silk as well.

Does this include silver or golden plated cars etc.?

The Muslim jurists differed in opinion regarding the ruling of gold-plated or silver-plated utensils and the like. The most preponderant opinion is that they are not permissible unless the plating is very slight to an extent that if it exposes to fire, nothing will remain of it. As the ruling as such in relation to gold plated items, if a car exposed to fire and its gold remains, then this use of gold is not permissible. The gold that used for that purpose is only a waste of money and this is the reason it is not permissible or forbidden to use silver-plated or gold-plated utensils. Thus, it includes all items that have been plated or covered with gold and silver. What more if it is made of solid gold.

Ibn Hajar Al-Haythami said:

'It is absolutely forbidden to cover utensils with gold according to Shafi'e school of thought, and if utensils have gold and after being exposed to fire, the gold still remains, then it is forbidden to keep the gold from such items or to use it. But if after being exposed to fire, nothing remains of it (gold) on these items then it is not forbidden to use them or wear them.' Allah only knows best.

Beautification and elegance permitted by Islam as per surah al-A'raf (7:32):

قُل مَنْ حَرَّمَ زِينَةَ ٱللَّهِ ٱلَّتِىٓ أَخْرَجَ لِعِبَادِهِۦ وَٱلطَّيِّبَـٰتِ مِنَ ٱلرِّزْقِ قُلْ
هِىَ لِلَّذِينَ ءَامَنُوا۟ فِى ٱلْحَيَوٰةِ ٱلدُّنْيَا خَالِصَةً يَوْمَ ٱلْقِيَـٰمَةِ كَذَٰلِكَ
نُفَصِّلُ ٱلْءَايَـٰتِ لِقَوْمٍ يَعْلَمُونَ ﴿٣٢﴾

"Say (O Muhammad): 'Who has forbidden the adornments of Allah which He has brought forth for His servants, and all kinds of lawful good things?' Say: 'They are, in the life of this world, for those who believe, exclusively for them on the Day of Resurrection'. Thus We explain the ayat (Islamic laws) in detail for people who have knowledge'".

Islam however, prohibited two kinds of adornment for men, while permitting them to women. These are first, gold ornaments and second, clothing made of pure silk. 'Ali reported that the Prophet (pbuh) took some silk in his right hand and some gold in his left, declaring that:

"These two are *haram (not permissible)* for the males among my followers." Hadith narrated by Ahmad, Abu Daoud, al-Nisai, Ibn Hayyan, and Ibn Majah who reports the additional phrase, 'but *halal (permissible)* for the females'.

Umar reported that he heard the Prophet (pbuh) said:

"Do not wear silk, for those who wear it in this life shall not wear it in the Hereafter." Hadith reported by al-Bukhari and Muslim. A similar *hadith* reported by them on the authority of Anas.

On another occasion, referring to a silken garment, he said:

"This is the dress of a man who has no character." Hadith reported by al-Bukhari and Muslim.

The Prophet (pbuh) once saw a gold ring on a man's hand. He immediately took it from him and threw it down saying:

"Does a person pick up a piece of burning coal and hold it in his hand?"

After the Prophet (pbuh) had left the place, someone asked the man:

'Why do you not pick it up and benefit from it?' He replied, 'No, by Allah! I shall not pick it up after the Messenger of Allah has thrown it away." Hadith narrated by Muslim.

The Prophet (pbuh), however, permitted men to wear silver rings. On the authority of Ibn 'Umar, al-Bukhari reported the former saying:

"The Messenger of Allah wore a silver ring. After him, Abu Bakr and then 'Umar and 'Uthman wore it until it fell off his finger into the well of Arees." (Hadith reported by al-Bukhari in the chapter on "Clothing" *(Al-Libas)*.)

As for other metals such as iron, there are no sound texts prohibiting them. In the *Sahih* of al-Bukhari, the Messenger of Allah (pbuh) advised a man who wanted to marry a woman to **"Present her with a gift, even if it be ring made of iron."** On the basis, this *hadith* al-Bukhari inferred the permissibility of iron rings.

The Prophet (pbuh) made concessions in the wearing of silken garments for medical reasons, as he gave 'Abd al-Rahman bin 'Auf and al-Zubayr bin al-'Awwam, both of whom suffered from scabies, permission to wear silk. (Hadith reported by al-Bukhari.)

On the wisdom of these two prohibitions, concerning men is that Islam's aim is to achieve certain noble educational and moral objectives.

According to Sheikh Yusuf al-Qaradawi that:

"Islam enjoined Muslim to jihad (striving) for the strength of Islam. Therefore, Islam must safeguard the manly qualities of men from any

show of weakness, passivity and lethargy. Allah has made the physique of the man different from that of the woman, and it does not befit a man to wear clothes made of fine material or to adorn his body with costly ornaments.

There is, however, a social aim underlying these prohibitions. The prohibition of gold and silk to males is part of a broader Islamic program of combating luxuriousness in living. From the Quranic point of view, luxurious living leads to weakness among nations and to their eventual downfall. The existence of luxury is also an expression of social injustice, as only a few can afford luxurious items at the expense of the deprived masses of people.

In addition to this, luxurious living is an enemy of every call towards truth, justice, and social reform. In surah, Al-Isra', verse (17:16) Allah said:

وَإِذَآ أَرَدْنَآ أَن نُّهْلِكَ قَرْيَةً أَمَرْنَا مُتْرَفِيهَا فَفَسَقُوا۟ فِيهَا فَحَقَّ عَلَيْهَا ٱلْقَوْلُ فَدَمَّرْنَٰهَا تَدْمِيرًا ﴿١٦﴾

"And when We intend that We should destroy a township, we permit its luxury-loving people (the good things in life). Then they transgress (commit wickedness) therein thus the word (of torment) is justified against it, We then destroy it utterly." In surah Saba': (34:34) Allah said:

وَمَآ أَرْسَلْنَا فِى قَرْيَةٍ مِّن نَّذِيرٍ إِلَّا قَالَ مُتْرَفُوهَآ إِنَّا بِمَآ أُرْسِلْتُم بِهِۦ كَٰفِرُونَ ﴿٣٤﴾

"And We did not send a warner to any township without its luxury-loving people saying, 'Assuredly we are disbelievers in that with which you have been sent.'"

119

In keeping with the spirit of the Quran, the Prophet (pbuh) forbade Muslims any indulgence in conspicuous consumption. He not only forbade the use of gold and silk to men but also forbade men and women alike the use of gold and silver utensils.

Finally, economic considerations also carry some weight here. Since gold is a universal medium of exchange, using it to make household utensils or ornaments for men does not make sense in economic terms."

Avoid wastage and be in simplicity in life is the teaching of Islam. The Quran warned against excessiveness and exaggeration in life. The Sunnah of Prophet also stressed that humility should be practised by all Muslims and avoid exaggeration, extravagance and the desire for fame or glory.

The principle of humility reflected practically in the life style of the Prophet whose bed was a layer of palm leaves or fibres covered with a simple fabric. The prophet house was also very basic and simple without any luxurious item. Even though he was the leader of the Muslims, his house was small and simple like other ordinary people.

Jabir reported that the Prophet said:

"There should be a bed for a man, a bed for his wife and the third one for the guest, but the fourth one is Satan."

According to Muslim jurists, the hadith explained that spending on big buildings unnecessarily or in excess of the needs of its owner is not rewarded. A house is to provide shelter from climate etc. but not to spend on construction of expensive houses with unnecessary rooms and ornamentations. Humility is not only for personal behaviour but for spending on building or other luxurious things too. To build a100-room house is a sheer extravagant, as an example.

Prophet Muhammad (pbuh) on arrival in Medina he firstly built a mosque instead of building a palace. That was the sign of his humility to Allah and to his followers.

The Messenger of Allah and his close companions strictly follow the Islamic way of life so much so many non-Muslims attracted to Islam and ultimately voluntarily embraced Islam. With the good image of Islam exemplified by Prophet Muhammad (pbuh) and his companions, Islam became highly revered and its followers accorded with much respect at that time. The Muslims at later stage, however, much transgressed and did otherwise. Their leaders abused their riches, live in opulent with big palaces and made use of government treasury for the benefits of their cronies and families.

Good and honest leaders are of rare breed. Thus, popular revolutions frequently did happen, as the world had seen, due to authoritarian and tyrant regimes.

Many verses in al-Quran began with the phrase: **"If you are believers or O you believers**" as a commandment to the Muslims to be true believers and truly fear Allah, not just mere saying without spiritual and physical commitments in the name of Allah.

Islam is not just performing the obligatory five times daily prayers only, but also must be the wholesome Muslims, that is, to carry on other general obligations, duties and responsibilities to other fellow human beings and the rest of the other creatures of Allah too. The Muslims have to see that justice and fairness done for the sake of Allah, not for the sake of fellow mortals.

Many Muslims wantonly ignored their obligatory duty towards Allah. As such, would these people sincerely take responsibility for other people's welfare since they themselves are not sincere and do not fear Allah?

It is little wonder, therefore, many instances of corruption, abuse of power, criminal breach of trust, adultery and other wrong doings committed by the Muslims themselves. Therefore, they are no difference comparatively with the non-Muslims. They are indeed disobedient and ungrateful Muslims. In this regard, the Muslims are the ones who humiliate and disservice Islam. Thus, do not expect the disbelievers will give due respect to Muslims and Islam.

In politic, many Muslim leaders before they gain their power seemed to be men of integrity and grateful to Allah but soon when they are in power, their attributes and personality gradually changed and degrading, resulting in many abuses of power and corruptions, hoarding tones of money in or outside the country. They become arrogant and ungrateful, but worst still they forget Allah. For political survival, they are willing to do anything, including cooperate with the non-Muslims rather than their Muslims counter parts. This is the element of hypocrisy as shown by some Muslim leaders, thereby directly contributes to the weakness of the Muslim ummah. Here again, the Muslims themselves humiliate Islam.

Throughout the Muslim world, as many times already stated, it is generally apparent that the Muslims had diminished in their Islamic faith because they are happy to accept the man-made laws rather than the Divine laws or syariah laws. They are much comfortable with the secular system because they feel that Islamic laws are rigid and limit their freedom.

Some of the liberal Muslims are even critical towards the Divine Revelations. They dare to question the sanctity of al-Quran, al-Sunnah and Islam itself. They are the destructive agents of Islam from within for they go against the very grain or fibre of Islamic principles.

The Muslims will stay in humiliation as they are as long as they do not repent and return to al-Quran and al-Sunnah. If the Muslims do not help themselves and always remained ungrateful to Allah, it is sunnatullah (the Will of Allah) that Allah will not help them.

CHAPTER 12. THE WRATH OF ALLAH

People keep on continuing committing wrong doings and evil deeds in this beautiful world without any limit and conscience. They have transgressed beyond limit against the commands of Allah.

The incidents of wars, revolutions, calamities, hunger, diseases and so on are ever presence and on the increase. These are the signs of wrath of Allah befallen on mankind for which they cannot escape, no matter how strong and powerful they are.

Any disaster or tragedy happening is a mean of warning and punishment of Allah over all to the human beings - believers or non-believer - as the result of their own doings. When it comes, the Will of Allah prevails. No human power can stop and avoid it.

Those who transgress beyond the limits set by Allah expose themselves to punishment in this life and the next. Many verses in al-Quran describing numerous past nations that rejected Divine guidance subsequently destroyed. These stories serve as reminders to humankind of the consequences of disobedient against the commandments of Allah. Allah gave a general warning, for example, in surah al-Anfal, verse (8:25) as follows:

وَٱتَّقُواْ فِتْنَةً لَّا تُصِيبَنَّ ٱلَّذِينَ ظَلَمُواْ مِنكُمْ خَآصَّةً وَٱعْلَمُوٓاْ أَنَّ ٱللَّهَ شَدِيدُ ٱلْعِقَابِ ﴿٢٥﴾

"And fear the fitnah (affliction, trial etc.) which affects not in particular (only) those of you who do wrong (but it may afflict all the good and the bad people), and know that Allah is severe in punishment."

With regard to the incident of calamities or misfortunes, Allah revealed in surah al-Syura, verse (42:30-31):

وَمَآ أَصَابَكُم مِّن مُّصِيبَةٍ فَبِمَا كَسَبَتْ أَيْدِيكُمْ وَيَعْفُواْ عَن كَثِيرٍ ﴿٣٠﴾

"And whatever of misfortune befalls on you, it is because of what your hands have earned. And He pardons much".

وَمَآ أَنتُم بِمُعْجِزِينَ فِى ٱلْأَرْضِ وَمَا لَكُم مِّن دُونِ ٱللَّهِ مِن وَلِيٍّ وَلَا نَصِيرٍ ﴿٣١﴾

"And you cannot escape from Allah (i.e. His Punishment) in the earth, and besides Allah you have neither any wali (guardian or protector) nor any helper".

In surah al-Ankabut, verse (29:40), Allah said:

فَكُلًّا أَخَذْنَا بِذَنۢبِهِۦ فَمِنْهُم مَّنْ أَرْسَلْنَا عَلَيْهِ حَاصِبًا وَمِنْهُم مَّنْ أَخَذَتْهُ ٱلصَّيْحَةُ وَمِنْهُم مَّنْ خَسَفْنَا بِهِ ٱلْأَرْضَ وَمِنْهُم مَّنْ أَغْرَقْنَا وَمَا كَانَ ٱللَّهُ لِيَظْلِمَهُمْ وَلَٰكِن كَانُوٓاْ أَنفُسَهُمْ يَظْلِمُونَ ﴿٤٠﴾

"So We punished each (of them) for his sins. Some of them were We sent hasiban (a violent wind with shower of stones as the people of Prophet Lot), and of them were some who were overtaken by assaihah (torment awful cry etc. as Thamud or Shu'aib's people). Some of whom We caused the earth to swallow (as Korah), and of them were some whom We drowned (as the people of Noah or Pharaoh and his people). It was not Allah Who wronged them, but they wronged themselves".

Therefore, if people keep on defying the command of Allah and continuing to commit many wrong doings or sins, disaster will beget upon them as stated in the above verses.

The glorious al-Quran gives enlightenment, guidance, lesson etc. for people to take cognisance. It also gives warning and injunctions to them not to commit evil or wrong doings.

Allah gives blessing and endowment to all, however there is a limit to it. When a country progresses and becomes rich, and its people live in opulent, more often than not, they start transgressing in extreme. Although they already possess many things and yet they long for more and subsequently they may become crazy in the search of vain desire and happiness.

Arising from human misbehaviour and inconsideration to this beautiful world like causing destructions to the earth, hills and mountains, forests, rivers etc. various catastrophes frequently ravaged the planet earth. Many properties destroyed and many people also lost their lives. Allah already said: *"And whatever of misfortune befalls on you, it is because of what your hands have earned."* These are all the Acts of Allah due to human wrong doings, but of course, many people may not believe about it. They instead blame global warming, climate change, natural disaster etc. That is true per se but who is behind it if not the Almighty Allah?

Some of the Muslims too even proudly without reservation said that they all have well prepared to meet any eventualities, as if they are so strong to prevent the catastrophes. Whereas Islam taught the Muslims to say humbly: "**Insya Allah (God willing)**" after all the preparations made as a sign of their humility.

Disaster may happen of a sudden without warning or it would slowly take place at the Will of Allah. Malevolent to the extreme may set in, and verily it would be disastrous and painful. No more mercy, no more benevolent but catastrophe of extreme nature would be fallen onto them like earthquake, typhoon, hurricane, devastating flood, tsunami, outbreak of plague, famine etc. These calamities, in fact, happened more frequently at the present time as transgression increased.

People may not take cognisance on this because of their arrogance for they have the power and the technology to contain any exigencies. Nay, wait and see the horrendous calamities when they come, soon or in future. No one can predict and escape from them. History will repeat itself, may be in different form according to time and environment. In the past, people of Noah, Thamud, 'Ad, Lot (LGBT people), Aikah etc. experienced disaster as described in the glorious al-Quran. They were wiped out in entirety from the surface of the earth because of their heinous sins and disobedient to Allah. Some of the remnant of the ruins, as examples, still until today standing and remained there as reminders for people to see. Nonetheless, Allah will not wipe out the ummah of the Prophet of Muhammad (pbuh) because of Allah's Blessing due to love and the prayer of the Prophet (pbuh) to Allah to save his ummah until to the end of the world.

Although Allah is the Most Benevolent, Most Merciful with all the endowments or provisions, but if people are not grateful to Him and keep on committing all kind of transgressions, Allah surely will punish them. Allah said in surah al-A'raf, verse (7:96-99):

وَلَوْ أَنَّ أَهْلَ ٱلْقُرَىٰٓ ءَامَنُوا۟ وَٱتَّقَوْا۟ لَفَتَحْنَا عَلَيْهِم بَرَكَٰتٍ مِّنَ ٱلسَّمَآءِ وَٱلْأَرْضِ وَلَٰكِن كَذَّبُوا۟ فَأَخَذْنَٰهُم بِمَا كَانُوا۟ يَكْسِبُونَ ﴿٩٦﴾

"And if the people of the towns had believed and had the taqwa (piety), certainly We should have opened for them blessings (with provisions) from the heaven and the earth, but they belied (the Messengers) so We took them (with punishment) for what they used to earn".

أَفَأَمِنَ أَهْلُ ٱلْقُرَىٰٓ أَن يَأْتِيَهُم بَأْسُنَا بَيَـٰتًا وَهُمْ نَآئِمُونَ ﴿٩٧﴾

"Did the people of the towns then feel secure against the coming of Our Punishment by night while they are asleep?"

أَوَأَمِنَ أَهْلُ ٱلْقُرَىٰٓ أَن يَأْتِيَهُم بَأْسُنَا ضُحًى وَهُمْ يَلْعَبُونَ ﴿٩٨﴾

"Or did the people of the towns then feel secure against the coming of Our Punishment in the forenoon while they play?"

أَفَأَمِنُوا۟ مَكْرَ ٱللَّهِ فَلَا يَأْمَنُ مَكْرَ ٱللَّهِ إِلَّا ٱلْقَوْمُ ٱلْخَـٰسِرُونَ ﴿٩٩﴾

"Did they then feel secure against the Plan of Allah? None feels secure from the Plan of Allah except the people who are the losers".

A nation may develop and progress well but if its people are not thankful and disobedient, it does not dwell well if moral decadent prevails in the society. Even if a country attains a developed and rich nation status, with its high-income per capita, it does not ensure that its society will be in peace and live in harmony if the people keep on disobeying Allah. Social problem or illness like drug abuse, freedom of sex like LGBT etc. will pervade the society, soon or later the society will become morally chaotic. When transgression goes beyond bound, then punishment of Allah will come at any time without due warning, either during the day or night.

One of the obvious examples described in al-Quran is in surah Sabaa', verse (34:15-16), in which Allah revealed:

لَقَدْ كَانَ لِسَبَإٍ فِى مَسْكَنِهِمْ ءَايَةٌ جَنَّتَانِ عَن يَمِينٍ وَشِمَالٍ كُلُواْ مِن رِّزْقِ

رَبِّكُمْ وَاشْكُرُواْ لَهُ بَلْدَةٌ طَيِّبَةٌ وَرَبٌّ غَفُورٌ ۝

"Indeed there was for Saba' (Sheba) a sign in their dwelling place, two gardens on the right hand and on the left (and it was said to them) "Eat of the provisions of your Lord, and be grateful to Him, (your country) a fair land and an Often Forgiving Lord".

فَأَعْرَضُواْ فَأَرْسَلْنَا عَلَيْهِمْ سَيْلَ الْعَرِمِ وَبَدَّلْنَهُم بِجَنَّتَيْهِمْ جَنَّتَيْنِ

ذَوَاتَىْ أُكُلٍ خَمْطٍ وَأَثْلٍ وَشَىْءٍ مِّن سِدْرٍ قَلِيلٍ ۝

"But they turned away (from the obedience of Allah, not grateful) so We sent against them sail al'arim (flood released from the dam), and We converted their two gardens into gardens producing bitter bad fruit and tamarisks and some few lote trees".

Sabaa' was the name of a country in Yemen in the olden days. It had fertile lands with abundant of fruit trees or orchards. They built dam to harness water from up streams for domestic use and to irrigate their orchards. They lived well and wealthy but later on they turned away from Allah. They became disobedient and Allah sent down big flood, thereby their dam collapsed. All their dwelling houses and orchards submerged and destroyed. The survivors, with much hardship, moved away because the lands became barren and infertile. The orchard produced bad and bitter fruits. In the olden days, people could move away to other fertile lands, but now the affected people have no choice but to stay put at the same place for they do not have any other place to move on.

Since the wrath of Allah will come hard upon people at any time at His disposal, be proud not on big and tall buildings, big dams etc. for they may come down crumbling beyond imagination in split seconds, no matter how strong and sophisticated the structures are. Hence, transgress not but be grateful and take a good lesson from the Pharaoh of Egypt who claimed himself as 'god' drowned like an ant in the Red Sea in pursuit of Prophet Moses.

Failure to abide to Allah's commands and failure to implement syariah laws had created many instances of power struggle, greed, corruption, abuse of power, criminal breach of trust, murders and what not in the society, country and the world at large. Mistrust with one another, spying and cyber espionage on other countries have become a norm in today's globalised world. Out of the mistrust, military and nuclear race in order to outdo one another is the order of the day. Military supremacy is the name of the game. One of these days, it cannot be discounted that accidental nuclear explosion may occur, destroying the whole world and with it goes the civilisation of man in this small planet earth.

No power in this world can outdo Allah's power. In this context, from Abdullah bin Abas that the Messenger of Allah said:

"I will tell you a certain wisdoms: Take care of Allah, Allah will take care of you, take care of Allah He will be in front or beside of you. When you ask for something, ask from Allah and when you need help, ask from Allah. Be known that if the whole ummah (community) want to help you, they will help you not unless written so by Allah for you. And if the whole community want to harm you, they will not unless written so by Allah. Pen (Qalam) has been lifted and the letter already dried". Hadith narrated by Imam Ahmad and at-Tarmizi.

What that has been destined for a person, it will be for sure to come true. Nevertheless, it does not mean that a person should stay idle and doing nothing. Notwithstanding, again it is the Will of Allah that will determine the outcome, good or bad, for it is all in the hands of Allah. Allah may change the course of anything or events without warning and therefore in the first place do not place the hope, the fate or be dependent on human beings, except Allah.

Allah has bestowed on mankind countless of blessings and graces. The most importance of these graces and blessings is the coming of Islam. This great blessing of Islam has no equal. Whoever follows it and thanks Allah for it will be a winner in this world and the world hereafter.

Allah said in surah Ibrahim, verse (14:34):

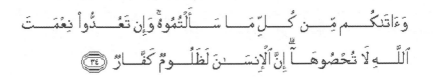

"And He gave you of all that you asked for, and if you count the Blessings of Allah, never will you be able to count them. Verily man is indeed an extreme wrong-doer - a disbeliever (an extreme ingrate, denies Allah's Blessings by disbelief, and by worshipping others besides Allah and by disobeying Allah and His Prophet Muhammad)."

Allah also said in surah at-Taghabun, verse (64:11):

مَآ أَصَابَ مِن مُّصِيبَةٍ إِلَّا بِإِذْنِ ٱللَّهِ وَمَن يُؤْمِنۢ بِٱللَّهِ يَهْدِ قَلْبَهُۥ وَٱللَّهُ بِكُلِّ شَىْءٍ عَلِيمٌ ﴿١١﴾

"No calamity befalls, but with the Leave [i.e. decision and Qadar (Divine Preordainments)] of Allah, and whosoever believes in Allah, He guides his heart [to the true faith with certainty, i.e. what has befallen him was already written for him by Allah from the Qadar] and Allah is the All-Knower of everything."

130

In surah al-Shura (42:30) and Fatir or al-Malaikah, verse (35:45)
respectively Allah said:

وَمَآ أَصَـٰبَكُم مِّن مُّصِيبَةٍ فَبِمَا كَسَبَتْ أَيْدِيكُمْ وَيَعْفُواْ عَن كَثِيرٍ

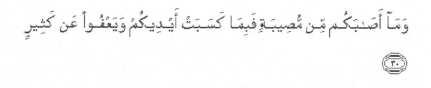

*"And whatever of misfortune befalls you, it is because of
what your hands have earned. And He pardons much."*

وَلَوْ يُؤَاخِذُ ٱللَّهُ ٱلنَّاسَ بِمَا كَسَبُواْ مَا تَرَكَ عَلَىٰ ظَهْرِهَا مِن دَآبَّةٍ وَلَـٰكِن
يُؤَخِّرُهُمْ إِلَىٰ أَجَلٍ مُّسَمًّى فَإِذَا جَآءَ أَجَلُهُمْ فَإِنَّ ٱللَّهَ كَانَ بِعِبَادِهِۦ بَصِيرًا

*"And if Allah were to punish men for that which they earned,
He would not leave a moving (living) creature on the surface
of the earth, but He gives them respite to an appointed
term, and when their term comes, then verily, Allah is ever
All- Seer of His slaves."*

In surah Qaf (50:36) Allah said:

وَكَمْ أَهْلَكْنَا قَبْلَهُم مِّن قَرْنٍ هُمْ أَشَدُّ مِنْهُم بَطْشًا فَنَقَّبُواْ فِى ٱلْبِلَـٰدِ هَلْ
مِن مَّحِيصٍ ﴿٣٦﴾

*"And how many a generation We have destroyed before
them, who were stronger in power than them, and (when
Our Torment came) they ran for a refuge in the land! Could*

they find any place of refuge (to save themselves from destruction)?"

The wrath of Allah will keep on coming and all the signs that happened in this universe that aroused sympathy like thunderbolts, fierce wind, big floods, earthquakes, tsunami etc. destroying everything on their wakes. Allah put trial and ordeal on His servants as a mean to frighten and to warn them to refrain from committing transgression and aggression.

It was reported that the number of big disasters happened in the eighties was 120 times yearly. In 2006, the disasters rose to 500 times yearly. While during the same period, weather-related disaster was 80 times yearly but it increased to 240 times yearly up to 2006. Arising from the disaster, millions people affected. In 1985-1994, 174 million people affected yearly, whereas in 1995 - 2004, 254 million people affected yearly. Certainly, in years to come more people will be affected.

In recent years, for example, big floods occurred in China and Bangladesh in 2010. In January 2011, the biggest flood in this decade hit Queensland, Australia, destroying about 20,000 houses. It will take years to rebuild. Also in 2010, the volcanic eruption hit Iceland, causing millions of monetary loss in tourism and aviation industries of the country.

On Friday, 11 March 2011, a big volcanic eruption followed by tsunami devastated Japan. The cost of destruction was estimated about 300 billion USD. Thousands of people perished. The worst thing was a few nuclear reactors destroyed, releasing contaminated radioactive waste into the air and sea. It was so scary like the Chernobyl nuclear disaster happened in Ukraine in 1986.

Before the tsunami in Japan, there was a big volcanic eruption in Indian Ocean hitting Aceh, Indonesia and the beaches of other surrounding countries on December 2004, killing 230,000 people, including 170,000 people in Aceh. This tsunami destroyed the town of Aceh and other places as well. Notwithstanding, with the Will of Allah a few mosques in Aceh withstood the impact and kept standing intact while the rest of the surrounding buildings destroyed by the ferocious tsunami. No one could ever explain the phenomena. Because of this miracle happening, some people converted to Islam.

Then in October 2012, a very strong Hurricane Sandy devastated the United States of America, only a bit lesser in violent than Hurricane Katrina in 2005. The Hurricane Sandy hit 24 states from Florida to Maine in the East Coast and in the West until Michigan and Wisconsin. The worst places affected were New York and New Jersey. Thousands of people evacuated. Overall, about 8.1 million houses and business premises were without electricity. Underground system of New York of 108 years old never hit by such a massive disaster, so much so the whole New York City was in the dark. Eqecat Firm estimated about 60 million people (1/5 of American population) affected and the estimated loss was about $20 to $50 billion. [*The Sun 31 October 2012 and Wikipedia*].

The point is that all these extraordinary catastrophes were only a small manifestation of Allah's punishment and warning to the people to refrain from committing excessive transgression and other despicable deeds in this planet earth. People will have to face more and more disasters in time to come if they keep on committing the wrong doings and other misdemeanours.

With regard to the catastrophes, Huzaifah bin al-Yaman reported that the Messenger of Allah said:

"Indeed my soul is in the hands of Allah, you should preach people to do good deeds and prohibit them from doing wrong deeds otherwise Allah will bring down on you punishment because of it. Then if you ask for help in your prayer, Allah will ignore your prayer". This hadith narrated by At-Tarmizi.

In surah al-An'am, verse (6:6) Allah said:

أَلَمْ يَرَوْاْ كَمْ أَهْلَكْنَا مِن قَبْلِهِم مِّن قَرْنٍ مَّكَّنَّهُمْ فِى الْأَرْضِ مَا لَمْ نُمَكِّن لَّكُمْ وَأَرْسَلْنَا ٱلسَّمَآءَ عَلَيْهِم مِّدْرَارًا وَجَعَلْنَا ٱلْأَنْهَٰرَ تَجْرِى مِن تَحْتِهِمْ فَأَهْلَكْنَٰهُم بِذُنُوبِهِمْ وَأَنشَأْنَا مِنۢ بَعْدِهِمْ قَرْنًا ءَاخَرِينَ ⑥

"Have they not seen how many a generation before them We have destroyed whom We had established on the earth such as We have not established you? And We poured out on them rain from the sky in abundance, and made the rivers flow under them. Yet We destroyed them for their sins, and created after them other generations".

In the modern world, as already mentioned earlier, people blamed global warming was the main cause of the disasters across the world. As of 2007, it was reported 410 disasters, 56 percent of which were weather-related, which is consistent with the trend of rising numbers of climate change-related disasters. People could not careless about man-made destruction of the environment on the excuse of development. For examples, people cut and burned down forest, cut hills, digging for mining indiscriminately thereby causing respectively smog, landslips, erosions etc. Factories, greenhouses, motor vehicles etc. produced excessive toxic gases into the air causing air pollution and consequently peoples' health suffer. Thus, the Will of Allah comes into play. Allah already warned people not to cause destruction to this beautiful earth but to take care of it, yet they abide not.

Apart from human greed that destroyed the ecology system, character and moral transgression and decadent in the society is also on the increase. Illicit sex and adultery become rampant, even in the Muslim countries. For example, in Malaysia, according to National Registration Department (JPN), children born out of wedlock in the year 2000-2008 were 257,000 or 2380 per month. This did not include abandoned children. This was alarming.

In the year 1999-2003, children born out of wedlock were 70,430 and out of which 30,978 (44%) were Muslim children. Clearly moral degradation among the younger generation is worsening, not much different between Muslims and non-Muslims. Unlike the Muslims, for non-Muslims, perhaps, it is of no concern because it is normal for them.

Mitigating the misdeeds is possible, God willing, if the Muslim ummah revisit al-Quran and al-Sunnah. Perhaps the following measures are relevant and helpful:

- Encourage single people to get married as per surah al-Nur, verse (24:32):

 نكِحُـوا ٱلۡأَيَـٰمَـىٰ مِنكُـمۡ وَٱلصَّـٰلِحِـينَ مِـنۡ عِبَـادِكُمۡ وَإِمَـآبِكُمۡ إِن كُونُـوا فُقَـرَآءَ يُغۡنِهِـمُ ٱللَّـهُ مِـن فَضۡلِـهِۦۖ وَٱللَّـهُ وَٰسِـعٌ عَلِيـمٌ ۝

"And marry those among you who are single (i.e. a man who has no wife and the woman who has no husband) and (also marry) the Salihun (pious, fit and capable ones) of your (male) slaves and maidservants (female slaves). If they be poor, Allah will enrich them out of His Bounty. And Allah is All-Sufficient for His creatures' needs, All-Knowing (about the state of the people)".

Nowadays, many young single people, males and females, do not take seriously about marriage. Social freedom and sexual freedom among them is the cause. Furthermore, getting married is also costly. High dowry has become a social norm or custom for the couple to get married. This custom, therefore, should be re-evaluated. The point is it is much better to have poor children with legally married status parents rather than illegitimate and abandon children without parents.

- Muslim women are to cover their body (aurat) to make them look decent and respectable. Allah said in surah al-Ahzab, verse (33:59):

بِسْمِ ٱللَّٰهِ ٱلرَّحْمَٰنِ ٱلرَّحِيمِ

يَٰٓأَيُّهَا ٱلنَّبِىُّ قُل لِّأَزْوَٰجِكَ وَبَنَاتِكَ وَنِسَآءِ ٱلْمُؤْمِنِينَ يُدْنِينَ عَلَيْهِنَّ مِن جَلَٰبِيبِهِنَّ ذَٰلِكَ أَدْنَىٰٓ أَن يُعْرَفْنَ فَلَا يُؤْذَيْنَ وَكَانَ ٱللَّٰهُ غَفُورًا رَّحِيمًا ﴿٥٩﴾

"O Prophet! Tell your wives and daughters and the women of the believers to draw their cloaks (veils over all their bodies). That will be better, that they should be known (as free respectable women) so as not to be annoyed or disturbed. And Allah is Ever-Forgiving, Most Merciful".

In this respect, do not the Muslimah (Muslim women) believe in the above verse? Why is that so difficult for some of them cover their bodies and their heads (the aurat)? Why a woman so cheaply wants to show off her body, flesh, beauty and ornaments for men to see? Is the body for sale? Thus, it will directly or indirectly lead to vice or immorality. However, secularists and liberalists claimed that this is an individual choice within the human rights. They argued that those who decently covered their bodies also raped by men, but in reality the incidents of rapes more frequently happened to those who scantly covered their bodies.

• Restrict the unnecessary freedom of socialising between men and women. At-Termizi narrated that Prophet Muhammad (pbuh) said:

"It is not a man and a woman together, except the third is Satan".

• Polygamy is permissible in Islam, but not in the style of the Shiite sect. As such, make it easier to practise polygamy for man. It is something that is legal, though not encouraged. Since Allah allowed a man to marry up to four women at a time, with certain conditions, there must be certain wisdom and safeguards behind it. Due to feminine rights and human rights pressure, non-believers created their own law to make polygamy illegal, yet certain countries legalise homosexual marriage. Some people see illicit sex and homosexual are better than polygamy. This is really out of logic. Now there are more women than men, therefore there is wisdom in polygamy to protect the women from exploitation.

It is obvious that mixing freely between different genders has brought about social misbehaviour, especially spending long hours in night- clubs, fiestas etc. where people mix freely, young and old. More often than not, drug and hard liquor are available which again may lead to trouble, misbehaviour or close promiscuity. The facilities are there available for them to enjoy. Nine months later after partying, they produce new babies born out of the wedlock.

Who are responsible for this immorality in the Muslim countries, the Muslim governments of the day for not taking measures to stop the sources of evil or the Muslims at large are ignorant of Islamic teaching? Deep critical thinking on the part of ulama (Muslim scholars) and the government of the day is of paramount important to mitigate this moral decadent in the societies.

This societal misbehaviour is a global problem. This moral misbehaviour had already pervaded into every society. In Western and other non-Muslim countries, it is rather their social norm acceptable by the society, but moral decadent has become a social problem in their societies much worst comparatively with that of the Muslim societies.

The above social misbehaviour such as excessive entertainments, liquor, illicit sex, cigarettes and drug abuse, LGBT, all kind of sports with scanty costumes, showing swelling private flesh, etc. are the common factors that lead to social misbehaviour. All those factors are against the Islamic way of life. Allah reminded them to behave accordingly. In surah Thaha, verse (20: 124-127), Allah said:

وَمَنْ أَعْرَضَ عَن ذِكْرِى فَإِنَّ لَهُ مَعِيشَةً ضَنكًا وَنَحْشُرُهُ

يَوْمَ ٱلْقِيَمَةِ أَعْمَىٰ ۝

"But whosoever turns away from My Reminder (i.e. neither believes in this Quran nor acts on its orders etc.) verily, for him is a life of hardship, and We shall raise him up blind on the Day of Resurrection".

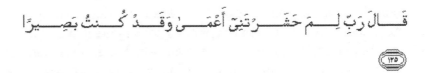

"He will say: 'O my Lord! Why have you raised me up blind, while I had sight (before)?'"

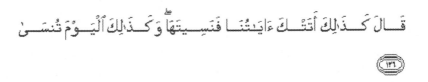

"(Allah) will say: 'Like this, Our ayat (proofs, evidences, verses, lessons, signs, revelations etc.) came unto you, but you disregarded them, and so this Day you will be neglected (without Allah's Mercy)'".

وَكَذَٰلِكَ نَجْزِى مَنْ أَسْرَفَ وَلَمْ يُؤْمِنْ بِـَٔايَٰتِ رَبِّهِۦ وَلَعَذَابُ ٱلْأَخِرَةِ أَشَدُّ وَأَبْقَىٰ ۝

"And thus We do requite him who transgresses beyond bounds and believes not in the ayat (proofs, evidences, verses, lessons, signs, revelations, etc.) of his Lord, and the torment of the Hereafter is far more severe and more lasting".

138

Allah will punish whoever disobeys Him in this world and in the life hereafter. While alive, these people seemed to be happy outwardly but inwardly they are surely not. Whether they are rich or poor, they will always feel scared, sceptic and unease of mind because their lives are empty and devoid of spiritual guidance. Al-'Aufy narrated a hadith from Ibnu Abas:

"Anything I give to My slaves, few or more, but they do not fear Me, they will never feel delighted and always live in difficulty".

The hard truth is that many Muslims have turned away from al-Quran and al-Sunnah. Their faith in Allah and Islamic principles are overall lacking. The leaders are busy wrestling for powers and wealth rather than helping Allah to look after the welfare of their people and guiding them to be God fearing citizens by being themselves, not only seem to be pious, but also leaders of integrity.

Young generation is the future leaders of any country. The moral behaviour of young generation will reflect either in the strength or weakness and true identity of a nation. A moral decadent nation will not be able to stand strong and progress, but sooner or later it will lead into a doom and socially chaotic society. Then the country will be in weak position to face any future challenges.

The manifestation of wrath of Allah as stated above is only part of the minor signs of doomsday (qiyamah), the time of which nobody knows except Allah. In the meantime, all human beings, Muslims and non-Muslims, while alive are under scrutiny or watchful eyes of Allah all the time of whatever they do in this world. The disbelievers and the rejecters can disobey the commands of Allah, and act in whatever way they like as they deem fit to satisfy the vain worldly desires. But, they should remember that they are not going to live forever. The Muslims are too of no exception, but the pious ones.

The final judgement of their deeds will come. Virtuous or otherwise, is measured on a weighing scale of Allah at the Day of Judgement before Allah in the world hereafter. In order words, each one would have one's own Report Card or Performance Card presented to him and it would be weighing accordingly before Allah. On the day, no one can escape from the assessment except those members of prophet-hood, the pious ones etc. with the leave and blessing of Allah.

The ultimate aim of the Muslims while in this world is to have clean slate or good performance cards. To have that, the only way for the Muslims is to adhere to Islamic teaching in full, not just to follow a certain portion of it only but in totality. For the disbelievers and others certainly they will have full of tainted or bad report cards.

Touching on Islamic principles and the commandments of Allah, many disobedient Muslims opt to take them lightly. Some of them are uncomfortable with the Islamic laws (syariah), even to the extent of against them. They prefer the secular system. To them Islam is an outdated religion that does not conform to modern norm of life as advocated by secularists and industrialised world. Probably, they wish to return to the life style of the ignorant before the advent of Islam and Islamic civilisation where evil life style and immorality like murders, LGBT etc. already existed and ruled the day then.

For those who are defiant to the commands of Allah and that of His Messenger will surely taste the wrath of Allah, either in this world or in the world hereafter.

CHAPTER 13.   THE FINAL VICTORY

All living creatures of Allah will die. Mankind would be resurrected again in the world hereafter to face the consequences of their deeds. The believers (Muslims) will live happily forever in the heavens of Allah. The disbelievers will also live but in sheer torment in hell fire forever.

In the meantime, the Muslims are looking for the real victory (al-falah), that is, to achieve a good life (hasanah fiddunia) in this world as well as good life in the next world hereafter (hasanah filakhirah) in the heaven of Allah. To achieve this, the Muslims have to honestly obey and summit to Allah in totality in accordance with the teaching of Islam as enshrined in the al-Quran and the Sunnah of Prophet Muhammad (pbuh).

Living in this temporal world is always subject to constant trial or test by Allah to abide to His rules. Everyone has to face the ordeals. For the Muslims they are in a constant struggle to conform to the path of Allah by choosing between the right against the wrong; between the truth and the falsehood. This struggle goes on at various stages of life until the time of death.

Thus, the struggle between the forces of right, virtuousness, justice, equality, purity and truth etc. and those of evil, falsehood, egoism, materialism, tyranny, selfishness, injustice, faithlessness, discrimination, corruption, infringement of rights, abuse of power etc. is ongoing to the end. Winning the struggle against the satanic evil deeds is the ultimate aim for Allah fearing Muslims.

Allah raised many Prophets in this world from time immemorial to awaken the hearts of potentially ready fellow human to accept the religion of

Allah (that is to believe in Islamic Monotheism) with different syariah at different times.

The last Prophet cum the messenger of Allah was Prophet Muhammad (pbuh). He brought glad tidings and the light of Islam to this world. His companions along with him preached Islamic Monotheism and its virtues against evil, ignorance etc. They continued to make gradual progress and did not falter at any stage in their struggle until the society underwent a basic change for the better in line with the Islamic way of life. Thus, belief in Allah, truth and justice had taken root in the various societies.

Some of the believers, however, while still maintaining the form of Islam also deviated away from the right path introduced by the Prophet (pbuh), but due to dedication of many ulama, many of them usually returned to the true Islam.

With the fall of Islamic empire and colonisation of Muslim countries by the West, secularism effectively weakened the Muslims. Western influence therefore succeeded in corrupting Islam with the introduction of secularism in the Muslims countries. Thus, a process of struggle between Islam and secularism continues.

Islam regarded falsehood - intrigue, hypocrisy, evil, misrepresentation of Islam and so forth - as froth of water without its roots and therefore is bound to disappear finally.

Allah said in surah ar-Ra'd, verse (13:17):

أَنزَلَ مِنَ ٱلسَّمَآءِ مَآءً فَسَالَتْ أَوْدِيَةٌۢ بِقَدَرِهَا فَٱحْتَمَلَ ٱلسَّيْلُ زَبَدًا

رَّابِيًا وَمِمَّا يُوقِدُونَ عَلَيْهِ فِى ٱلنَّارِ ٱبْتِغَآءَ حِلْيَةٍ أَوْ مَتَـٰعٍ زَبَدٌ مِّثْلُهُۥ

كَذَٰلِكَ يَضْرِبُ ٱللَّهُ ٱلْحَقَّ وَٱلْبَـٰطِلَ فَأَمَّا ٱلزَّبَدُ فَيَذْهَبُ جُفَآءً وَأَمَّا

مَا يَنفَعُ ٱلنَّاسَ فَيَمْكُثُ فِى ٱلْأَرْضِ كَذَٰلِكَ يَضْرِبُ ٱللَّهُ ٱلْأَمْثَـٰلَ

١٧

142

"He (Allah) sends down water (rain) from the sky and (water) flows the valleys according to their measure, but the flood bears away the foam that mounts up to the surface, and (also) from the (ore) which they heat in the fire in order to make ornaments or utensils, rises a foam like unto it, thus does Allah (by parables) show forth truth and falsehood. Then, as for the foam it passes away as scum upon the banks, while that which is for the good of mankind remains on the earth. Thus Allah sets forth parables (for the truth and falsehood, i.e. belief and disbelief)."

Thus, Islam - its virtue and truth - always maintains its positive position over falsehood and its effect on individual or society is tremendous. However, when the falsehood threatens the truth, it needs supporters to defend it. In this regard, Muslims play the very role in supporting it. Without their efforts, struggle, perseverance and faith in fighting or jihad to bring about a social justice, evil and falsehood will always prevail in the society. In this struggle, in the end the truth and justice will prevail and be victorious. Every form of wrong doings, falsehood, oppression and tyranny will be annihilated finally.

The clash of civilisations between the East and the West had produced crises of values and identity. Polarisation between the secularists and liberalists with the fundamentalists and the traditionalists is continuously ongoing. It appears that the conservative is losing ground.

Western culture is now thriving well and dominant in the Muslim world. More and more younger generation attracted to the free life style of Western culture. Disobedient to Allah had become more wide spread. This is the real contemporary challenge that haunted the fundamentalists and the traditionalists.

The enemies of Islam are too happy to see the degrading of Islamic morality by the Muslim themselves because moral decadent and corruption of Islamic religion is the linking bridge in bringing down the Islamic fundamental in the Muslim society.

However, the faithful Muslims and the pious ones will not feel the fear because they trust only in Allah for Allah will protect them at the Day of Judgement. They are the best peoples ever created by Allah as per surah Ali imran, verse (3:110) as follows:

كُنتُمۡ خَيۡرَ أُمَّةٍ أُخۡرِجَتۡ لِلنَّاسِ تَأۡمُرُونَ بِٱلۡمَعۡرُوفِ وَتَنۡهَوۡنَ عَنِ ٱلۡمُنكَرِ وَتُؤۡمِنُونَ بِٱللَّهِ ۗ وَلَوۡ ءَامَنَ أَهۡلُ ٱلۡكِتَـٰبِ لَكَانَ خَيۡرًا لَّهُم ۚ مِّنۡهُمُ ٱلۡمُؤۡمِنُونَ وَأَكۡثَرُهُمُ ٱلۡفَـٰسِقُونَ ﴿١١٠﴾

"You (true believers in Islamic Monotheism and followers of Prophet Muhammad and his Sunnah etc.) are <u>the best of peoples ever raised up for mankind</u>; you enjoin al-ma'ruf (i.e. all good deeds that Islam has ordained) and forbid al-munkar (polytheism, disbelief and all that Islam has forbidden), and you believe in Allah. And had the people of the Scripture (Jews and Christians) believed, it would have been better for them; among them are some who have faith, but most of them are al-fasiquun (disobedient to Allah and rebellious against Allah's command)".

Being the best peoples ever raised, Allah will protect the true Muslims that uphold and adhere to the teaching of Al-Quran and al-Sunnah.

Why are the Muslims the best people ever created by Allah? Because they enjoin people to do righteous deeds and to refrain or forbid from doing anything that Allah prohibited. In order to achieve as the best ummah ever created by Allah, the Muslims have to fulfil three basic conditions as stated in the verse:

i)   Believe in Allah only (Islamic Monotheism),

ii) Enjoin the righteous deeds and

iii) Abstain from doing anything bad or evil deeds that Allah forbad.

These three ingredients are essentials and are complementary to one another that move in unison to make Muslims as the best ummah. Failing to observe one of them, particularly with regard to faith or belief in Allah (Islamic Monotheism), Muslims will become the worse ummah just like the people of the book, the Jews and the Christians. The Jews claimed that they are the chosen people by Allah. True the Jews were once the chosen people, but they disobeyed Allah and ungrateful lots and therefore they had become the worst ummah or community without a country.

People who have faith in Allah are free from any negative influence of others because all the others are creatures of Allah as well. Belief in Allah will make people feel free from fear. That is the real freedom and dynamism in life that lead to freedom of want, freedom of positive and creative thinking for the good of human race within the parameter of Islam.

With the freedom, no one can prohibit the Muslims from doing the righteous deeds for the development of human race. Any wrong doings that Allah prohibited can be contained accordingly within the syariah. When people know their limit they will live harmoniously and peacefully. That is the aim of Islam as a religion of universal peace. It is an ideal one. It is achievable provided the Muslims are led by leaders of integrity.

It is a reality in life that people usually dislike criticism pointing at them especially it involves people of authority unless they are open hearted persons. Though it is a positive criticism on something of the public interest, often than not, it may be construed as bad and incriminating by others. Thus, criticism on certain wrong doings may be taken as a serious offence against the government of the day, particularly the autocratic regime, even though the critique is a positive one. That is why many people become 'yes man' or lackey to the leaders lest they would face unnecessary trouble. There are, of course, a few daring ones but they usually will face prosecution and risk of being put in jail.

In the past, pious and Allah fearing people, for example the four well known Imams (Muslim scholars), Imam Abu Hanifah (80-150 A.H), Imam Malik (93-179 A. H), Imam Shafie (150-204 A.H) and Imam Ahmad bin

Hambal (164- 241 A.H), faced prosecution and subjected to tortures for their stands against the wishes of the Caliphs. In this regard, there is no difference between the olden days and in the contemporary Muslim world because there are many scholars imprisoned and tortured or even killed for strongly voicing criticism directly against the government of the day. Those people were actually the real winners for they had many followers and were remembered for long time to come.

Oppressive government has resulted in the loss of fighting spirit on the part of many of the current scholars, though they are not lacking in their faith. Most of them more often than not will just remain silent or keep their frustrated feeling in their hearts to avoid from being prosecuted by the people in authority.

Allah sent Prophet Muhammad (pbuh) to make Islam as the exclusive religion of Allah over and above the other religions. However, many people disagreed about it especially the religious pluralists and liberalists. Allah said in surah as-Shaff, verse (61:9) as follows:

هُوَ ٱلَّذِىٓ أَرْسَلَ رَسُولَهُۥ بِٱلْهُدَىٰ وَدِينِ ٱلْحَقِّ لِيُظْهِرَهُۥ عَلَى ٱلدِّينِ كُلِّهِۦ وَلَوْ كَرِهَ ٱلْمُشْرِكُونَ ۝

__"He it is Who has sent His Messenger (Muhammad) with guidance and the religion of truth (Islamic Monotheism) to make it victorious over all (other) religions__ even though the musyrikuun (polytheists, pagans, idolaters, and disbelievers in the Oneness of Allah and in His Messenger Muhammad) hate it".

The above verse is clear that Islam is the only religion of truth and is above and over other religions. The perception that Islam is inclusive of other religions is not right for there is no substance to substantiate it. Therefore, it is the duty of Muslims to protect the image and the sanctity of Islam because Islam is supreme over others. It is an on-going jihad for all Muslims to safeguard Islam and their territories.

146

Earlier in the same surah, verse (61:8), Allah said:

$$يُرِيـــدُونَ لِيُطْفِئُـــواْ نُـــورَ ٱللَّـــهِ بِـــأَفْوَٰهِهِمْ وَٱللَّـــهُ مُتِـــمُّ نُـــورِهِۦ وَلَـــوْ كَـــرِهَ ٱلْكَٰفِـــرُونَ ۝$$

"They intend to put out the Light of Allah (i.e. the religion of Islam, al-Quran, and Prophet Muhammad) with their mouths. But Allah will complete His Light even though the disbelievers hate (it)."

Although the disbelievers want to distinguish Islam, Allah will protect it. In the verse (61:9) above, Allah ensured Prophet Muhammad that He would guide him in making Islam as a true religion over and above other religions, including Judaism and Christianity. The Jews and the Christians deviated from the origin of the true religion of Islamic Monotheism. The Christian religion Christianity as such was not known during the time of Prophet Jesus. It emerged later on after the 'demise' of Prophet Jesus. Prophet Jesus was himself a Muslim.

Since the history of the advent of Islam in Mecca, the Meccan Quraish pagan, the Jews in Medina and the Christians and others tried to distinguish Islam, but they were not successful. Islam is always the winner.

The pagan and barbaric Tatar and Mongol ransacked Baghdad and Islamic Abasyiah Caliphate. They killed thousands of Muslims and burning thousands of books of knowledge. King Ferdinand and his consort in 1492 defeated the Muslim ruler of Granada. They also killed thousands of Muslims who refused to convert to Christianity and chased all of them for good from Spain. The infidel Kemal Attartuk of Turkey abolished the caliphate of Turkey and turned Islamic state into secular government. The Muslims in Turkey under Attaturk lived under duress and oppression. The communist regimes of Russia and China killed many thousands of Muslims as well and suppressed Islamic practice inordinately. Notwithstanding of their suppression, Islam keeps on spreading.

147

The Western Christian colonists did their best to stifle the growth of Islam in the countries they colonised. They brought in secularism as an alternative. Their orientalist scholars misrepresented about Islam and they always propagated negatively about Islam to make people shun away from Islam. They also failed in their mission.

In the Southeast Asian archipelago, that is Indonesia, Malaysia and Brunei, once dominated by Hinduism, but with the introduction of Islam there, the population almost in entirety converted to Islam. When the Portuguese, the British and the Dutch colonised those countries, they tried hard to convert them to Christianity, but they miserably failed.

When Alfonso de Albuquerque conquered Melaka, he proudly planted a steel cross and said that with the fall of Melaka the way to Mecca blocked forever.

The above shows that the disbelievers failed in their attempts to stifle the growth of Islamic faith. Thus, it proved that Islam is victorious all the time. It cannot be wiped out from the surface of this earth because Allah always protects Islam.

Therefore, it is certain that no matter whatever challenge Islam is facing, Islamic fundamental is to stay and the Islamic principles and virtues would remain intact. Ultimately Muslims will win over their enemies and would rule the world with Islamic syariah. Nonetheless, many people do not subscribe to this prediction because the Muslims for so long have been in weak position all the way until to this present moment. They considered this as a fantasy that would never be realised in this modern globalised world. Never mind, be rest assured the victory day for the Muslims will come despite of the fact that the disbelievers will never ever stop in trying to extinguish the light of Islam. Allah is All-Knower, All-Powerful, and His wrath as promised by Him will come hard on all the disbelievers and the hypocrites.

Again, it is a fact that the Muslims faced many challenges but Islam keeps on spreading and growing everywhere in this world, be it in Europe, United States of America, Russia, China and so forth. Thus, Islam is already in a victory mode throughout the world. Now Muslim population has grown approximately about or more than 1.6 billion people worldwide. However, whether their leaders or the Muslim masses overall adhere to the Islamic principles in full or not is not the issue but Islam keeps on growing and a force to reckon with because of its sheer large number of followers.

With such a big force, they can shake the world political scenario if they unite as brothers in Islam and uphold Islamic teaching in totality as shown by the great Muhammad al-Fateh, the conqueror of Constantinople. For this very reason, the Western Christian powers, and for that matter any non-Muslim powers in the world, are trying their very best to contain and to break up the Muslim power and unity so that the Muslims will not be a threat to their supremacy again.

They covertly planted their agent net-works to spy other countries -Muslim and non-Muslim, friendly and non-friendly alike, but more so in the Muslim countries - to undermine them. They played political games, supporting friendly opposing sides or parties with material and financial help so that the Muslims will quarrel among themselves, thus directly destabilise the countries. The quagmire in the Middle East, Afghanistan and elsewhere was the result of their military interference and political intrigues to destabilise them. Thus, Muslims would be busy fighting among themselves instead of consolidation. That is their forte as to how to maintain their supremacy over others.

Allah commanded Muslims to be united and always be prepared in defending Islam. However, in the battle of Uhud, the Muslims were defeated for they disobeyed the command their leader, the Prophet Muhammad (pbuh). After the battle, Muslims were listless, weak and sad. Prophet Muhammad (pbuh) himself was injured and his uncle, Hamzah, died martyr. As a consequence of which Allah said in surah Ali Imran, verse (3:139):

$$وَلَا تَهِنُوا۟ وَلَا تَحْزَنُوا۟ وَأَنتُمُ ٱلْأَعْلَوْنَ إِن كُنتُم$$

$$مُّؤْمِنِينَ ۝١٣٩$$

"So do not become weak (against your enemy) nor be sad and you will be superior (in victory) if you are indeed (true) believers".

The essence of this revelation is that the Muslims must be 'true Muslims', that is to have complete faith in Allah and His Messenger, only then they would be victorious. The true Muslims should not feel scared in facing their enemies because Allah will always be with them.

In surah Muhammad, verse (47:7) Allah said:

$$\text{يَٰٓأَيُّهَا ٱلَّذِينَ ءَامَنُوٓاْ إِن تَنصُرُواْ ٱللَّهَ يَنصُرْكُمْ وَيُثَبِّتْ أَقْدَامَكُمْ ٧}$$

"O you who believe if you help (in the cause of) Allah He will help you, and make your foothold firm".

Helping Allah does not mean that He is weak and needs help - Allah is Most Powerful. Allah's help will come on the precondition that the Muslims firstly must help in upholding Islam; that is the meaning and spirit of the above verse.

To be strong, Allah reminded Muslims not to quarrel among themselves. Allah said in surah al-Anfal, verse (8:46):

$$\text{وَأَطِيعُواْ ٱللَّهَ وَرَسُولَهُۥ وَلَا تَنَٰزَعُواْ فَتَفْشَلُواْ وَتَذْهَبَ رِيحُكُمْ}$$
$$\text{وَٱصْبِرُوٓاْ إِنَّ ٱللَّهَ مَعَ ٱلصَّٰبِرِينَ ٤٦}$$

"And obey Allah and His Messenger, and do not dispute (with one another) lest you lose courage and your strength depart, and be patient. Surely, Allah is with those who are as-sabirin (the patient ones)".

The core of Islamic faith is to believe in Allah alone and to obey Him and His Messenger. The faithful should not quarrel but be united and patient in facing any eventualities.

The message is very clear. After all the hard works and struggle, then the Muslims have to leave it to Allah with full of conviction, patience and wait for His decision. Whatever the result is, good or bad, accept it accordingly. Be grateful to Allah if the result is good. If the result is not as expected, accept it patiently with open hearth without remorse for there would be a blessing in disguise or something to learn from it. Islam does not recognise disappointment but to place trust and hope in Allah. Keep on shouldering the responsibilities as usual, insya Allah (God willing) it will bear fruit ultimately.

Prophet Muhammad and his companions in many battles against the enemies of Islam lacked of weaponry and soldiers comparatively with their enemies, yet they won all the battles because his followers had strong faith and conviction in Allah and him as a supreme leader. For example, in the first and most important battle in Islam against disbelievers (kufar Quraish) of Mecca, that is, the **Battle of Badar** the small army of Prophet Muhammad won the battle because Allah helped them by sending troop of angels, though invisible to them, to fight the disbelievers. In the **Battle of Ahzab**, Allah helped the Prophet by sending strong storm to destroy the disbelievers. An exception was in the **Battle of Uhud,** where the Muslims lost the war because some soldiers disobeyed the Prophet's command. That was a lesson for the later Muslims to learn from it.

Nevertheless, it does not mean that strong military personnel with good weaponry etc. are not important as per Allah revelation in surah al-Anfal, verse (8:60) as already mentioned earlier.

Allah also said in surah al-Ma'idah, verse (5:54-56) as under:

يَـٰٓأَيُّهَا ٱلَّذِينَ ءَامَنُواْ مَن يَرْتَدَّ مِنكُمْ عَن دِينِهِۦ فَسَوْفَ يَأْتِى ٱللَّهُ بِقَوْمٍ

يُحِبُّهُمْ وَيُحِبُّونَهُۥٓ أَذِلَّةٍ عَلَى ٱلْمُؤْمِنِينَ أَعِزَّةٍ عَلَى ٱلْكَـٰفِرِينَ يُجَـٰهِدُونَ

فِى سَبِيلِ ٱللَّهِ وَلَا يَخَافُونَ لَوْمَةَ لَآئِمٍ ذَٰلِكَ فَضْلُ ٱللَّهِ يُؤْتِيهِ مَن

يَشَآءُ وَٱللَّهُ وَٰسِعٌ عَلِيمٌ ﴿٥٤﴾

"O you who believe, whoever from among you becomes apostate (turns back from his religion Islam), Allah will bring a people whom He will love and they will love Him; humble towards the believers, stern towards the disbelievers, fighting in the way of Allah (jihad), and never afraid of the blame of the blamers. That is the Grace of Allah that He bestows on whom He will and Allah is All-Sufficient for His creatures' needs, All-Knower".

إِنَّمَا وَلِيُّكُمُ ٱللَّهُ وَرَسُولُهُۥ وَٱلَّذِينَ ءَامَنُواْ ٱلَّذِينَ يُقِيمُونَ ٱلصَّلَوٰةَ

وَيُؤْتُونَ ٱلزَّكَوٰةَ وَهُمْ رَٰكِعُونَ ﴿٥٥﴾

"Verily, your wali (Protector or Helper) is Allah, His Messenger and the believers - those who perform solat (prayer) and give zakat (obligatory alms) and bow down (submit themselves with obedience to Allah in prayer)".

وَمَن يَتَوَلَّ ٱللَّهَ وَرَسُولَهُۥ وَٱلَّذِينَ ءَامَنُواْ فَإِنَّ حِزْبَ ٱللَّهِ هُمُ ٱلْغَـٰلِبُونَ

﴿٥٦﴾

"And whosoever takes Allah, His Messenger and those believers as Protectors then the party of Allah (the Muslims) will be the victorious".

From the above verses, the Muslim ummah only will win provided they observe, among other things, the following:

- They love none others but Allah. They fear none but Allah to achieve the highest adulation of Allah.

- They love and help other fellow Muslims as brothers in Islam for the sake of Allah, not for the sake of others. They are humble towards brother Muslims and strict toward the disbelievers.

- They unite and fight in the way of Allah (jihad) in defending Islam. They are not traitors in the cause of Allah.

- They are not afraid of the blame of the blamers.

- They fear not of the enemies of Islam. To Allah alone they submit or surrender themselves. Allah is the only Protector and He alone they seek help. They seek help not from the disbelievers or make alliance with them.

- They have firm faith in Allah and His Messenger and choose good Muslims as their leaders.

- They take only Allah, His Messenger and the believers as protectors in any struggle. Only then, they will be victorious.

- They must have all the necessary machinery of war - military, weaponry etc. - to show off their strength to the enemies or would be enemies as per Allah's revelation in surah al-Anfal, verse (8:60).

The Muslims should be humble or moderate, but then it does not mean that they should ignore any wrong doings. In a hadith narrated by Imam Ahmad from Abu Said al-Khudry that Prophet Muhammad (pbuh) said:

"Do not make yourself humble among you if you see some wrong doings in the way of Allah that make you refrain from saying about it. Allah will ask you about it during the Day of Judgement:

'What stops you from saying about it?' He replies:

'He is afraid of man'. Allah says:

'I am the One you should rightfully be scared of'".

The genuine Muslims have the attributes of loving Allah and His Messenger more than anything else, including that of their own selves. The true Muslims will not trade-off their faith with material world and riches because all those worldly things would be perished eventually.

As stated in verse (5:56) above *that whosoever takes Allah, His Messenger and those believers as Protectors then the party of Allah (the Muslims) will be the victorious* is the core points to be observed. This is in the underlying principles that the Muslims should strongly uphold in their faith against the Satan, the taghut, the enemies, the vain desire and all the evils from their life.

The real victory or success (al-falah) is to win in upholding the faith, truth, justice and the sanctity of Islam. Muslim leaders that are lacking in integrity and self-worth will not be able to lead the Muslims or country to victory. These are the 'taghut leaders' for they have betrayed the trust of Allah and His Messenger and their people.

This kind of leaders or people when they are in trouble they turn immediately to Allah for help but during happy time, they conveniently forget Allah. This analogous to a hadith narrated by Imam Muslim and Imam at-Tarmizi that Messenger of Allah said:

> **"There was a traveller from a faraway place with his hair and cloth covered with full of dust. He put up his hands to the sky saying: 'O my Robb (God), my Robb' but his food, his drink and his cloth were haram (illegal or not permissible). He was raised-up with haram food too. How could Allah accept his prayer?"**

The above hadith is very much relevant in this modern contemporary world. Look honestly at own self, look at the people in power etc. how

154

many can confidently dare to say that they have not been raised from 'haram' money as stated in the hadith? The truth is that many of them since generations were raised and lived on millions of haram money or income obtained by cheating and corruption. So, would Allah accept their prayers? Hopefully they would repent before they die because Allah is ever forgiven to those who repent.

One also could see around when calamity happened, say big devastating flood or downing of a plane killing all the passengers, many people cried and prayed to Allah but during happy time where are all these people - in the night-club, in the golf course or in the mosque? Except the pious ones, they accepted it calmly and with full of patient for they knew it was the Will of God. They trusted Allah, come what may life has to go on without much remorse. But the rest keep on cursing, unnecessarily blaming and finding fault on other people since they could not accept the fate. Fine enough, everybody naturally feels sad on the incident but let the due process of investigation going on without hassle and much criticism.

Due observance of the Islamic principles is a prerequisite for a real success and happiness. Success is not only based on material achievement but also in upholding the virtue of Islam for without which life will not be complete. Money alone cannot bring happiness.

Imaging in the scenario where the power is obtained through illegal means, for example by election rigging, money politics, coup d'etat etc. It is for sure the government so formed is unclean and its governing members are unclean too. They are governed by a bunch of rogue and untrustworthy people. Success is no doubt, but then the riches they earn, the food and drink they take, the house they occupy and the clothes they wear and so forth are also illegal (haram). Would they be happy? Would Allah accept the prayer from this kind of people who follow the footsteps of Satan?

In this connection, Allah said in surah al-Baqarah, verse (2:208):

يَـٰٓأَيُّهَا ٱلَّـذِينَ ءَامَنُـوا ٱدْخُـلُوا فِـى ٱلسِّـلْمِ كَآفَّـةً وَلَا تَتَّبِعُـوا خُطُوَٰتِ ٱلشَّيْطَـٰنِ إِنَّهُۥ لَكُمْ عَدُوٌّ مُّبِينٌ ﴿٢٠٨﴾

"O you who believe, enter perfectly in Islam (by obeying all the rules and regulations of the Islamic religion) and follow not the footsteps of Satan. Verily he is to you a plain enemy."

When a person accepts Islamic faith, he should completely follow all the tenets of Islam. If for the time being, for example, he may not be able to follow it in entirety, he should not go against or object the Islamic syariah or the maqasid (purpose) of Islamic syariah but he should endeavour hard to conform to it in order to attain the highest achievement, that is, 'husnul khatimah' (happy or good ending) in the world hereafter. Similarly, if a Muslim country presently is unable to implement Islamic syariah or laws exactly to the letter, it should slowly endeavour to upgrade it by slowly doing away with the secular laws. It should not accept and protect the secular laws.

As Muslims they should truly and sincerely submit to Allah alone completely until death. He should die as Muslims (believers). In this regard, Allah said in surah Ali Imran, verse (4:102):

يَـٰٓأَيُّهَا ٱلَّذِينَ ءَامَنُوا ٱتَّقُوا ٱللَّهَ حَقَّ تُقَاتِهِۦ وَلَا تَمُوتُنَّ إِلَّا وَأَنتُم مُّسْلِمُونَ ﴿١٠٢﴾

"O you who believe, fear Allah (by doing all that He has ordered and abstaining from all that He has forbidden) as He should be feared, and die not except in a state of Islam (as Muslims)."

The above verse is always recited in every Friday sermon to remind Muslims to adhere to Islam and die as Muslims. True Muslims will never abandon Islam. This is indeed the purpose of life. The most important victory or success for the Muslims is to obtain blessing, reward or benefit from Allah in the everlasting world hereafter. For this purpose, the Muslims always pray to Allah, especially after solat (worship) by reciting the following verse (2:201) in surah al-Baqarah:

"And of them there are some who say: 'Our Lord (Robb)! Bestow us good life in this world and in the Hereafter, and save us from the torment of the Hell Fire!'"

The ultimate aim of Muslims is to get forgiveness of sins from Allah, to get blessing and rewards from Him. Thus, the apex of all success is indeed to attain the genuine victory (al-falah) as revealed by Allah in surah al-Mu'minun, verses (23:1-10), already stated in Chapter 10.

The Muslims cannot achieve victory, in the first place, without having to face challenges or obstacles. Likewise, a nation cannot attain victory or supremacy without going through sacrifice and struggle to develop the country spiritually, economically, militarily etc. in preparation to face its adversaries and other challenges.

Similarly to attain success in the context of 'al-falah' (victory) the Muslims must have a strong faith (iman) in Allah. Other than performing obligatory worship (solat) in earnest five-time a day, many other general obligations are required on the part of the Muslims to perform, especially with regard to human relationship between fellow human and other creatures of Allah such fauna and flora. Hills and forests should not be unnecessarily destroyed in order to maintain safe environment and so forth.

Islam never stops calling for victory every day in line with the call for solat (prayer) – "Hayya 'alal falaah" (Come let us race for victory). However, many Muslims ignore this call and to emulate its meaning.

A true Muslim, therefore, is happy and convinced that if he were to die he will inherit the "jannatul Firdaus" (Paradise or Heaven). However, whoever believes in Allah superficially and without the virtuous practical deeds will not to be able to achieve the al-falah (victory) in the true sense of the word.

To achieve highest success, it requires highest sacrifice and jihad to maintain one's piousness and devotion to Allah and also to protect the sanctity of Islam. This is the key of success as shown by the Prophet Muhammad (pbuh) in his devotion to Allah in facing Muslim adversaries. Nonetheless, one should remember that achieving success through extremism in any form whatsoever is outside the context of Islam. This directly would tarnish the good image of Islam because extremism is not the teaching of Islam.

Islam is a progressive religion. It teaches its followers to have vision and mission to progress forward, outreach the world globally to give light of Islam and to pioneer in every sphere of life as leaders, not to be as it is now being followers of disbelievers (kufar). True Muslims are neither the slave of power and riches nor afraid of non-believers but only Allah, even though in doing so they may sacrifice their life.

Without doubt, 'al-falah' is the genuine success. This is the jihad or struggle for self-righteousness. Al-Falah stresses the principle of genuine faith, fearing Allah, high morality and integrity, never give up in any endeavour and always place great hope in Allah only, because success or failure is solely in the hand of Allah. In essence, anything done must be in the name of Allah and for Allah. Doing anything that is not in the name of Allah is not acceptable to Allah, no matter how noble the deed seems to be. This holistic Islamic understanding and spirit is the only way to enhance the image and the working culture of Muslims overall.

Allah said respectively in surah at-Taghaabun, verses (64:11-13) as follows:

مَآ أَصَابَ مِن مُّصِيبَةٍ إِلَّا بِإِذْنِ ٱللَّهِ وَمَن يُؤْمِنۢ بِٱللَّهِ يَهْدِ قَلْبَهُۥ وَٱللَّهُ بِكُلِّ شَىْءٍ عَلِيمٌ ﴿١١﴾

"No calamity befalls, but with the leave [i.e. decision and Qadar (Divine Preordainments)] of Allah, and whosoever believes in Allah, He guides his heart and Allah is the All-Knower of everything".

وَأَطِيعُوا۟ ٱللَّهَ وَأَطِيعُوا۟ ٱلرَّسُولَ فَإِن تَوَلَّيْتُمْ فَإِنَّمَا عَلَىٰ رَسُولِنَا ٱلْبَلَـٰغُ ٱلْمُبِينُ ﴿١٢﴾

"Obey Allah, and obey the Messenger (Muhammad), but if you turn away, then the duty of Our Messenger is only to convey (the message) clearly".

ٱللَّهُ لَآ إِلَـٰهَ إِلَّا هُوَ ۚ وَعَلَى ٱللَّهِ فَلْيَتَوَكَّلِ ٱلْمُؤْمِنُونَ ﴿١٣﴾

"Allah La ilaha illa Huwa (none has the right to be worshipped but He) and in Allah (alone) therefore let the believers put their trust."

The above verses are the guidance for the true Muslims to adopt and emulate. The Muslims should not be fidgety and scared when calamity befalls on them because it is the Preordainments (Qadar) of Allah. It is the sixth Pillar of Faith (iman) in Islam. Whoever obeys Allah and His Messenger, will accept any eventualities - good or bad, happiness or sad - with thankfulness and patient because anything is from Him because He is All-Knower of everything.

In surah at-Taubah, verse (9:51) Allah also said:

قُـل لَّـن يُصِيبَنَـآ إِلَّا مَـا كَـتَبَ ٱللَّـهُ لَنَا هُـوَ مَوْلَنَـاۚ وَعَلَـى ٱللَّـهِ

فَلْيَتَـوَكَّلِ ٱلْمُؤْمِنُـونَ ۝

"Say: Nothing shall ever happen to us except what Allah has ordained for us. He is our Maula (Lord, Helper and Protector). And in Allah let the believers put their trust."

A Muslims is, therefore, to accept whatever happened because it is the Will of Allah since He is the Lord and the Protector of the universe. Nevertheless, Allah also commanded humankind to work hard first before leaving the fate to Allah. The guiding principle is trust in Allah after doing everything honestly and to the best of one's ability. Success, failures, difficulties or calamities is the preordainment of Allah. Though as human, one may feel sad and remorse but one should never lose hope, sense of bearing and self-worth.

Death and disaster may come at any time, so why brood or feel remorse about it. For all the happenings, there are hidden blessings that no one can predict or knows about it. Therefore, one should pray to Allah asking for forgiveness (istighfar) by always uttering as simple as: *'O Allah, please forgive me for all my wrong doings or sins'.* This is because no one, as human, is free from mistakes or sins except the Prophets and the Messengers of Allah.

It is as simple as the above doa (prayer for forgiveness) to seek for Allah's mercy for He is the Most Merciful and Most Forgiven. However, one should never ask for pardon from mortal being. A fasiq (disobedient) Muslim may not get mercy and blessing from Allah unless he repented. Therefore, during and after effect of any bad incidents, there is no point harping, blaming and 'crying blood' for what had happened is gone for good. Feeling sadness is human, but what that had lost will never come back and therefore asking forgiveness from Allah is the only one's solace as mortal beings.

Material success and spiritual accomplishment are the two complements for self-righteousness that a good Muslim is longing for. This is the holistic ideal because success in material wealth only without spiritual attainment would make life incomplete and empty. Wealth alone will not make a person's life happy. Life without spiritual fulfilment just like a person living without purpose and may become crazy for loneliness at the end of the day. Nevertheless, material wealth is essential to up keep good living and to make good investment for the world hereafter. Therefore, both sorts of wealth are important to have a sane and noble life but again it should be in moderation and always be grateful to Allah.

Whoever believes in Allah, His Messenger and His Book (al-Quran) will have the guidance and enlightenment from Allah. Allah said in surah al-A'raf, verse (7:157):

الَّذِينَ يَتَّبِعُونَ الرَّسُولَ النَّبِيَّ الْأُمِّيَّ الَّذِي يَجِدُونَهُ مَكْتُوبًا عِندَهُمْ فِي التَّوْرَاةِ وَالْإِنجِيلِ يَأْمُرُهُم بِالْمَعْرُوفِ وَيَنْهَاهُمْ عَنِ الْمُنكَرِ وَيُحِلُّ لَهُمُ الطَّيِّبَاتِ وَيُحَرِّمُ عَلَيْهِمُ الْخَبَائِثَ وَيَضَعُ عَنْهُمْ إِصْرَهُمْ وَالْأَغْلَالَ الَّتِي كَانَتْ عَلَيْهِمْ ۚ فَالَّذِينَ آمَنُوا بِهِ وَعَزَّرُوهُ وَنَصَرُوهُ وَاتَّبَعُوا النُّورَ الَّذِي أُنزِلَ مَعَهُ ۙ أُولَٰئِكَ هُمُ الْمُفْلِحُونَ ﴿١٥٧﴾

"That is those who follow the Messenger, the Prophet who can neither read nor write (i.e. Muhammad) whom they find written with them in the Taurat (Torah) and the Injeel (Gospel). He commands them for al-ma'ruf (all good deeds that Islam ordained); and forbids them from al-munkar (disbelief, polytheism of all kinds and all that Islam prohibited). He allows them as lawful at-taiyibat (all good and lawful as regards things, deeds, beliefs, persons, foods, etc.) and prohibits them as unlawful al-khaba'ith (all evil and unlawful as regards things, deeds, beliefs, persons,

foods, etc.). He releases them from their heavy burdens (of Allah's Covenant) and from the fetters that were upon them. So those who believe in him (Muhammad), honour him, help him, and follow the light (the Quran) which has been sent down with him, it is they who will be successful".

At the end of the verse above, Allah said that whoever believes in (i) the Messenger of Allah (Prophet Muhammad pbuh), (ii) honours and helps him and (iii) accepts and follows al-Quran sent down through him will be successful in life in this world and hereafter. That is the promise of Allah.

When a person believes in Allah and His Messenger (Prophet Muhammad, pbuh) he is a Muslim. It is undeniable notwithstanding, many Muslims do not reflex this in practice because they do not follow the full teachings of Islam. They follow Islamic teachings or rituals only as they deem fit at their own convenience. Thus in this context, they do not diligently help the religion of Allah and the Prophet. Their faith have been diminished and some of them do not follow the Sunnah of Prophet (his sayings, actions etc.) and do not love and honour him. Some of them even went against him like those who are anti-Sunnah or Hadith whereas Allah clearly commanded the Muslims to follow his Sunnah and to honour him by always praising (solawat) him.

Throughout Islamic history, many caliphs, governors and army commanders were Allah fearing people. They were good leaders and respected by many. To name a few, they were Abu Bakar al-Siddiq, Umar al-Khatab, Othman, Ali, Khalid al-Walid, Umar Abd Aziz, Thariq bin Ziyad, Solehuddin al-Ayyubi (Saladin), Muhammad al-Fateh etc. were exemplary leaders in their respective time. They were famous for their valour and yet they were humble. During the height of Muslim power, the Muslim empire was strong and no power on earth then could challenge them. Europe at that time was still in the Dark Age under feudal kingdoms and the authority and clutches of Christian churches.

The basic strength of Muslim ummah of the past had strong faith, adhere to Islamic syariah and anything done was in the name of Allah. There is no two ways about it – meaning that it cannot mix or merge the secular and Islamic systems into one system. Islamic syariah is supreme above all the other systems. It is above the man-made secular constitution. Without such conviction, belief in Islamic Monotheism is incomplete.

Is it necessary to declare or to name a country an Islamic State? Some opined that it is not be necessary so as long as the syariah system is established and implemented in totality in the state because the entire world would know about it any way. What is there in name if some of the practices in the country are not in line with Islamic syariah. It is a mockery to Islam itself to declare as an Islamic state if abuse of power, cruelty and injustice are still prevalent in the country. Again it is a mockery to Islamic syariah or laws if the head of state is above the law. There are countries declared as Islamic states but the government are not transparent and abuse of power and corruption etc. reigned supreme. Some of the leaders are above the laws and living in opulence and extravagance which do not reflex at all the virtue of Islam and the life style of Prophet Muhammad (pbuh) and his glorious companions.

Islamic law is very fair and applicable to all without exception. Whether the kings, sultans or presidents etc., they are subject to the same laws. No one is above the law, no one is immune from it, whether committed inside the country or outside; no one has the right to pardon any criminals; and there is no special court or council to try the accused elite leaders. That is the beauty of Islamic laws for no one is exempted from it. If a supreme leader, for example, exempted from syariah laws, then it is not an Islamic state despite of it being declared as Islamic State.

Allah will defend the believers as per His revelation in surah al-Hajj, verse (17:38):

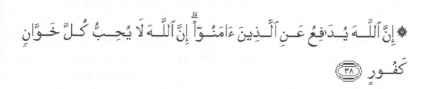

"Truly, Allah defends those who believe. Verily Allah likes not any treacherous ingrate to Allah (those who disobey Allah but obey Satan)".

According to al-Qurtubi the above verse was revealed for the Muslims in Mecca to be patient without retaliating although they were severely suffered at the hands of the pagan disbelievers (kufar) of Mecca because they were weak at that time.

Some of the followers of Prophet Muhammad (pbuh), for example the mother of Ammar bin Yasir was cruelly killed by impaling a stick into her, Bilal was put under the sun with heavy stone on him and some others were beaten simply because they believed in Oneness of Allah. They also wanted kill the Prophet. Finally, with the blessing of Allah, Prophet Muhammad (pbuh) migrated (hijrah) to Medina in 622 AD.

Then in Medina when the Muslims became stronger, Allah gave them permission to fight the disbelievers as per verse (17:39) of the same surah al-Hajj:

أُذِنَ لِلَّذِينَ يُقَـٰتَلُونَ بِأَنَّهُمْ ظُلِمُوا ۚ وَإِنَّ ٱللَّهَ عَلَىٰ نَصْرِهِمْ لَقَدِيرٌ ﴿٣٩﴾

"Permission to fight is given to those (i.e. believers against disbelievers) who are fighting them because they (believers) have been wronged, and surely Allah is able to give them (believers) <u>victory</u>".

Allah assured the Muslims that He would help them. Thus, in the Battle of Badar on 17th Ramadan 2AH (3rd March 624 AD), the most important and the first war with the pagan Quraish of Mecca, the Muslims won the war with the help of Allah although they were less in number.

Then, in the sixth year after Prophet Muhammad migrated to Medina, Prophet Muhammad (pbuh) in March 628 AD (Zulkaedah 6 AH) decided to perform Umrah (the lesser pilgrimage or little hajj) in Mecca. There were fourteen hundreds of his companions joined him. He ordered them not to carry any weapons of war, but allowed a sword that was customary for the travellers to carry for protection against any caravan raids.

The Quraish of Mecca (Pagans or Idol worshipers) refused to allow the Prophet and his entourage to enter Mecca. They closed all access to the city. The Prophet then reached a place called Hudaibiyah, on the precinct of the sacred territory of Mecca, and halted there. The Quraish tried to provoke Prophet's companions to fighting. However, upon finding the pilgrims in their Ihram (pilgrim's garb) and their intention was not to fight, the Quraish abated and agreed to negotiate with the Muslims. Having agreed by the Quraish to negotiate with the Muslims was actually a blessing to them because they treated the Muslims all this while as foes and refugees. Despite of robust and recalcitrant attitude by the Quraish negotiators, with the heavenly subtle diplomacy by Prophet Muhammad (pbuh), the 'Treaty of Hudaibiyah' was however finally agreed and penned down accordingly. Earlier during the negotiation, some companions of Prophet resented about the text and the terms of the treaty. They were not happy on the distasteful attitude of the Quraish negotiators shown towards the Prophet, but they relented after Prophet Muhammad insisted on the agreement.

Among the text of the agreement, inter alia, both parties agreed to lay down the burden of war for ten years. During the time, each party should be safe, and neither should injure nor damage the others but uprightness and honour should prevail between them.

The Muslims, in the meantime, had to return to Medina without performing the Umrah for the year. In the following year, however, Prophet Muhammad and his followers only would be able to enter Mecca. That was the big winning point for the Muslims as the result of the intelligence and political diplomacy in the negotiation by Prophet Muhammad (pbuh). The Prophet declared that the treaty was a victory and his companions accepted it on the conviction that Allah and His messenger knew best.

After the signing of the agreement, the Muslims began to feel its blessing because everyone felt safe and at peace from harassment from the kufar Quraish. They could mix around without fear and at the same time took opportunity to propagate Islam to the non-believers. Many of the non-believers or pagan Arabs willingly embraced Islam after they found out its virtues.

There were many lessons could be inferred and learned from the success of the Hudaibiyah Treaty. At the first instance, it was obvious that the treaty was unfair towards the Muslim side but the hidden Divine Power and Blessing planned and destined by Allah was already in the process towards the conquest of Mecca in the immediate future. This was the initial strategic key indicator of success arranged by Allah as a prelude to the victory of Islam. The Messenger of Allah already knew about this on his way back to Medina when Allah revealed to him His revelation in the al-Quran, surah al-Fath, verse (48:1) as hereunder, for which his companions did not know.

إِنَّا فَتَحْنَا لَكَ فَتْحًا مُّبِينًا ۝

"Verily, We have given you (O Muhammad) a manifest victory".

Finally in the month of Ramadan in the 8th year AH (630 AD), Prophet Muhammad (pbuh) entered and occupied Mecca with little resistance and bloodshed and thus Mecca came under the jurisdiction of Islam. Prophet Muhammad entered Mecca with humility without any pompous for the victory.

It should be emphasised that Allah would defend and help Muslims provided they help Him in upholding Islam. For instance in the current scenario, even though Muslim population is large, significant of them have abandon Allah and therefore Allah will not help them to victory. Practically Muslim countries of today do not adhere to Islamic syariah. Some are autocratic regimes while others practise secularism or quasi-Islamic government.

In order words, they have transgressed or deviated from the Islamic syariah. The failure of Muslims to return to the command of Allah as enshrined in al-Quran and al-Hadith is the underlying cause of their failure.

Since many Muslims had abandoned Allah, probably in near the future a new batch of pious and Allah fearing peoples will soon emerge to replace the current disobedient Muslims, to help Allah in upholding the religion of Islam. With that, with the Will of Allah the victory of Islam is certain. By then, perhaps the end of the world will set in or is very near.

As mentioned earlier, Allah created all Jinn and human beings as His servants to submit and worship Him alone without associating Him with anything. Humankind is also the caliph of Allah to manage this world accordingly in accordance with Islamic syariah. Finally they will die and return to Him to face the Day of Judgement. Therefore, human beings should behave well for they are mortal creatures. The most honourable peoples beside Allah are the pious and devoted ones, not the rich neither the powerful.

Whatever the position of Muslims is in now, the Muslims ummah will be victorious ultimately when they return to al-Quran and al-Sunnah of Prophet Muhammad (pbuh). Muslims will be victorious because Allah promised it. When would it be? Only Allah knows best.

Touching on the Day of Judgement or Doomsday, it would be relevant to cite briefly with regard to the minor signs before the coming of greater signs that would happen before the actual time of Doomsday. They are happening now. There are many collections of Hadith mentioned about them.

Islamic scholars classified the signs of doomsday into two headings: the lesser signs and the greater signs. The primary minor or lesser signs that manifested are in the form of the general diminishing of Islamic religious observance by the Muslims, the increase of immorality and cruelty in the world. The general minor signs are, though not exhaustive, as follows:

- Al-Quran and al-Sunnah of Prophet Muhammad (pbuh) ignored by most people. The knowledge of Islam will gradually disappear with the death of many of the genuine and honest Islamic scholars (ulama). There may be some scholars that are left but most them are bad Islamic scholars. Majority of the people will cease to obey Allah.

- Sexual depravity and adultery will become prevalent, even doing it in the public like animals. Increase in the consumption of alcohol and other vices; and also increase in the number of women over the number of men.

- The children not only do not respect their parents but also desert them; and the wives also do not respect their husbands. Men will be submissive to women.

- False Prophets emerged. People will claim to be Prophets even though Prophet-hood ended with the last Prophet Muhammad (pbuh).

- Time passes quickly. Time will pass very swiftly, so much so that a year will slip away like a month, a month like a week, a week like a day while a day will fizzle out in a fleeting moment.

- Entertainments, namely music, singing and dance become popular. Artists become celebrity and respected more than the ulama (Islamic scholars).

- Falsehoods and lies regarded as truthful. Mean and ignorant people become leaders and live in opulent and in big mansions.

- People compete to construct tall buildings in most part of the world.

- Increase in frequency of earthquakes and other calamities.

- Increase in murders, bloodsheds and the appearance of fitnah (sedition, mischief etc.). The incidents of war and anarchy, religious or otherwise, are omnipresent throughout the world.

- War breaks out between the Jews and the Muslims.

- Mosques decorated as a matter of pride and competition. Expensive and big mosques built but empty and not fully utilised.

- Women appear naked despite their being dressed, meaning that women do not dress properly according to Islamic attire or code of dress.

All the above minor signs are already appearing and prevailing. The world is now waiting for greater signs to come. It would appear definitely, if not soon it would not be too far in a distance future.

Some of the signs related in the hadith were observable as predicted since more than a thousand year ago by Prophet Muhammad (pbuh), but that were just the minor signs as precedents to the period of major signs leading to the End Time of the universe. In this regard, Prophet Muhammad said:

"Signs follow one another like the pieces of a necklace falling one after the other when its string is cut". Hadith narrated by Imam at-Tirmizi.

The following hadith is interesting as the fighting between the Muslims in Palestine and the Jews is ongoing. Probably, it would finally lead to ultimate fighting between the Muslims and the Jews before the coming of the Doomsday. In the hadith, the messenger of Allah said:

"Qiamah (doomsday) will not happen until the Muslims fight all the Jews. They will kill the Jews. The Jews have to run for their lives by hiding behind the big stones or trees, but even the stones or the trees speak: 'O Muslims, here behind me are the Jews, come and kill them' except only the gharqad tree will not tell about the hiding Jews". Hadith narrated by Imam Muslim.

The signs that the Prophet (pbuh) described are occurring one after the other in every corner of the world. The hadith painted a perfect portrayal evident of our time. Every sign that occurred is to remind people that the Doomsday or the Day of Reckoning or Judgment is very near. It is a day when people will give account of themselves whatever they did in the world in the presence of Allah, whether big or small as an atom.

In this modern world, sophisticated military technology - nuclear, biological, chemical weapons etc. – is on the increase and unstoppable. With the development of such dangerous weapons of mass destruction by many nations, should a third world war happen again or nuclear explosion simultaneously happens accidently in the world, it would be hell and probably be the end of the world as well.

In surah al- Rum, verse (30:40-41) Allah said:

اَللَّهُ ٱلَّذِى خَلَقَكُمْ ثُمَّ رَزَقَكُمْ ثُمَّ يُمِيتُكُمْ ثُمَّ يُحْيِيكُمْ هَلْ مِن

شُرَكَآئِكُم مَّن يَفْعَلُ مِن ذَٰلِكُم مِّن شَىْءٍ سُبْحَٰنَهُ وَتَعَٰلَىٰ عَمَّا

يُشْرِكُونَ ۝

"Allah is He Who created you, then provided food for you, then will cause you to die, then (again) He will give you life (on the Day of Resurrection). Is there any of your (so-called) partners (of Allah) that do anything of that? Glory be to Him and Exalted be He above all that (evil) they associate (with Him)."

ظَهَرَ ٱلْفَسَادُ فِى ٱلْبَرِّ وَٱلْبَحْرِ بِمَا كَسَبَتْ أَيْدِى ٱلنَّاسِ لِيُذِيقَهُم بَعْضَ

ٱلَّذِى عَمِلُوا۟ لَعَلَّهُمْ يَرْجِعُونَ ۝

"Evil (sins and disobedience of Allah) has appeared on land and sea because of what the hands of men have earned (by oppression and evil deeds etc.) that Allah may make them taste a part of that which they have done, in order that they may return (by repenting to Allah, and begging His Pardon)."

In surah Ghafir, verse (40:59) Allah said:

إِنَّ ٱلسَّاعَةَ لَآتِيَةٌ لَّا رَيْبَ فِيهَا وَلَٰكِنَّ أَكْثَرَ ٱلنَّاسِ لَا يُؤْمِنُونَ ۝

"Verily, the Hour (Day of Judgement) is surely coming, therein is no doubt, yet most men believe not."

The above verses are clear for mankind to take note. That is the truth. Every mortal, big or small, has to go through it.

Whether people believe or not, the cycle of life will come to an end when the Doomsday comes for which no one can predict but cannot avoid. Mankind in this world began with Adam that Allah created from clay. Subsequently human beings through Adam and Eve (his consort from his rib) developed. Their off springs and descendants spread to every corner on the surface of this planet earth. Then they die and would be alive again on the Day of Resurrection in the world hereafter to face Allah at the Day of Judgement for their deeds in this present world. At that time, their fate depends on the virtuous deeds that they did in the world. Nobody can help them except the mercy and blessing of Allah.

Currently, the world becomes more developed and progressed, but the trade-off is that people live in uncomfortable environment and life, inhaling and drinking toxic air and water respectively and so forth arising from pollution from uncontrolled factories, destruction of hills, forests, rivers etc. Global warming, unexpected climate changes, famine due to lack of food and water, and newfound diseases are also inflicting on human race. Verily, people are now tasting or sampling all the fruits of their misdemeanours.

Finally, when the Doomsday comes, all living creatures will face tremendous upheaval and destruction beyond imagination. Allah described the occurrence of the Doomsday as per surah al-Zalzalah, verse (99:1-8) as follows:

إِذَا زُلْزِلَتِ ٱلْأَرْضُ زِلْزَالَهَا ①

"When the earth is shaken with its (final) earthquake (with terrible force and upheaval)."

وَأَخْرَجَتِ ٱلْأَرْضُ أَثْقَالَهَا ②

"And when the earth throws out its burdens."

وَقَالَ ٱلْإِنسَٰنُ مَا لَهَا ﴿٣﴾

"And man will say: "What is the matter with it?"

يَوْمَئِذٍ تُحَدِّثُ أَخْبَارَهَا ﴿٤﴾

"That Day it will declare its information (about all what happened over it of good or evil)."

بِأَنَّ رَبَّكَ أَوْحَىٰ لَهَا ﴿٥﴾

"Because your Lord has inspired it."

يَوْمَئِذٍ يَصْدُرُ ٱلنَّاسُ أَشْتَاتًا لِّيُرَوْاْ أَعْمَٰلَهُمْ ﴿٦﴾

"That Day mankind will proceed in scattered groups that they may be shown their deeds."

فَمَن يَعْمَلْ مِثْقَالَ ذَرَّةٍ خَيْرًا يَرَهُ ﴿٧﴾

"So whosoever does good equal to the weight of an atom (or a small particle) shall see it."

وَمَن يَعْمَلْ مِثْقَالَ ذَرَّةٍ شَرًّا يَرَهُ ۝

"And whosoever does evil equal to the weight of an atom shall see it."

There are many other verses Allah revealed in the al-Quran explaining the terrible occurrence on the Doomsday. Among other verses are such as in surah al-Ma'arij, verses (70:8-15), al-Qiamah, verses (75:8-14) and surah al-Takwir, verses (81:1-29) in which Allah said respectively, and translation of which, without Quranic verses, are as following:

Surah Ma'arij, verses: (70:8-15):

8. *The Day the sky will be like the molten silver.*

9. *And the mountains will be (flying) like flakes of wool,*

10. *And no friend will ask of a friend (because everybody is thinking of his fate).*

11. *Although they shall be made to see one another (i.e. on the Day of Resurrection), the Mujrim, (disbelievers, criminal, sinner etc.) would desire to ransom himself from the punishment by his children.*

12. *And his wife and his brother,*

13. *And his kindred who sheltered him,*

14. *And all that are in the earth, so that it might save him.*

15. *By no means, verily it will be the Fire of Hell.*

Surah al-Qiamah, verses (75:8-14):

8. *And the moon will be eclipsed (lost its light).*

9. *And the sun and moon will be joined together (by going one into the other or folded up or deprived of their light etc.)*

10. *On that Day man (who did not believe the Doomsday) will say: 'Where (is the refuge) to flee?'*

11. *No! There is no refuge!*

12. *Unto your Lord (Alone) will be the place of rest that Day.*

13. *On that Day man will be informed of what he sent forward (of his evil or good deeds) and what he left behind (of his good or evil deeds).*

14. *Nay! Man will be a witness against himself [as his body parts (skin, hands, legs etc.) will speak about his deeds].*

Surah al-Takwir, verses (81:1-21):

1. *When the sun Kuwwirat (wound round and lost its light).*

2. *And when the stars shall fall;*

3. *And when the mountains shall be destroyed (flying like dust in the air);*

4. *And when the pregnant she-camels shall be neglected;*

5. *And when the wild beasts shall be gathered together;*

6. *And when the seas shall become as blazing Fire;*

7. *And when the souls shall be joined with their bodies;*

8. *And when the female (infant) buried alive (as the pagan Arabs used to do) shall be questioned.*

9. *For what sin she was killed?*

10. *And when the written pages of deeds (good and bad) of every person shall be laid open;*

11. *And when the sky shall be stripped off and taken away from its place;*

12. *And when Hell-fire shall be kindled to fierce ablaze.*

13. *And when Paradise shall be brought near,*

14. *(Then) every person will know what he has brought (of good and evil).*

15. *So verily, I swear by the stars (planets),*

16. *And by the stars (planets) that move swiftly and hide themselves,*

17. *And by the night as it departs;*

18. *And by the dawn as it brightens;*

19. *Verily, this is the Word (this Quran brought by) a most honourable messenger (Gabriel), [from Allah to the Prophet Muhammad].*

20. *Owner of power, and high rank with (Allah) the Lord of the Throne,*

21. *Obeyed (by the angels), trustworthy there (in the heavens).*

22. *And (O people) your companion (Muhammad) is not a madman;*

23. *And indeed he (Muhammad) saw him (Gabriel)] in the clear horizon.*

24. *And he (Muhammad) withholds not knowledges of the unseen.*

25. *And it (the Quran) is not the word of the outcast Shaitan (Satan).*

26. *Then where are you going?*

27. *Verily, this (the Quran) is no less than a Reminder to (all) the 'Alamin (mankind and jinns and all that exists).*

28. *To whomsoever among you who wills to walk straight path (Islam),*

29. *And you will not, unless (it be) that Allah wills, the Lord of the 'Alamin (mankind, jinns and all that exists).*

That is it. When the explosion of the universe occurred, everything will be destroyed and the earth disembowelled out its contents. The sky and all the planets disappeared, falling down in total destruction. It is not a fantasy but a reality when the day comes. There is no place of refuge. No one will be able to help or protect.

On the day of Judgement, Allah will adjudge accordingly whatever one does in the world, good or bad, according to the weighing scale of Allah. Nothing will miss out even as small as an atom. One's body will speak out about one's deeds, virtuous or otherwise. Nobody can escape. With the blessing of Allah, whoever gets heavier measurement of virtuous deeds will go to heaven, while the others with heavier wrong doings or sins shall go to hell. The disbelievers and the hypocrites will straight away go to hell into the blazing hell fire indefinitely while the hypocrites will be at bottom of it. The disobedient Muslims will be put into the hell too, but finally only with the blessing and grace of Allah they will enter the heavens as well.

As it is now, the world is experiencing the smaller signs of the Doomsday and they are happening every day. It does not matter whether one believes it or not, but at the end of the world or the Day of Judgement they will have a taste of it. Then the greater signs of Doomsday will be forthcoming. At that time, every living creature will die. All mankind finally will meet Allah at the "Padang Mahsyar or Plain of Mahsyar" (The huge plain where mankind are assembled after death and the end of the world in front of Allah to be weighed for their sins and good deeds) for His judgement.

In this world before the Doomsday, the Muslims will be definitely the ultimate victor in the end with the emergence Imam Mahadi. Then the Prophet Jesus (Isa) would also emerge. He would rule the world for some times with Islamic syariah.

About the Muslim victory, many hadith reported that Imam Mahdi and Prophet Jesus al-Maseh (who is Muslim and not a Christian as believed by the Christians), with the Will and Grace of Allah, will emerge as saviours of Muslim ummah. Thus, it completes the final supremacy of right and justice of Islam over falsehood. During the time, an ideal Islamic society would be established. Then soon afterwards, the end of the universe or Doomsday will be forthcoming as determined by Allah.

Without an iota of doubt, Islam will be the ultimate victor and rule the world. It will certainly happen.

CHAPTER 14. ENDLESS TRAGEDY

The crises among the world civilisations and religions would be there and never end. It will continue indefinitely until the end of the world, although some people believed otherwise.

In the current globalised world, many latest and fresh ugly incidents that are affecting the Muslim ummah in particular and the others in general are happening. However, the Muslims in general seem to be at the losing end. It is difficult for them to meet the challenges because, aside their spiritual strength has been weakened their strength in military etc. is also non-existence vis-à-vis of the big powers.

Until and unless the Muslims return to the Islamic way of life, they cannot stand the ordeal of life. They would easily crumble under worldly pressure, whatever pressure it may be. Since they have no spiritual strength, disintegrated and disorganised as a group, they would easily succumb to others. To a certain extent, Iran may be an exception, but again its faith is outside the majority Sunni Muslim faith, so this little strength of Shiite sect is discounted from the main Muslim group.

Muslims nations are in dearth of charismatic, capable and credibility leaders to lead and to steer the Muslims to close ranks, unite and work hard together to protect Islam and their turf against the ever hostile Muslim adversaries. They need the leaders that dare to sacrifice together to uphold justice for all in facing the vagaries of the villains. Then only Allah will help them accordingly. Until then, the wrath of Allah will be fallen on them.

While the Sunni Muslim world is in a state of dilemma and at loss of its focus and vision in the world politics vis-à-vis the ever powerful and domineering Western powers, out of sudden in its midst an extremist and ferocious of the so-called Islamist group ISIS emerged to usurp and claim territories in Iraq and Syria. Now, the whole world is directly or indirectly involved against the ISIS. Had the ISIS is not an extremist organisation probably the scenario would be different altogether.

Why does the ISIS come into the picture and it happen in the heart of the Middle East in the first place? Is it the sign of wrath of Allah as punishment and as an ordeal on the inordinate fasiq (disobedient) Sunni Muslims vis-a-vis the infidel Shiite sect in this once the heart and the cradle of Islamic civilisation? Only Allah knows best.

Who is **ISIS**? ISIS or ISIL is the 'Islamic State of Iraq and Syria or the Levant' or simply 'IS'. Its formation is rather obscure and unexpected, emerged out of sudden in the insane man-made hell in the area. Its extreme and draconian actions are beyond imagination in the modern world and definitely are very much un-Islamic. Is its formation a proxy of the world powers to destroy the Muslims in general? Again, Allah only knows best.

It came into being, right or wrong, perhaps, out of vengeance after the long inordinate suffering of Arabs Sunni Muslims at the dirty hands of the Shiites and the Americans and their allies in Iraq and Syria. Thus, the whole of the Middle East had become more chaotic than ever before. The Sunni Muslims were helpless in those areas soon after the United States of America unilaterally with the Great Britain invaded Iraq to punish the not-so-innocent Saddam Hussein. Their intention, perhaps, was not only to destroy Saddam Hussein but also to destroy the Muslims as a whole from resisting them.

Saddam Hussein, whether people like him or not was a 'Sunni hero' who at least managed to maintain stability of Iraq then despite of Sunni minority comparatively with the majority Shiites. Saddam Hussein was recalcitrant Muslim leader who dared to defy the hawkish Western powers. The proud Saddam Hussein sacrificed his life with dignity for this and some people said he died martyr for defending Islam.

Ironically, the whole Muslim world then, especially the Iraq Arab neighbours, did not dare to lift a finger to help him. Some Muslim Arab countries even connived with the invading forces. It was a shame, indeed, for the Muslims not help fellow Muslims under attack by the disbelievers.

In surah al-Maidah, verses (5:51-52) Allah said respectively:

﴿يَـٰٓأَيُّهَا ٱلَّذِينَ ءَامَنُوا۟ لَا تَتَّخِذُوا۟ ٱلْيَهُودَ وَٱلنَّصَـٰرَىٰٓ أَوْلِيَآءَ بَعْضُهُمْ أَوْلِيَآءُ بَعْضٍ وَمَن يَتَوَلَّهُم مِّنكُمْ فَإِنَّهُۥ مِنْهُمْ إِنَّ ٱللَّهَ لَا يَهْدِى ٱلْقَوْمَ ٱلظَّـٰلِمِينَ ۝﴾

"O you who believe, take not the Jews and the Christians as Auliya' (friends, protectors, helpers, etc.), they are but Auliya' to one another. And if any amongst you takes them as Auliya', then surely he is one of them. Verily, Allah guides not those people who are the zalimun (polytheists and wrongdoers and unjust)".

﴿فَتَرَى ٱلَّذِينَ فِى قُلُوبِهِم مَّرَضٌ يُسَـٰرِعُونَ فِيهِمْ يَقُولُونَ نَخْشَىٰٓ أَن تُصِيبَنَا دَآئِرَةٌ فَعَسَى ٱللَّهُ أَن يَأْتِىَ بِٱلْفَتْحِ أَوْ أَمْرٍ مِّنْ عِندِهِۦ فَيُصْبِحُوا۟ عَلَىٰ مَآ أَسَرُّوا۟ فِىٓ أَنفُسِهِمْ نَـٰدِمِينَ ۝﴾

"And you see those in whose hearts there is a disease (of hypocrisy), they hurry to their friendship (Jews and Christians), saying: 'We fear lest some misfortune of a disaster may befall us'. Perhaps Allah may bring a victory or a decision according to His Will. Then they will become regretful for what they have been keeping as a secret in themselves".

In the following verses (5:55-57) also from surah al-Maidah, Allah said:

إِنَّمَا وَلِيُّكُمُ ٱللَّهُ وَرَسُولُهُ وَٱلَّذِينَ ءَامَنُواْ ٱلَّذِينَ يُقِيمُونَ ٱلصَّلَوٰةَ وَيُؤْتُونَ ٱلزَّكَوٰةَ وَهُمْ رَٰكِعُونَ ۝

"Verily, your Wali (Protector or Helper) is Allah, His Messenger and the believers - those who perform solat and give zakat, and they bow down (submit themselves with obedience to Allah in prayer).

وَمَن يَتَوَلَّ ٱللَّهَ وَرَسُولَهُ وَٱلَّذِينَ ءَامَنُواْ فَإِنَّ حِزْبَ ٱللَّهِ هُمُ ٱلْغَٰلِبُونَ ۝

"And whosoever takes Allah, His Messenger and those who have believed, as Protectors then the party of Allah will be the victorious".

يَٰٓأَيُّهَا ٱلَّذِينَ ءَامَنُواْ لَا تَتَّخِذُواْ ٱلَّذِينَ ٱتَّخَذُواْ دِينَكُمْ هُزُوًا وَلَعِبًا مِّنَ ٱلَّذِينَ أُوتُواْ ٱلْكِتَٰبَ مِن قَبْلِكُمْ وَٱلْكُفَّارَ أَوْلِيَآءَ وَٱتَّقُواْ ٱللَّهَ إِن كُنتُم مُّؤْمِنِينَ ۝

"O you who believe take not for Auliya' (protectors and helpers) those who take your religion for a mockery and fun from among those who received the Scripture (Jews and Christians) before you, nor from among the disbelievers; and fear Allah if you indeed are true believers".

Literally from the above verses, Allah prohibited for Muslims to take disbelievers to be their leaders or protectors. As such, those who are in cahoot with the Jews and Christians are part of them. They actually fall into the vicious trap of the belligerent disbelievers.

With the defeat of Saddam Hussein, Iraq is in ruin, causing untold misery to the Iraqis that were very much worst then under President Saddam Hussein.

What had happened in Iraq is a pure reminder to the Sunni Muslims to unite and consolidate and take heed of the above verses.

It is for certain that the ISIS would not surface if President Bush and Tony Blaire did not attack Iraq. As it is now, the ISIS extremist is causing the whole furore and havoc in the region and elsewhere.

The dirty tactics and political intrigues of the West, had plunged all countries in the Middle East in a state of instability, thus their economies are not developed and in a situation of very bad shape. The upheaval in Syria and Iraq is an added burden with the emergence of extremist jihadist of the ISIS. The situation is really chaotic and out of control. The West and the Jews had played their games well with subtlety to set the traps to annihilate the Muslims.

The Western powers led by the United States are hectic, using air power bombing the ISIS targets that killed many people, mostly innocent, on the ground. Likewise, Russia also came in to support the tyrant Bashar al-Assad Shiite regime against the ISIS and the other insurgents, especially after the downing of the Russian civilian airline by the ISIS in Sinai Peninsula, Egypt. The situation has accentuated to become worst ever. But those killed and displaced were mostly the Sunni Muslims and also the other innocent minority groups.

The whole world gang-up against the ISIS as if it is a war between the Cross and the Crescent of the olden days except with the difference in which the listless Muslim world seemed to have no choice but reluctantly to take side with the Cross to hunt down the extremist ISIS. They are using air power rather than deploying ground troops. Probably they value the life of their soldiers more than the others, so they are not fighting directly on the ground to face the ferocious ISIS extremists. Again here, the West works smart in the sense that the real front soldiers that would be killed are the Iraqis or the Syrians.

The conflict, if broadly looking at the bigger picture, is between Muslims of different groups and sects. It has nothing much to do with the Western powers, but politically and economically, as always, they have interest in those areas. Therefore, they are readily available to interfere at the invitation of the beleaguered parties. Even if they do not have invitation, they would find excuse somehow to interfere. The consequence of their dirty games, thousands or millions of the innocent Muslims and others suffered and displaced.

The West and Zionist Israel like this sort of quagmire game where the Muslims killing each other. In the end, the warring Muslim parties somehow or other would be crawling to the West or the East for help. Thus, the big powers of the divides keep on dominating the Muslim world.

Turkey, a key NATO ally, is also playing a role in the conflict. Some critiques accused Turkey of playing a double role, depending on the circumstance, that is beneficial to it. The ISIS is fighting against anti-ISIS Kurdish militia and Shiites to acquire for more territory. The hard-line Kurdish militia movement also fought Turkey for its independence or autonomy. Turkey branded them as a terrorist group and it already battled the Kurdish guerrillas for decades. Turkey vowed to wipe out the Kurdish guerrillas, including the ISIS nuisance at its borders.

With the downing of Russian warplane by Turkey on November 24, 2015 in Syria's Bayirbucak region, near Turkish-Syrian border - one of the world's most volatile regions - roiled the relationship between Turkey and Russia. Turkey said it hit the plane after it violated Turkey's airspace for which Russia vehemently denied. The tension between them is damaging their diplomatic relationship – politically and economically - for both sides.

The Western military intervention against the ISIS is a sure thing, like pouring gasoline on to the fires, creating greater escalation of conflict in the Middle East. With the Russians joining in the 'hunting' game, the situation is indeed becoming more complicated and dangerous, not much to them but to the Muslims and others on the ground.

The mind boggling question is: How and why the ISIS emerged out of a sudden and so explosively happened?

Many opined that this could be the result of continuous inordinate atrocities committed on the local Sunni Muslim population there in Iraq and Syria by the Shiites and the Americans; and elsewhere in the Muslim world by the West. Since the Sunni Muslims had been suffering for so long, this ISIS fighting group that was part of al-Qaeda decided to take action to retaliate and revenge against those perpetrators, though they had certain covert understanding with them before.

The ISIS vengeance has come out like an 'angry volcano' and without warning. It came out with full of force and steam, releasing its fiery anger, barbaric or not is none issue for the jihadists, because the cruelty committed by the perpetrators were no difference in atrocity or no lesser than them. The difference is that the ISIS jihadists are the extremist Sunni Muslims whereas their perpetrators are the Christians and the Shiites.

The Sunni Muslims and the ISIS particularly regarded the Shiites as infidels, but the extremist ISIS jihadists went too far by branding the moderate the Sunni Muslim world is not Islamic enough in their practise, and therefore they go against them as well.

The ISIS has messed-up the whole things. The Arab countries and other Muslim world as well feel nervous, particularly Saudi Arabia, when its borders had already been breached many times by the ISIS jihadists with the bombing incidents against the Shiite community there.

The whole world as well as the Muslim world presently seemed to be very edgy, trying to contain the belligerent ISIS extremist issue. The Muslim countries are nervous and wary because they are being targeted sporadically by the ISIS. As stated above, in the eyes of the ISIS, the other Muslim countries are not Islamic enough except themselves, although their terrorism and philosophy are absolutely a far cry from the true teaching of Islam. They are targeting everybody who does not subscribe to their extremist philosophy or their brand of Islam. But the 'lambs' being sacrificed in the conflicts are mostly the ordinary and innocents Sunni Muslims and other minorities as well.

The ferocious ISIS quickly gained control of certain swath of territories of Iraq and Syria that was large enough to form a state. It affiliates also operates in eastern Libya, the Sinai Peninsula of Egypt and other areas of the Middle East, North Africa, Southern Asia and in the Southeast Asia as well. They have had many sympathisers throughout the world, although not significant, perhaps.

The ISIS leader is Abu Bakr al-Baghdadi. He was once an associate of al-Qaeda. However, on 3rd February 2014, he broke rank with al-Qaeda and declared 'Caliphate' on 29th June 2014 and that he is the caliph. The atrocities committed by the ISIS widely criticized and condemned throughout the world for its brutality in the name of Islam. As mentioned above, its extreme action does not reflect the very teaching of Islam thereby affecting the good name of the Muslims as a whole.

In this shrouded conflicts, some critiques opined that the ISIS group is not Sunni Muslims in view of its barbaric actions but a masquerade in the name of Islam. The critiques went further to speculate that a certain 'powers', including the Jews, are covertly supporting behind it in order to destroy or to divide the Muslims. They also said that Abu Bakr Al-Baghdadi is the Mossad agent of Israel Jews. However, they do not have solid basis on it. Only God knows best.

Whatever it is, Islamofobia has become more and more prominent in the West and is spinning throughout the world.

This extremist group, as reported by some, initially was a 'baby' created by the US and its allies, including Saudi Arabia, as a special vehicle for political game intrigues to maintain their controlling position. However, eventually the groomed 'baby' had grown up by its own accord and turned out to be as a ferocious 'monster' against its creator. This is actually a pure blowback from the Western imperial incompetency in handling the Middle East debacle or perhaps, purposely created by the West to perpetuate instability in the region. Thus, the ISIS emerged and is acquiring by force for more territories of its own.

In Washington's wave of thinking, this group when initially established was supposed to be composed of "moderates", a short-lived, easily controlled force that expected to overthrow the hated Syrian regime. What really transpired behind the back of this political proxy and conspiracy in this high stake of political chess in the Middle East cauldron is of anybody's guess. Nonetheless, it is quite certain that this whole episode of conflicts was due to the long dirty work of the Western imperialists to instigate the Muslims among themselves to fight against one another in order the contain and to weaken the Muslim ummah from emerging again as their rival in this world and at the same time to exploit oil riches in the Middle East.

Therefore, it might not be wrong to say that the emergence of the ISIS is due to the result of the filthy work of the Saudi Arabia and the United States of America in the political intrigue in the Middle East as stated above. The Royal Saudi Arabia has been quietly occupied by the United States for quite a long time since there are some thousands American advisors, technicians and contractors serving the oil industry and the military. There are also secret United States military bases in Saudi Arabia. Israel is also a secret ally of the Saudi royal family. The American CIA, FBI and other military intelligence are protecting the Royal family of Saudi Arabia or the House of Saud.

As often in the past, the Saudis sought to use militants as a tool to vent revolution away from its borders. Saudi Arabia is in a very unstable and volatile situation. Thus, the Wahhabi Saudis and the United States are in cahoot, so anything goes for their own mutual interest. However, what is interesting is that the ISIS quickly ran out of their control and turned against its creators mercilessly, whoever they are. So far, the mess created by the ISIS is unimaginable.

While the world recoiled in horror at the merciless and fanatical ISIS jihadist beheadings of its prisoners, the Saudis also cut off the heads of its prisoners at the same time – without much notice and condemnation from the Western media.

In retrospective, the whole scenario before the advent of the ISIS, the sectarian conflict between Sunni Muslim and Shiite sect was infamous since the olden days. The conflict became further widen in the rift between Sunnis and Shiites in Iraq soon after the United States, the imperial warlord, invaded Iraq in 2003. The United States, an expert in the imperial divide, made an alliance with the Shiite majority against the nation's Sunni minority in Iraq. The strategy was initially highly successful in keeping control of Iraq against the Sunni insurgents. Washington even quietly and subtly aligned itself with Tehran over Iraq.

Many atrocities inflicted on the Sunnis by the Shiites. Death squads were unleashed; torturers used electrical drills, acid etc. to make prisoners talk and break the anti-Shiite and anti-US resistance. The United States funded and abetted this dirty torture and the war. The United States protégé, Israel, provided much useful advice.

Turning Shiites against Sunnis stabilised Iraq for certain period only, but the hatred and tension dangerously intensified across the Muslim world all the way east to Pakistan. The long proxy war between Saudi Arabia and Iran intensified. That was the reality that the West targeted at to disunite and weaken the Muslim world.

As religious hatred is being fanned, then out of blues from the bowels of the Middle East emerged the ferocious ISIS, ostensibly claiming to be waging jihad war against Shiites and the hated Assad Alawite regime of Syria. But so far the ISIS does not dare enough to touch Israel regime, another United States protégé, thereby people speculated that there could be some sort understanding or connection with the Israel regime.

ISIS is rich in cash, has many staunch followers worldwide and has many weapons. With the strength, it turned on against the US-installed regime in Iraq and routed its 'toy' soldiers.

Thus, it is evident that the conflict in the Middle East is the war of proxies between the world big powers of the divides – the West and the East – where the pawns are the 'naive' Muslims, so to speak crudely.

The fanatic ISIS group is very fierce fighters because it is in thirst of blood for revenge. The fury for the vengeance is probably due to the following underlying factors:

- Firstly, the Western colonial powers entered and directly or indirectly occupied the whole of the Middle East, and in the process killed untold numbers of Muslims for a century. They exploited the Arab world oil riches. The ruthless tyrant rulers as overseers, supported by the United States, suppressed the people under the banner of fighting insurgents and terrorism.

- Secondly, they are the sons of the aborted "Arab Spring" that had withered and died under Western and Saudi counter-revolution. They are the 'cousins' of the 9/11 hijackers who were mostly from Saudi Arabia. Al-Qaeda members too are naturally a part of them. Foreigners who believed in the jihadist cause are also included in the group.

- This group is desperate and willing to die for revenge as martyr because they felt that the Muslims at large, including the OIC member states, are incapable of defending them and the sanctity of Islam.

ISIS uses the idiom of Islam, but their so-called brutality action is very much un-Islamic and this has stirred up intense 'Islamophobia' in the West. Ironically the brutality of the West killing thousands of innocent Muslims and the so-called 'Muslim terrorists' around the world is not stirring up the free world because the victims were the Muslims.

Whatever it is, thus far, ISIS seemed to remain quite strong and rather organised group. Their ambition is clear, that is to create an Islamic state of their own under their own brand. Evidently, without outside interference of the foreign forces, definitely they might have already attained their objectives in carving certain regions of the Middle East firmly in their hands. However, of late it appears that the ISIS lost certain swath of territories due the heavy bombing from the allied forces and the Russians, and the ground forces of Assad's and Iraq's soldiers.

Arising from the injustice, conflict and civil wars, it might be right to say that terrorism is a by-product of or response to the global injustice faced by Muslims or otherwise worldwide. Some Muslims are, whether misled or not, attracted to the "call of jihad" after hearing news after news about injustices inflicted on Muslim people in the countries such as in Palestine, Iraq, Egypt, Syria, Afghanistan and so forth.

These people have no alternative choice and desperate for justice, and therefore they choose to fight extremism with extremism and terrorism with terrorism. That was how the ISIS ideology so fast successfully spread out because people in those affected countries deprived of justice.

People can blame them, but for some fanatic inclined people, they are willing to sacrifice for the Islamic State that promises them justice for all the Muslims. Most cases of terrorism committed today are "reactive violence and vengeance". Although Islam prohibits extremism whatsoever, not all of its followers subscribe to it when they themselves are subject to injustice and cruelty.

Where does the ISIS get its weapons? It appears that it has got the weapons and ammunition manufactured from many different countries, notably from the United States, including Russia, China etc. The militant groups also possessed many of the weapons they captured on the battle fields, most of the weapons came from those countries.

It shows that the Islamic State relatively has had little difficulty in getting the supply of weapons from the huge pool of armaments in the conflicts in Iraq and Syria, supplied by the world big powers.

At the same time, the group's income from the sales of oil and other sources is high enough to buy additional weapons directly from the dealers that take advantage to exploit the strife to make easy profit from the conflicts. Indeed, the weaponry dealers of the big powers are too happy to trade the weapons, not only to make more profit but also to see more Muslims killed in the sectarian conflict.

Some of the weapons also frequently changed hands between the rival forces captured or recaptured as the case may be during the battles.

As the consequence of brutal civil war in Syria and Iraq, the atrocities of the ISIS and the air bombardment by the United States and Russia, a new world humanitarian crisis emerged, that is the refugees. This has become a world problem facing humankind in the modern era.

According to the Syrian Observatory for Human Rights that about 330,000 people (probably much more) died since the Syrian civil war which began in March 2011.

According to the United States Agency for International Development, an estimated figure of 7.6 million people had been displaced internally, and four million people fled the country altogether to some of the countries like Turkey, Lebanon, Jordan, Egypt and Europe, particularly Germany, etc. This does not include millions of people that need humanitarian assistance in Syria.

As the war keeps on escalating, more and more Syrians become desperate. Thousands have tried to reach Europe by taking land or sea routes sailing across the Mediterranean, often deadly, after paying their life savings to smugglers. Many of them have not made it. A few thousands of them died or missing while making the journey. Those who survived face rising hostility from the European countries concerned due to security, religion etc.

In this current upheaval and human tragedy, retrospectively one could point out to two persons behind it that initiated the cause of this misery and carnage. They were no other than the ex-President George Bush of America who unilaterally invaded Iraq in 2003, and his friend, the ex-Prime Minister Tony Blair of Britain that supported him.

The President of France, Jacques Chirac, then warned them not to do so because it would destabilise the Middle East and inflict dangers to Europe arising from it. While, President Saddam Hussein of Iraq also warned that an American invasion would ignite the **"mother of all battles and would open the gates of hell"**.

Now their warnings turned out to be very right as confirmed by the waves of desperate Middle East refugees flooding into Europe due the rampage of ISIS and others, and also the air bombardment against the ISIS by the Americans and Russians. Thus, this is the mother of debacle of the modern time being faced by the innocent or otherwise people of Iraq and Syria and yet both culprits, Bush and Blair, are still enjoying life unscathed. That is the fruit of the so-called the 'democratic system of the free world'.

Whatever it is, this kind of carnage is much to the delight of the Israel regime, the West and the Russians as well. Russia disliked Islam too because the Muslims in the Caucasian Mountains used to fight against them for years for their freedom, notably the Chechens. Thousands or millions of Muslims there had been killed by the Russians. Many Muslims from the areas came forward to fight alongside the ISIS as well.

As hell broke loose in Syria with its civil war, it destroyed or ruined most of the cities to rubble after more than four years of urban warfare. Out of Syria's population of about 23 million, roughly about 16 million people have been displaced, become homeless and refugees to other countries. This is really the sign of the wrath of Allah be fallen on the Muslims as an ordeal on them for being disunited and disobedient Muslims.

Unless the ISIS power can fast be contained - amicably or otherwise - the misery and the killing of people, innocent or otherwise, will continue for some time to come. Most probably, the ISIS can withstand the severe blow of the onslaught of the world powers in this senseless sandy desert warfare. Thus far, it remains fairly intact despite of the frequent air bombardments by both parties of the divides – America and Russia - though it has lost some the areas it captured. Time only will tell of the consequences but it may take a long time to subdue the jihadists in this kind of hit and run warfare. Probably, another Afghanistan is in the making.

While the world cries on the current tragedy in Syria and Iraq and the refugees crisis, ironically people conveniently tend to forget that there are still five million stateless Palestinian refugees in diaspora due to the ethnic cleansing of Arab Palestine population in 1947-48 by Israel regime which was directly supported both by the imperial powers of the United States and the Soviet Union.

Those are the endless tragedies being faced by the Muslims in the Middle East at the hands of the big powers. Would they honestly want to solve the current crisis in Syria, Iraq and Palestine? The pessimist critiques say that they would just prolong the conflict for their own geo-economic-political advantage so that they can continue controlling the whole Middle East.

As to the Israel Jews regime, they become more arrogant and aggressive in Palestine. They are taking the opportunity to annihilate further the Palestinians as a mean to distract world attention due to the chaotic situation in Syria and Iraq. Almost every day the Palestinians are being killed by the Jews without much attention by the world but the atrocities of the ISIS.

The conflicts in the Middle East rightly had created much world attention, but nonetheless people ignored for so long the suffering and inhuman treatment of the Muslim Rohingyas in Myanmar (Burma) in the Southeast Asia.

The Buddhist Myanmar regime refused to recognise them as its citizen. Prosecution and discrimination against the dark skin Rohingyas (Bengalis Muslim) in Arakan Coast (Rakhine State) had been going on for years, in fact, over a half century since 1945. Myanmar regime seems determined to expel the Muslim Rohingyas for good. This is indeed an ethnic cleansing or genocide by the Buddhist government of Myanmar. The so-called free world again failed to resolve and protect these minority unwanted people.

Due to atrocities and ill-treatment committed by the Buddhist regime, many of the Rohingya became refugees, flooding other ASEAN countries like Thailand, Malaysia and Indonesia.

Human traffickers took the opportunity to exploit the situation. It is pathetic to see, time and again, the plight of thousands of Muslim Rohingya in overcrowded boats left adrift in the waters of Andaman Sea without food, water and shelter from the burning tropical sun. Some of them perished in the sea. Some of them were found to be held in guarded cramped camps deep in the jungle borders between Thailand and Malaysia by human traffickers to smuggle them into Malaysia.

In this regard, it appears that ASEAN is hopeless association due to its non-interference policy. It is of late only, due public pressure, the countries like Malaysia, Thailand and Indonesia, on humanitarian ground helped easing the situation by accommodating some them on temporary basis. Bangladesh whose people are involved cannot do much since it cannot even feed its own starving people. In fact, thousands of its people are seeking for better future by working in other countries like Malaysia, a country that is shortage of labour force to work in the oil palm plantations etc.

The West does not concern much about the suffering of the Rohingyas, except the United States voices some displeasure. Probably, as some people said, the West does not want to offend Myanmar because it has bigger economic agenda for want of doing business there. Burma is rich in unexploited natural resources, including oil. The Western darling, Aung San Suu Kyi also does not say anything on the prosecuted Rohingyas affairs in order to avoid antagonising the staunch Buddhist voters. Her strong stand on human rights and democracy has disappeared into the thin air. On the other side of political divides, Russia and China also keep mum on this issue.

The thesis of Samuel P. Huntington on the 'Clash of civilisations' is again appears to be true but in a more complicated fashion. The bloody borders are happening. The Western powers are ever ready to face any eventuality whereas the Muslim world prepares nothing, but in nightmarish day dream and quarrelling among themselves.

Arising from the ISIS issue and its 'lone wolf' of the jihadist carnage, for instance the incidents like the massacres in Paris – Charlie Hebdo satirical magazine office and concert hall and national stadium etc., suggested that the Middle East's mayhem and killings have come to doorstep of Europe. The incidents massacre in United States, and elsewhere, including in Indonesia etc., the downing of civilian airline of Russia-jet-airline Airbus A321 by ISIS in Sinai, Egypt, create panic everywhere throughout the world. But the poor innocent minority Muslims in Europe, America and elsewhere bear the consequences and inconvenience. The backlash of the anti-Islamist such as physical harassment, burning of mosques and al-Quran, spitting on the face, baring the Muslim bearded men and women adorning veils from boarding plane etc. is really scary. The call by certain xenophobe syndrome people for banning Muslims from entering the United State is really racist and panicky religious bigot of the 21st century of a democratic country. Nevertheless, it may be good too that all the Muslims in the world would not visit the country so that the Muslim tourists should not spend money there but elsewhere in Asia and Europe. But for the multi-ethnic and multi-religious, peace-loving, English speaking, charming and warm-hearted people and also a stable country in the South East Asia like Malaysia may benefit more from the call so that more people, especially from America, to visit **Malaysia**. **"Malaysia boleh"** or **"Malaysia can"** as the slogan says.

This is a trying period for the innocent moderate and minority Muslims in those non-Muslim countries. The worst fear is that if the terrorist could inflict injuries to them, the anti-Islamist can do the same likewise towards the Muslims. It is scary indeed! Nevertheless, the true and innocent Muslims should fear nothing but always be patient and have trust in Allah, insya Allah (God willing) they will be safe.

Committing crime, in whatsoever form and whoever they are, is a criminal act. That is fine but to brand a section of people and their religion as whole as terrorist is not acceptable. Terrorist has its own cause, valid or not is another issue, but committing terrorism on the innocents should be condemned by all. But what about the act of sporadic bombing, missing the targeted foes in the process, that killed the innocent people is not it an act of terrorism as well?

As to the ISIS, its members and its affiliate will go on fighting against any country that attacked or condemned them. But, how long will it persist? It all depends as to whether the ISIS is defeated by all-out war or a resolution to the conflict is amicably settled. In the meantime, more and more people will get killed. The ISIS jihadists will keep on going to attack their adversaries and whoever does not subscribe to their extremist brand of Islam wherever and whenever there is opportunity for them to do so in every corner of the globe. Thus, the world should not blame the whole Muslim communities per se as extremists because they do not subscribe to the ISIS brand of ISLAM.

While the world is concerned on the war in Syria and Iraq and the atrocities of the ISIS, it had been reported by the media that Angola, a Christian state in Africa, also had discriminated and prosecuted its minority Muslim population.

According to most sources, the estimated Muslim population in Angola is only about 90,000 to 100,000 although some gave a higher figure. Most Muslims in the country are Sunnis. Majority of them are foreign migrants from West Africa and the Middle East, although a few are local converts. The Association of the Development of Islam in Angola is the primary organisation proselytising Islam for which Angolans are chary about. As of late 2013, the Angolan government did not legally recognise any Muslim organisations and as a result, mosques in the country faced restrictions. Many mosques, schools and community centres were shut down by the authorities. Some Angolans resorted to burning of certain mosques. However, Angolan officials denied that the government had a policy to close down mosques or preventing their constructions.

According to the Islamic Community of Angola, the government had closed sixty mosques, mostly outside of Luanda, in 2013. Voice of America reported seeing a video that showed the demolition of a mosque in Saurimo.

It was also reported in 2013, Angola had become the first country in the world to put a ban on Islam that is practised by some 1% of its population.

There are conflicting reports about the prosecution of Muslims in Angola. It is also reported that Angola has banned Islam, but some officials denied it.

Who was telling the truth? The alleged ban sparked controversy around the world especially in the Middle East where some countries reportedly burnt down Angolan flags. There was uneasy calm in Angola itself.

Local reporters frequently reported that series of clashes in the hinterlands of the country between Christians and Muslims which barely reported to the outside world. Tension is gradually building up between

Angola as a nation and the Muslim community, but the African Union, the United Nations and other so-called conflict resolution bodies have turned a blind eye on it, probably as always the case, because the victims were the Muslims. Again, this naturally would be a fertile ground for the ISIS or al-Qaeda type groups to slowly gaining foothold with local support.

In another scenario, the conflict between the Shiite sect and Sunni Muslims in Yemen is a heart-aching affair, but then the power struggles do not recognise or are colour blind between brothers because the countries since the olden days was always at loggerhead between the two sectarian divides. But again, this is a proxy war between Iran and Saudi Arabia with the help of West for which, as always, they interfere to actuate the quagmire, just like in Syria and Iraq.

Thus, looking at overall, the spark of the 'Clash of Civilisations' as predicted by S. P. Huntington has begun and is unstoppable.

EPILOGUE

In conclusion, with due respect to other religions, Islam is the only the true religion of Allah. It is an exclusive religion for there is no other religion acceptable to Allah. Islam is not an inclusive religion accommodating other faiths. Thus, polarisation between civilisations and religions are unavoidable, but its degree of division and misunderstanding may be mitigated by mutual understanding and respect of the differences. Therefore, the linking bridge must be established between different races and religions to foster good relationship and mutual appreciation of the good values of one another.

The conflicts are real for they had happened all the time between Islam and other faith since the advent of Islam, either in small or large scale only. The fact is the non-Muslims or disbelievers hate and dislike Islam forever since its birth. Nevertheless, some of the optimist critiques believe that this clash of civilisations will not occur in this era of modern globalised world. However, with current scenario of tension and bloody conflicts of proxy wars, religious or otherwise, in the Middle East and elsewhere, the clashes are ongoing and would be protracted into the unforeseeable future.

The fundamental differences between religions and cultures are one of the underlying factors that would never be able to compromise, notably with the Islamic religion. In fact, the Islamic Monotheism cannot be compromised whatsoever with any other religions because it involves the basic faith or belief. Compromising on Islamic faith and its syariah or laws is a form of deviation which is absolutely not permissible in Islam. Therefore, proponents for liberalism and pluralism in Islamic religion to be in conformity with the universal human rights are absolutely not workable for it is outside the parameter of Islam. Notwithstanding, with more cross-cultures, open dialogues, tolerance and understanding, hopefully the tension between the religions may cool off accordingly.

Although the fault lines and culture differences are too great to reach a converging point, co-existence in plurality or diversity is possible provided there is no religious bigot among them. Conforming to one's true religion is not fanatic provided there is no element of force in them to influence on the others.

The world had enough experienced to go through the conflicts between civilisations, religious and non-religious wars for territorial and economic expansion, revolutions and so forth. The world also had seen deployment of large military forces and personnel by the belligerent powers to colonise the weaker nations, to rake their economies or riches since time immemorial. Thus far, the World War 1 and World War 2 were the greatest human tragedy suffered untold misery to millions of human kind due to human craziness and greed for power etc. in the modern history. Most probably, the war will continue into the future as it is still happening today, although in a smaller or moderate scale. Hopefully, people will be sober enough not to activate nuclear warfare.

The colonial masters of yesterday are still pursuing their 'divide and rule' policy in wanting to maintain their domain as far as possible as before. They will find ways and means to exploit the world economies etc. to maintain their status quo and supremacy.

Secularism, democracy, capitalism, communism, liberalism, modernism, pluralism and whatever brought about by the West and Russia had permeated into global societies, including the Muslim societies. Their influence had severely affected the Muslim world, resulting in the weakening and diminishing of the traditional or fundamental Islamic belief. This has resulted in misunderstanding of Islamic virtue and values among the modern Western educated Muslim intellectuals, thus it creates divisions among the Muslims. The West, thus far, had successfully tamed and harnessed down most of the Muslims to conform to their way of thinking and life style of living. Certainly, they wish to weaken the Muslim tradition further to ensure that the Muslims will follow the

Western culture and their way of life completely. If the Muslims are willing to compromise and transform the Islamic principle into the cauldron of secularism and liberalism of the West, probably there would be no more 'fault lines' or 'bloody borders' between them.

Will it happen? Islamic fundamental faith of Monotheism as enshrined in the al-Quran and al-Sunnah is not a subject to compromise or bargain because overall Islam is already a religion of moderation within the parameter of Islamic principles. To protect Islamic faith, majority of the Muslims would be willing to sacrifice anything, including life, to invoke jihad in the way of Allah.

The Muslims will keep on holding-fast to the al-Quran and al-Sunnah of the Prophet Muhammad (pbuh) on the following principles as per surah Al-Kafirun, verse (109:1-6):

قُلْ يَٰٓأَيُّهَا ٱلْكَٰفِرُونَ ۝

لَآ أَعْبُدُ مَا تَعْبُدُونَ ۝

وَلَآ أَنَا۠ عَابِدٌ مَّا عَبَدتُّمْ ۝

وَلَآ أَنتُمْ عَٰبِدُونَ مَآ أَعْبُدُ ۝

لَكُمْ دِينُكُمْ وَلِىَ دِينِ ۝

1. *"Say (O Muhammad) to the al-kafirun (disbelievers).*
2. *I worship not that which you worship.*
3. *Nor will you worship that which I worship.*
4. *And I shall not worship that which you are worshipping.*
5. *And nor will you worship that which I worship.*
6. *To you be your religion, and to me my religion (Islamic Monotheism)."*

The above verses are clear that it is misleading and very wrong to accuse that Islam is a religion of force to convert people to Islam. Of course, once a person had embraced Islam, he or she is prohibited to abandon Islam or be apostate. The punishment for this is severe, that is, death penalty.

The revelation of the above verses to Prophet Muhammad (pbuh) was to ensure that he would not compromise whatsoever Islamic faith (Islamic Monotheism) and that the Muslims would have to worship only Allah alone. The Quraish idol worshipers of Mecca at that time were very much against Islam and the Prophet Muhammad (pbuh) for keeping on proselytising Islam to them despite of their hatred.

As they could not stop Prophet Muhammad (pbuh) from preaching Islam, they finally decided to meet the Prophet to compromise. They proposed that they would agree to worship Allah on the condition that Muhammad would also agree to worship idols. It would be a win-win situation for both parties.

Soon after the proposal, Prophet Muhammad (pbuh) received the above revelation from Allah. Thus, it is clear that as far as Islamic faith (aqidah) is concerned, it is not a subject of negotiation.

In surah al-An'am verse (6:153), Allah said as follows:

وَأَنَّ هَٰذَا صِرَٰطِى مُسْتَقِيمًا فَٱتَّبِعُوهُ وَلَا تَتَّبِعُوا۟ ٱلسُّبُلَ فَتَفَرَّقَ بِكُمْ عَن سَبِيلِهِۦ ذَٰلِكُمْ وَصَّىٰكُم بِهِۦ لَعَلَّكُمْ تَتَّقُونَ ﴿١٥٣﴾

"And verily, this is My Straight Path (Islam), so follow it, and follow not (other) paths, for they will separate you away from His Path. This He has ordained for you that you may become the pious and God fearing ones".

Obviously, there is no religion but Islam. Allah sent down Muhammad as His Messenger to preach humankind about Islam as the true religion of Allah. Allah provided human beings with mind to think and to choose between the straight and the wrong path; between the truth and the falsehood. If they are sincere to want to follow the straight path, that is to become Muslim, insya Allah (God willing), Allah will bless them with His guidance.

Despite of all the differences, Islam respects other religions. Allah commanded the Muslims to live and co-exist with the others in peace and harmony on the concept of:

"*To you is your religion and to me my religion.*"

However, if a person is already a Muslim this concept does apply. He cannot get out from Islam or renegade Islam and the punishment is death.

Mutual respect and understanding of each other of the differences in religions, ethnics and cultures is the core of living in harmony and peace among fellow mankind if they can emulate in earnest the following philosophy:

"It is not differences that cause disunity and disharmony but fanaticism, extremism and non-tolerance of differences that lead to disunity and violence".

In the current era of globalisation, though the world becomes closer and peoples can interact faster and better than ever before, it seems that the benefit of cross-culture interaction does not lead to peace and harmony. The thought of nationalism and even fanaticism towards one's own religion and ethnic origin easily nullify the goodwill arising from the good international relationship. The bad attributes of the uncivilised world of the olden days are being carried forward into the modern civilised world where the differences are often settled by wars. The war of the jungles is being practised in which the strongest wins the day.

The world had seen the hostility between the Christians and the Muslims since the advent of Islam. It is transparent that the hatred towards Islamic religion and its followers has been ongoing and become an obsession on the part of the Christian West, just like in the olden days but more dangerously with different subtlety. Propaganda of hates in the form Islamophobia towards Islam through mass-media, electronic or otherwise has conspicuously become a norm in the West especially after 9/11 incident and the emergence of the ISIS.

The West seems not to admit that the extremism and terrorism that burdened the world, Muslim or otherwise, was and is the result of colonisation, interference and atrocities inflicted for centuries on the Muslims in the various Muslim countries until to the present day. The root cause of the emergence of the al-Qaeda and the ISIS and the other radical groups was the result of the Western very political intrigues in the Middle East and elsewhere. The West plays politics and dirty games by blaming others except themselves. Thus, the whole world suffers and will keep on suffering.

The thesis on the 'Clash of Civilisations' by Samuel P. Huntington, the policy papers of Cheryl Benard etc. that applied by the United States towards the Muslim countries seemed to be bearing fruits – sweet or bitter as the case may be. However, despite of the long and inordinate misrepresentation and campaign against Islam, more and more people in the West embraced Islam.

The Western powers are ever ready to interfere in any area that they have interest, especially in countries rich in oil resources like the Middle East. However, more often than not, instead of finding solution, they created more problems like that had happened in Iraq, Syria, Yemen, Libya, Afghanistan, Africa, etc. They used to collaborate with the internal subversive elements to destabilise the country concerned, and then they install a friendly puppet government that tows along the lines of their policies.

The globalised modern world now seems to be more chaotic, unsafe and unstable than ever before. It turned people to become either smarter or crazier with wicked ideas, and thus it becomes the medium ground for heartless people, greed, cheat, falsehood, evil, immorality and so forth.

It has been an experience now that secularism, liberalism, capitalism, communism etc. would not be able to bring peace and better life to people universally. The world is not safe; life has become more difficult instead of becoming better place to live in for all. The systems could not function well save the Islamic system, but then in the modern world the Muslims themselves too do not fully subscribe to the Islamic principles in their system of government and their daily way of life. Thus, the Muslims always live in transgression for not governing their countries accordingly in the way of Allah.

The mission of Islam is to bring peace and harmony in this temporal world. However, since many people rejected Islam, its vision and mission is not accomplished, but it is also the Will of Allah that not all mankind will accept Islam other than those Allah bestowed guidance on them.

Morally, people do not subscribe to the virtues or good values of Islam. Many of them are free thinkers or godless people. Human rights principles coined and promulgated throughout the world, preaching and giving the people the freedom passports to do whatever they think right without restriction. For instance, LGBT is on the rise and marriage institution has become of no more importance to the modern families. People can stay together, without marriage, like that of husband and wife. Perhaps, they can even stay with animals or have sex with them, who cares. This unrestricted freedom has led to moral decadent in most of the modern societies. The world has become mad, moral order becomes crazier and some people become uncivilised and behave just like animals.

In contrast, in Islam there is no such thing as unlimited freedom in this world. Everything that is mortal has a limit. People who think that freedom is unlimited are crazy ignorant bunch indeed, because they are mortal. When they are sick, weak or on death bed, then only they would know what life is all about. They are powerless to fight the Preordainment of Allah. By then it is too late for them come back to the right path of Allah or to repent. When the Day of Judgement comes, they will be sent to Hell, only then they will know the severity of the blazing Hell Fire.

The challenge for the true Muslim ummah is to struggle hard to put things right into the correct perspective of Islam. The Muslims therefore are duty bound to close ranks and work in cohesion to fight the negative influence currently being facing by the overall ummah or community.

The Muslims have to lead the way by example by living in the righteous way of life, most importantly the people in the leadership echelon. There is no point pointing fingers and condemning others, no point having long sermons and prayers, no point getting angry with the Jews, Christians etc. if the Muslim themselves misbehave and not acting in line with the principles of Islam. The Muslims are the followers of Prophet Muhammad (pbuh) and called themselves brothers in Islam and yet their actions and behaviour do not speak well about them. They quarrelled and killed one another due difference of understanding, philosophy and ideology and for the sake of temporary worldly power and riches like in the ignorant days of the past. Some resorted to extremism or radicalism without due regard to humanity, in transgression of the real teaching of Islam.

It is being repeated, again and again, that the Palestinians are fighting for survival against the illegitimate Israel Zionist Jews regime. They are helpless and their Arab Muslim brothers suffocated them as well as if these Arab people do not have the moral conscience to be proud of and be part of Islam. To accuse them of being ignorant of al-Quran, al-Sunnah and jihad is unfair but they fear the powers of disbelievers rather than Allah. They love mere meagre perishable material world rather than Allah, al-Quran and al-Sunnah and their other brother Muslims.

Allah said in surah Fatir (al-Malaikah), verse (35:45) as follows:

وَلَوْ يُؤَاخِذُ ٱللَّهُ ٱلنَّاسَ بِمَا كَسَبُواْ مَا تَرَكَ عَلَىٰ ظَهْرِهَا مِن دَآبَّةٍ وَلَٰكِن يُؤَخِّرُهُمْ إِلَىٰ أَجَلٍ مُّسَمًّى فَإِذَا جَآءَ أَجَلُهُمْ فَإِنَّ ٱللَّهَ كَانَ بِعِبَادِهِۦ بَصِيرًا

"And if Allah were to punish men for that which they earned, He would not leave a moving (living) creature on the surface of the earth, but He gives them respite to an appointed term and when their term comes (Allah will punish them fairly), then verily, Allah is Ever All-Seer of His slaves."

Allah is the most Benevolent, Merciful and Almighty, and therefore He gives chance for people who committed wrong doings or evil deeds in this world to repent, but if they do not, a time will come for them to face the torturous punishment for their sins. No human power can avoid or surmount the power and the Preordainment of Allah. Just for examples, should Allah stop the rain or just pull the earth away from the sun etc. all living creatures will either die from thirsty or cold respectively, but in the meantime, out of His mercy and blessing Allah postpones the bane and punishment until a predetermined time best known to Him only.

At the time of judgement, nothing can escape from Allah – the rich or the poor; the powerful or the weak etc. shall be accounted for fairly before Allah. Happiness or sorrow; in heaven or hell in the world hereafter is solely depending on one's own deeds, virtuous or evil in this world.

The Muslims of the contemporary world are all in sins because they do not uphold the Islamic principles in full in managing their affairs. They betrayed the trust given by Allah to manage this world as the servants and caliphs of Allah. The Muslims had let secularism and liberalism out done Islamic fundamental and tradition vis-à-vis the disbelievers. In other words, the Muslims had let down Islam. Jihad in the way of Allah has lost of its importance thereby making Muslims being so weak, economically and militarily, by allowing the non-believers to control them for umpteen years. Being the best people ever created by Allah, the Muslims should lead the world in every aspect of life – religiously, culturally, economically and militarily. Since they are not, Allah abandons them simply because they do not help Allah and His Messenger in up-holding Islam. Thus, the Muslims become weak and Islam has become a stranger again, despite of having more than 1.6 billion of Muslim people.

The Muslims are the underdogs. They do not have creditable leaders to lead. Their Islamic faith is in diminishing syndrome. The secularists and liberalists are already in the winning mode even in the government of the day. This is unhealthy development for Islam. They are also in control of the businesses and education etc. The 'true Muslims' are put to shame - just look and see like the 'defunct' OIC.

To this end, the Muslim world need charismatic and calibre leaders of integrity that have the moral fibre and will power to work and to stand up together to protect their own turf. The Muslims do not need the extravagant leaders wearing or adorning in gold and silk, travelling in specially crafted aircraft and bullet-proof limousines. The Muslims need leaders of integrity that can take the lead to close rank and to 'jihad', that is to work hard and sacrifice together for Allah to uphold justice for all in facing the vagaries of the villains.

The Muslims will remain in humiliation as they are until all they realise the importance of jihad - religiously, educationally, economically and militarily - in up-holding the teaching of Islam and in defending of its supremacy. Even economically the Muslims do not have enough food to feed themselves, let alone to face the onslaught of its adversaries. May Allah bless the Muslims by bringing down a new breed of pious Muslims to lead the world in the path of Allah. Amin!

.............OOOOOOO.............

REFERENCES

Al-Quran – translated by Dr. Muhammad Taqî-ud-Din Al-Hilâlî & Dr.Muhammad Muhsin Khân

Al-Quran -Tafsir Al-Azhar – HAMKA

Al-Quran -Tafsir Ibnu Kathir

Manusia dan Islam – Dr. Harun Din dan lain-lain.

Tanbihul ghafilin (Peringatan Bagi Yang lupa) – Abu Laits As-Samarqandi.

Islam Liberal, isu dan cabaran – Published by P.U.M.

Hakikat Hikmah Tauhid dan Tasawuf (al-Hikam by Ibnu Athaillah Askandary) –syarahan terjemahan oleh Dr. K.H. Muhibbuddin Waly.

Fiqh & Perundangan Islam (Dr. Wahabah AL-Zuhaili) – Terjemahan Dr. Ahmad Shahbari Salamon et. al.

The Challenge of Islam – Edited by Altaf Gauhar - Islamic Council of Europe, London.

Issues in the Islamic Movement – Edited by Kalim Siddiqui of the Muslim Institute, London.

The Islamist: Why I joined Radical Islam in Britain, What I saw inside and why I left' - Ed Hussain (2007).

Nasihat Agama dan Wasiat Iman – Imam Habib Abdullah Hadad.

Hakikat tasawuf – Syaikh Abdul Qadir Isa.

Islam & Demokrasi – Abdul Hadi Awang.

Asal usul Aliran Inkarus Sunnah (Anti-Hadis) - Prof. Dr. Shahrin Muhammad (UTM).

Ancaman dan Tentangan Terhadap Islam dan Muslim - Prof. Dr. Idris bin Zakaria (UKM).

Idea-idea Islam Liberal, 2 Sept 2005 - Dr Muhammad Nur Manuty.

Tuntutan Agama Dalam Membuat Perancangan Harta - Abdul Muhaimin Mahmood (JAKIM).

Pembangunan Modal Insan dari Perspektif Pengurusan Islam – Fadilah Mansor dan Tg. Sarina Aini Kasim – UM.

Cabaran akidah: Pemikiran Islam liberal - Muhammad Ariffin Ismail.

Ancaman Nasionalis Sekular Ekstrim (2002) - Abdul Basir Alias.

Islam Liberal: Ancaman kepada Aqidah dan Jati-Diri Ummah (2009). Amad Adnan Faszil.

Islam and Secularism. Wikipedia.

The Objectives (Maqasid) of The Islamic Divine Law (Syariah) – Mashahad al-Alif.

Kitab 'Ash-syifa'. Qadi Iyad (1083-1149).

A World Without Islam - Graham E. Fuller.

Confession of an Economic Hit man - John Perkins.

Al-Iman - Dr. Muhammad Naim Yasin, Aman, Jordan.

Islam, Politik dan Pemerentahan - Dr. Abu al-Maati Abu al-Futuh, Cairo.

Art of Deception - Jerry D. Gray, ex-USAF.

The Clash of civilizations and The Remaking of world Order (1996. – S. P. Huntington.

Civil Democratic Islam: Partners, Resources and Strategies (2003) - Cheryl Bernard

Terror and Liberalism - Paul Berman.

The Clash of Ignorance - Edward Said (Arab-Christian).

The inevitablity Clash of Civilisation - Hizb ut-Tahrir (Al-Khalifah Publication), May 2002.

'What Went Wrong? - The Clash between Islam and Modernity in the Middle East' - Bernard Lewis:

Liberal Islam – Charles Kurzman

Internationalisation of the Political Islamic threat to the New World Order – Abdullah Y. S. & Hamed H. Al-Abdullah (Kuwait University).

Towards an Islamic Reformation (1989) - Abdullahi Ahmed An-Na'im

Islam & Secular State – Abullahi Ahmed An-Na'im.

Jahiliyyah Abad Dua Puluh (Ignorant in the 20th Century) - Muhammad Qutb

'Al-Islam Wa Usul Al-Hukm' (Islam and the Foundations of Governance) 1925 - Ali Abdel Raziq (1888-1966).

Speech by ex-Foreign Minister of Malaysia (Tan Sri Dato' Syed Hamid Albar): Organisation of Islamic Countries (OIC) - Perception and Achievement.

Wikipedia.

WRITER'S BIOGRAPHY

Born: Kuala Trengganu, April 12 1942. Descendant of Syarief Sheikh Abdul Malik bin Abdullah (1089H-1149H – also known as Datuk Pulau Manis, Kuala Trengganu) whose ancestors were from Baghdad.

Education: UM.

Career: Government civil servant for a few years in Kuala Trengganu. Then moved on to private sector in Insurance and banking industry in Kuala Lumpur.

Career training: Singapore, Tokyo, Sydney and London.

Last post: Senior Manager – Insurance Operation and Regional.

Religious Study: Islamic Law (syariah) and Usuluddin, UMCCed.

First book: Memperkasa Semula Islam and Memertabatkan Bangsa Melayu - 2010 (self-publisher).

Printed in the United States
By Bookmasters